WITH A POEM IN MY POCKET

WITH A POEM IN MY POCKET

THE AUTOBIOGRAPHY OF

Patience Strong

FREDERICK MULLER LIMITED
LONDON

First published in Great Britain in 1981
by Frederick Muller Ltd, London NW2 6LE

British Library Cataloguing in Publication Data

Strong, Patience
    With a poem in my pocket.
    1. Strong, Patience   2. Poets, English—
    20th century—Biography
    I. Title
    821'.912   PR6037.T847

ISBN 0-584-10613-0

Photoset by Rowland Phototypesetting Ltd, Bury St Edmunds, Suffolk.
Printed in Great Britain by Biddles Ltd, Guildford, Surrey.

CONTENTS

ILLUSTRATIONS
& ACKNOWLEDGMENTS

The publishers wish to thank Patience Strong for the photographs which will be found between pages 40 and 41, 120 and 121, 168 and 169.

1
PLAYING FOR TIME

ANY OF my readers through the years have asked me for details of my life. I have never kept a diary except in a spasmodic way but I have often wished to set down the record of certain events and to give my impressions of people with whom I have been in contact. What follows is not a detailed, chronological account of my life but rather a gathering-together of memories and a statement of my beliefs.

A book that is worth writing should write itself, propelled forward by its own momentum. I have opened my copy of *Alice in Wonderland* and there under my nose is just the inspiration required by all who sit in a verbal vacuum waiting for the first sentence to shape itself in the mind. I might have known Alice would come up with something.

"Where shall I begin, your Majesty?" said the White Rabbit adjusting his spectacles. "Begin at the beginning," the King said gravely, "and go on till you come to the end."

How simple! We usually discover that there is a simple solution to a problem and all too often the discovery is made after we have exhausted ourselves in unravelling the twisted threads of futile argument.

The trouble is that invariably we are too close to the facts to see them clearly. It is sometimes necessary to stand back from a picture in order to see the detail in the right perspective. The simple answer is usually the right one. So, without further ado I shall take the advice given by the King to White Rabbit and begin at the beginning.

2
STRANGER THAN FICTION

$\mathcal{S}$O HERE I AM, pen in hand on the last day of the seventies. After a crisp cold night this morning was like the gate of heaven, the sea outside the window suffused in a rosy haze, and as the mist rolled back with the risng sun a blue sky arched over the Channel from Beachy Head to the far horizon curving east. It was, I felt, a good omen for my personal project, though news filtering through the transistor radio at my elbow continued to pull me back from the past into the grim realities of the present.

Several false starts had already been made and the matter laid aside for various reasons. The first effort to rescue the past from oblivion was made aboard the *Edinburgh Castle* over four years ago on the homeward voyage from South Africa. I was half-way through the second chapter when my thoughts went scampering off in another direction. The urge to write about the poem in my pocket had spent itself, seeming unimportant in the light of recent experiences in that comparatively new land of Southern Africa so that the two chapters were laid aside and I commenced the book which was published soon afterwards called *The Other Side of the Coin**, and I am glad that I did so at that particular time because it was the

*published by Bachman & Turner

3

right time. But the days of procrastination now lie behind and I must plunge in at the deep end. My friend and literary mentor, the novelist, Neil Bell once wrote to me, "Don't paddle around in the shallows of life, dive in at the deep end", but the deepest depths are not always where things begin or end and I must bear in mind the instructions given to the White Rabbit, to begin at the beginning. And what is the beginning? Can anyone really isolate and pin down the first memory? How far back into the dim caverns of memory can the mind be stretched? "I give you the end of a golden string," said the poet, Blake. Tug as you will at that string or loosen your grip on it to ease the tension, it can never be traced to its full length. Childhood recedes as the years press forward.

Few can resist the temptation to talk or write about childhood memories, wandering in a fantasy land of irrelevant details. So that form of self indulgence must be avoided so far as is possible. I invariably skip the introductory chapters of an autobiography because they throw little light upon the main subject. If I had unlimited time with nothing else to do I can imagine no more delightful task than to commit all my childhood memories to paper, purely for my own satisfaction. I could write a full length novel from any of the incidents to be recorded here, for they are included only because they tie up in some way to the main point which is to bring out the simple proposition that everything leads on to something else, by the law of cause and effect, and is therefore a part of the whole having a significant place in the so far unformed pattern of the jigsaw-puzzle of life.

Wordsworth suggests that we come into the world "trailing clouds of glory," presupposing a life prior to birth. Be that as it may, my life began at the very moment I would have chosen if I had been able to choose with foresight: the period between the end of the Edwardian sunset and the accession to the Imperial Throne of the King-Emperor George V in 1911; being thus placed I can remember two world wars, at a time when the third now looms on the horizons of possibility.

My mother told me that I was born in fifteen minutes. The days before the outbreak of that first war were days of delight, or perhaps it only seems so viewed from a distance. Children have infinite capacity for enjoyment and joy turned into pure rapture in the simple pleasure to be had from bowling a hoop in the park, riding high on the painted horses of a merry-go-round, climbing trees and running home triumphantly with a few tadpoles in a jam jar. On Fridays the Italian organ grinder used to play by the lamp post when the children ran out of school. A scarlet coated monkey used to sit on his shoulders as we children danced around the barrel organ, flinging a halfpenny or a farthing into the cloth cap placed on the kerbstone. The streets then were busy with people doing their various jobs, the onion-seller, the chair-mender, the pedlar, the rag and bone man, the muffin man, the gypsies selling pegs and lavender, chimney sweeps, policemen and postmen on foot, the hand drawn milk cart and the horse drawn baker's van.

What pleasure we children enjoyed in the pre-television era. Life revolved around the public library, the local park, the swimming bath and, chiefly for me, the Sunday school. Every year there was the Christmas treat in the corrugated iron shed attached to the Baptist Church, known as the Tin Hall, where there were magic-lantern shows and lectures, mainly about missionary work in Africa, China and India. Names like Hudson Taylor, Livingstone and William Carey were household names. Each child had a missionary box in which it was expected to place a penny once a month to help feed 'the heathen', and propagate the Gospel. Since one halfpenny a week was the customary dole received by most children that missionary box represented a sacrifice that hurt. Every year there was a Christmas party at which each child received a small gift and an orange. In June there would be a summer outing to Hayes Common or the Shirley Hills by brake or train.

I do not remember very much about summer holidays, during the period when my father was away in Egypt or France, but I can hazily recall one or two years when we went to Ramsgate and Folkestone with Mrs Earl and Margery. I remember that if you knelt on the cliffs with your ear to the ground you could hear the vibration of the guns across the Channel. After the war we had a yearly holiday of a week in Brighton and the ecstasy of those days in Brighton defies description. I can still recapture the sheer joy of running barefoot along the ribbed sand when the tide was ebbing leaving an expanse of sand between the pebbled beach and the sea. Running towards the sunset on wet sands which glittered crimson and gold with reflected light was like running over the edge of the world. Even today, with a long stretch of years between, when ever I hear the tide dragging at the shingle it evokes the Palace Pier, the West Pier, the Downs, hokey poky, Pierots and Volk's Railway—oh what bliss it was to be alive and to lie under the elevated lines at Paston Place watching the trains pass over our heads! The thunder of the wheels matched the thunder of the surf piling along the shelving beach.

We stayed in lodgings over a pet shop owned by a Mrs Soper in the Queens Road. One of the highlights was to be taken by bus to Rottingdean and shown the house where Kipling had lived before moving to Batemans. Walks over the chalky downs at poppy time would be remembered for many a day after we had returned to London.

Brighton was magic and still is magic for me in spite of changes for the worse. You can still turn a corner and catch a glimpse of Regency Squares with their gracious houses and beautiful Georgian windows. And there is always the Royal Pavilion embowered in trees which come alive in the Spring when the wallflowers bloom warm and glowing around the fountain and the lawns in front of the Pavilion are golden with daffodils. During the 14-18 war it was used as a convalescent home for Indian soldiers. No wonder Brighton Pavilion always conjures up a motley procession of unrelated characters whenever I allow my imagination to get out of control under the gilded domes. Turbaned figures float by in hospital blue. The Prince Regent races his coach along the Stein and Mrs Fitzherbert makes her ghostly presence felt against a background of pillared splendour and Chinese wall-paper.

The stretching of memory to the farthest point of its elasticity takes me back to the days when I used to walk part of the way to the station with my father every morning except Sundays. Half-way to the station he would stop at the sweet shop on the corner and stooping to kiss me would say "Run along home now." Sometimes he would give me a farthing and before going home I would go into the shop and spend the precious farthing on a strip of liquorice or a quarter of a pound of jelly babies, cachous or acid drops. Time spent at the window agonising over the choice was half pleasure half pain, because this did not happen every day. It was all the more exciting because it was only an occasional treat and not something that could be taken for granted. My father went off to some mysterious place referred to as the London office and I ran home, eating my sweets as I jumped over each paving stone.

Suddenly this delightful ritual was interrupted. There was talk about something called "the war". Strange names cropped up in every conversation and became familiar; Kitchener, Belgium, Bonar Law, Bonham Carter, Lord Roberts, Viscount Grey of Falloden, the Kaiser. One never-to-be-forgotten day my father, a few months after the declaration of war, appeared dressed as a soldier, wearing khaki, a bandoleer across his shoulder and puttees on his legs. I remember kneeling by the chair watching his hands unwind the brown puttees. In his hat there was the regimental badge of the Royal Engineers. The following morning he went away with a heavy kit bag slung over his back. It was all very strange and secret.

Instead of going to London he was bound for a port of embarkation, destination unknown. We did not know it then because he did not know himself where he was going. We knew later; it was Egypt, Alexandria, aboard the *Euripides*.

We went with him as far as the front gate. My mother was crying, my baby brother, not yet a year old, in her arms. My sister and I waved to him until he reached the end of the road. We could not understand why he did not stop and wave before turning the corner. It was the beginning of a war and the end of our world as we knew it. It was to be three years before we saw him again when he came home on a fourteen day leave before embarking for France.

My paternal grandfather had fought in the Zulu War with the 17th Lancers. It was his custom to recite Tennyson's *Charge of the Light Brigade* every Christmas when all the family came together in the tall narrow house in Forest Hill. We would always stay for Christmas night and I can remember lying with my sister in the big brass bedstead with its deep feather mattress and hearing the screech of the trams as they rounded the bend by Brockley Rise. Yes, even on Christmas night the trams were there if required. Public services were maintained in those days under all conditions.

My father was the eldest of ten children so I had four aunts, two of whom are still alive, and five uncles; four joined up at the outbreak of war with the exception of Charles who failed his medical because of a heart condition. Uncle Ben was a gunner with the infantry, Uncle Percy who died in 1980 at the age of 82 was in Egypt, Palestine and France, and with the West Kents during the Allenby campaign in which we British-Israelites believe the Biblical prophecies in the book of Daniel were fulfilled to the very day.

STRANGER THAN FICTION

Uncle Ernie was a mere boy of sixteen when he volunteered, giving a false age. He was a sensitive, dreamy type and I remember hearing Grandma read one of his letters aloud to my mother. It was written from a trench in France. "Dear Mum," she read, "As I write this to you I'm crying because I'm so frightened. Don't tell anybody." The voice wavered. I remember, child though I was, feeling a sudden awareness of the tragedy of the war. Ernie, my youngest uncle, came back, but never settled to anything again. He was a roamer and a recluse to the end of his days, the youngest of the soldier uncles and the first to die in middle age while shovelling snow away from the doorstep of his remote cottage in Somerset. After the war he toyed vaguely with the idea of a chicken farm. It petered out and he joined the Black and Tans in search of adventure. A few years later he worked his way across Australia.

A few more memories intrude and clamour for their place in this story before I leave the old house in Forest Hill. My grandmother was tall and dignified but possessed a keen sense of comedy. My grandfather was also a wit and their love of fun was passed on to their family in good measure. There was always an undercurrent of irrepressible merriment in the house in spite of their reduced circumstances and the expense of raising a large brood. There was a funny side to everything—or so it seemed when I rang the bell pull at the front door to which at first I had to be lifted. It had been decided to leave the garden to the designs of nature and the consequence was an all-summer display of self-sown marigolds and nasturtiums—a wild but living tapestry of yellow, orange and gold. I must remember this when I feel I can no longer cope with my own wilderness of unmanageable weeds and self-sown flowers thrusting in at the wrong places.

There was a large old Collard grand piano in the parlour under which I loved to sit when the aunts performed on special occasions. Tunes such as *Washington Post, Poet and*

Peasant, The Blue Danube and *Over the Waves* were played on those old yellow ivories and I used to love seeing the shoes peeping out from the long frilly skirts as the pedals were worked.

One Sunday evening, during the war, when we were aiming to catch the ten o'clock tram home, my Uncle Charles said to my mother, "What's wrong with that child?" I was sitting nursing my arm grizzling with misery. "Take no notice," said my mother, "She is playing for sympathy in the hope that she can stay away from school in the morning." At this I let out a howl of protest the like of which had seldom been heard in that merry household. "A girl pushed me over in the park," I moaned, "Her name was Letitia Cass." My sister, my senior by two years said, "I think that is a very peculiar name." By this time Uncle Charles was across the room and struggling into his overcoat. My father, his elder brother, being away at the war he felt it his duty to keep an eye on his family. "Get your coat on," he said, "I'm taking you to the Miller Hospital at Greenwich on the tram." It was late on Sunday evening—but prompt attention was given to us in the out-patients department. I yelled when the nurse dabbed the arm with something that made it smart, but worse was to come. The doctor appeared, examined the abrasion, then suddenly gave my arm an almighty wrench, after which there was more dabbing followed by bandaging and instructions to attend the hospital every morning at 8.30 to have the arm redressed. As we left the doctor said, "Young lady—do you realise that you owe your right arm to your Uncle. You had a dislocated shoulder and an open graze on your arm which had turned septic. Had it been left until morning we should have had to amputate." I did not understand what the word meant but I imagined it to mean something awful.

My poor mother had to leave baby brother with a neighbour, pack our breakfast which we consumed in the tram and attend the Miller Hospital with a fractious child who made no secret of her resentment of the way in which the nurse tore off the bandage. This went on for more than a month.

A different turning my life would have taken if Uncle Charles had not called at Forest Hill that evening. Life without swimming, dancing, playing the piano and typing would have been only half a life. How thankful should all be who can lift up two arms in welcome to life.

Shortly after the beginning of that first war we were taken to Hounslow to stay for a month with Aunt Louise and Uncle Reuben, the sister and brother-in-law of the grandma at Forest Hill. I remember there were three framed photographs of their sons; young soldiers, over the mantelpiece in the living-room. They had been killed, all three, during the first few months of the war. I was taken to see aeroplanes at Heston, a novelty in those days.

Other memories with a 1914-18 war-time background filter through. One of the pleasures of life in those days was the cinema, where children were allowed to sit on the floor in the side gangways for three pence. I wonder if the present generation of young children could imagine the intensity of enjoyment the cinema gave to people of all ages in those early days. Drama, excitement, thrills, pathos, comedy, adventure, they were all there on those silent black and white screens. Names like Theda Bara, Charlie Chaplin, Pauline Frederick, Douglas Fairbanks, Nazimova and Mary Pickford, my favourite, starred our firmament. After seeing *Rebecca of Sunnybrook Farm* and *Daddy Long Legs*, I plucked up courage and wrote to Mary asking for a photograph. Imagine my rapturous surprise on receiving this from America duly signed.

On certain evenings of the week an instalment of the current serial would be shown, *The Perils of Pauline*, *The Exploits of Elaine*, *The Red Circle*, and various films in which Creighton Hale, Craig Kennedy and Pearl White held us enthralled.

Sometimes the picture would be interrupted by an air raid warning flashed onto the screen with the words: Patrons are warned that enemy aeroplanes have crossed the Channel. You are given twenty minutes to leave the cinema. The management regrets that it is unable to refund money paid for tickets.

These were the nights when a full moon meant Gothas. We, my sister and her friend Margery who lived opposite and sometimes my friend Ouida would be amongst the last to leave, feeling we wanted to have our money's worth. This meant running home to reach shelter before the gunfire started. There was an anti-aircraft gun in an emplacement nearby, known as Screaming Lizzie. Margery's mother and mine were friends, both husbands serving in Egypt at the time. Margery and her mother always came over to our place during a raid as it was not considered safe to take my brother across the road since he was usually sleeping peacefully in his basket under the kitchen table.

I was terrified when Screaming Lizzie started up, and knelt under the table in earnest prayer for our safe deliverance. I remember making a bargain with the Almighty promising that if He would spare us yet again I would go to school early in the morning and preach a sermon in the bicycle shed, appealing to the girls to repent and be saved. As good as my promise I mounted a box in the shed next morning to discover that I was in fact not as good as my word. I had meant it at the time, but courage failed as the girls came bustling in with their cycles and I slunk away feeling like a worm. When the warning went the next night I was down on my knees again imploring God to overlook my weakness and stretch forth the hand of His mercy upon us, undeserving though we were.

My sister and I shared a passionate love of poetry as well as a bedroom and here we would recite our favourites long into the night. Connie favoured Tennyson and the Brownings. I passed through many phases but

Shakespeare was my idol. We had erected a small stage between the dressing-table and the chest of drawers. It was really only an inverted orange box but it served our purpose. I would spring out of bed at any time of night and read lengthy passages from *Macbeth*, *The Merchant of Venice*, *The Tempest* and my favourite, *A Midsummer Night's Dream*. My mother used to knock on the wall and tell us that we must go to sleep. There were occasions when, her patience exhausted, she would open the door and threaten to write and tell Dad that we were being very naughty. Her parting shot was always "You won't be so bright in the morning." And we weren't. Getting up was agony after a night of Camelot and Arden.

When my father went to the war I was sent to a school a few minutes' walk from home. Connie was already launched at the local grammar school equipped with gym slip, hockey stick, tennis racquet and bicycle. My brother was still in the go-cart stage. I often think how lucky it was for me that I was at that school, it was exactly right for me. Several times in the year we were taken to the Old Vic for a Shakespeare session presented by the Ben Greet or Frank Benson's Players. My special friend at these performances was Win Payne.

We shared the same brand of humour, the antics of Bottom, Snout, Starveling, Flute, Snug and Quince would reduce us to a state of near hysteria. Win and I shared our delight in the *Dream* up to the time that she died a year ago. Pyramus and Thisby never lost their power to unseal the springs of laughter. I suppose it was these excursions to the Old Vic and the happy accident of living a mere tram ride from the Waterloo Road which fed my imagination and turned me into a single-minded worshipper at the Shakespearian shrine.

An annual pilgrimage to Stratford has always been a necessity for me. Life can hold nothing more exciting than to walk by Avon waters watching the swans, and to stroll along Sheep Street telling myself that this very street would have known the step of the boy who was not only on his way to school but on his way to a destiny which was to make him one of the greatest writers the world has ever known: England's gift to all men for all time. It was surely not by chance that William Shapespeare was born and died on the day which commemorates the martyrdom of George of Lydda, England's patron Saint.

One of the memories which cling around this particular period is of an October morning when the teacher made the announcement that Russia was no longer an ally. The Russian Revolution had begun. It was the beginning of something more catastrophic than a political and social upheaval.

I shall never forget my dismay when we were told that the Russian anthem would not in future be included in the customary singing of the anthems of the allies for this had been my favourite:

> "God the all terrible, King who
> ordainest
> Great winds Thy clarion and
> lightning Thy sword,
> Show forth Thy pity on high where Thou
> reignest
> Give to us peace in our time, O Lord."

3
CONSTANCE CAMELIA

ANOTHER MEMORY of that period floats up to the surface and cannot be ignored because it ties in with my belief that life is a series of stepping stones from one thing to another, all connected by Blake's "golden string"; nothing is isolated, all is providential unless we have struck out relying solely on our own strength doing something wholly out of character and wildly irrational. If a thing is meant to be it will happen to no matter how we strive to swim against the tide of circumstances.

I think I had always known about Constance Camelia so that when her moment came it was as if I had experienced it before long ago in a dream or in some fantasy world of my own. This is how it came about. My mother and her sister Ada were left motherless when she was four and her sister three. The inevitable happened. When the two girls had been sent from pillar to post living with various relations, the day came when mother's father announced that he had re-married and was able to have his two daughters at home again. The name of their stepmother was Emma. I was named after her; she was a reserved, unapproachable woman. She lacked glow. It was the old story of a woman who had married a widower only to discover that he needed only a housekeeper.

In such circumstances it was inevitable that feelings on

both sides should harden between stepmother and the two pretty little girls on whom her husband doted.

I had no clear recollections of Emma Mason until Grandpa developed cancer of the throat. He had been a pipe smoker; in those days they had little or no knowledge of the causes of this killer disease. They know now but still cannot find the cure.

Grandpa had an operation at Guy's Hospital and I remember Auntie Ada taking me to see him in their large icy house in Tressillian Road, Brockley. His neck was bandaged and when it was time to go he insisted on walking with us as far as the tram stop; that is my only memory of him, standing there under the lamplight in the wintry dusk, a tall figure wearing a black overcoat and bowler hat, the bandages concealed by a white silk scarf. He watched us until the tram was out of sight. I noticed that Auntie Ada had tears in her eyes when the conductor came for our fares. It was a long time ago but that was my only recollection of Grandpa Mason.

The war was still dragging on and my father was still away, but after Grandpa died I remember being taken by my mother once a week on a brief formal duty-visit to her step-mother. Connie and I sat wondering what to say, looking at the stern lifeless face of the woman in the high necked blouse, a cameo brooch at the throat. The gaslit room was full of shadows. It was a relief when we reached up to that parchment-wrinkled face to place a goodbye kiss on the cold cheek. She never' came to our house. Perhaps she was never invited, but one day my mother received a letter from her in which she asked if she could be allowed to take Connie and me on a visit to her sister Kate who lived in a cottage in Prestwood, Buckinghamshire. The matter was discussed at length over the breakfast table by my mother and Auntie Ada who was unmarried and living with us during my father's absence. Connie kicked me under the table. We were holding our breath, terrified of being sent away for a whole week with someone who was almost a stranger and of whom we were a little afraid.

At last mother said, "I think I'll say yes. After all, it's the only favour she has ever asked of us." It must have gone against the grain with my mother, a loving kindly soul to all who knew her but there seemed to be something which touched a root of bitterness in her where Mrs Mason was concerned. Perhaps children never quite forgive a widowed father for marrying again, and being incapable of seeing the situation from all angles except their own, take their revenge upon the unfortunate woman who appears to have taken the place of their own mother.

I shall always be grateful to my mother for being generous over this invitation though at the time Connie and I were unco-operative, even rebellious. When I found that tears were of no avail I began to realise that the situation might be turned to advantage and possibly lead to the acquisition of a new dress.

In those days dress material was on display in rolls outside, as well as inside, the linen draper's. For weeks I had had my eye on some pale mauve muslin, described on the ticket as heliotrope, at a shop I passed several times a week going to and from the swimming baths. It was one penny and three farthings a yard in the summer sale. I took a great pleasure in clothes and was determined that if we were to go to Prestwood I should be able to appear in a different dress every day of that week; so I set to work on my long-suffering mother and she, exasperated by my persistence, at last opened her purse, giving me the three pennies and a halfpenny needed for the two yards of material. I ran as fast as my legs could carry me through the park and down the hill to the shop on the main road. My mother made the dress that evening on her Singer treadle sewing machine, and we set out next morning to meet Grandma at Vauxhall Station.

There she was, waiting on the platform at the time

arranged looking sombre in dark clothes and carrying a basket-work travelling bag. We kissed mother tearfully and waved goodbye from the window of the train. It was our first parting. When we were clear of the station, a silence fell between us. I looked up and into Grandma's face. She smiled at me and her dark eyes were dancing as if she were enjoying her own thoughts. Presently she laughed outright and reaching for her bag said, "Now let me see what I can find." The bag was opened and she produced a tin of toffees. Surprisingly we were friends from that moment. She was a different person from the Grandma we had known. The years dropped away from her face like a falling mask. She was real and suddenly surprisingly young as she sat there outlining the plans for the week ahead, exciting us with the prospect of a visit to the Chiltern Hills, the neighbouring villages of Little Missenden and Great Missenden and, which seemed to her to be the most wonderful thing of all, we should be able to go to the farm up the lane every day to fetch milk in a jug instead of from the local dairy in a metal can.

I know now that she was a countrywoman born and bred and that this was her first return to fields and woods after twenty years of exile, first in Brockley and later as a London widow in a dark little house near the docks. When we were old enough to understand Connie and I felt sorry we had not done more to bring happiness into the narrow life of this lonely country-starved soul. As the train was nearing Aylesbury Grandma murmured something about Constance Camelia which tantalised us beyond endurance. "Shall we meet Constance Camelia?" we clamoured, scrambling up into the seat beside her agog with interest. "Possibly. She comes and goes," came the teasing reply, or words to that effect. "She came often when I used to sleep in that room."

I must not linger over the details of our arrival, the first sight of the cottage or the enthralment of that first evening visit to the farm, jug in hand, to fetch eggs and milk. The path from the lane led across a meadow where the silky flanks of the cows caught the rosy flush of sunset light. Tired with travelling and the excitement of our first sight of real country, we were taken at last up the steep staircase to the attic bedroom with its low ceiling and tiny dormers.

Grandma put us to bed and kissed us goodnight. The once cold cheek was warm and glowing. Before leaving she lit a candle which stood in a brass candlestick on the washstand beside the jug and basin. "What about Constance Camelia?" I cried. "She'll come and dance on the wall when you are asleep" came the reply. We had only a minute to wait before the secret of Constance Camelia was revealed. The candlelight falling across jug and basin produced a shadow in the form of a girl wearing bonnet and crinoline, and when the flame moved under the breath of draught from the half open door, the shadow curtsied and whirled. I have never forgotten that fascinating display of shadow and candlelight. Many years later I wrote a book of children's verses *Nursery Versery* and the one I most enjoyed doing was one drawn from that old memory. Here is its ending.

But now she does not come at all
To spread her skirts upon my wall,
It's only in a dream at night
That she returns by candlelight
And dances with the dancing flame,
The lady with the lovely name:
Constance Camelia.

Perhaps I have lingered too long over this little episode in my life but it left a lasting memory of someone I never really knew existed until it was too late, and I cannot let it go without its epilogue.

My mother met us at Vauxhall Station on our return from Buckinghamshire and the next day there came a message that her stepmother had died early that morning.

CONSTANCE CAMELIA

It was as if Emma Mason having pre-knowledge of what lay in store, had contrived to combine the two things that meant most to her in her meagre life; the longing to give expression to her love for her two step grand-daughters and to revisit her old home in the country. She had made the two pleasures coalesce and could say her Nunc Dimittis, departing in peace, but not into oblivion. I, for one, should never be able to forget her or her fantasy child, Constance Camelia, who was no more than a dancing shadow.

But there is a strange little epilogue to add to the epilogue of her lonely demise in that dark house on the edge of London's dockland. Nearly thirty years later when my own mother, Emma Mason's step-daughter, lay dying in the beautiful blue twilight of a February evening in the first year of the second world war, it was the unloved and unlovely Emma Mason who seemed to stand between the bed and the window caught in a rosy shaft of sunset light, remaining with me as a very real presence during the whole of that long, sad week. And it is she who seems to walk with me at times when I am afoot in the lanes as we walked together in the Prestwood days. From where do these strong impressions come if not from somewhere outside our own consciousness? They come unbidden, unsought as from a world beyond our knowing. I believe in guardian angels, and I like to think that this step-grandmother whom I never really knew in life has not forgotten or forsaken me. It is in the times of crisis that we feel the tightening of the invisible cobwebs of memory in which we are enmeshed and from which we can never escape even if we would. Forward we press into the future through these webs of delicate threads woven by time into an intricate pattern of seemingly unrelated circumstances.

4
OUTSIDE ONLY

A DISASTROUS HOUSE MOVE the year before last in which
many of my treasured diaries and files seemed to
disappear has left me with no alternative but to rely on
memory for piecing together the jumbled jigsaw puzzles of
past events; but so much was crowded into that particular
period that some of the recollections may not be strictly in
their right order. For instance, I cannot recall whether the
night of the delivery of the piano came before or after the
Prestwood adventure, but I must have been about four
because I had not yet started school.

Connie and I had been packed off to bed at what
seemed to us to be an early hour. On hearing a knock on
the front door followed by a commotion in the hall we
sprang out of bed and hung over the banister demanding
to know what was happening. This brought an immediate
response from my harassed mother and the promise that
we should see in the morning.

Next morning which was a Sunday, I was the first to
rush downstairs to find a brand new piano installed in the
parlour complete with music stool which had a hinged lid
upholstered in green velvet upon which I sat, still in my
nightgown, and played the latest popular song *Everybody's
Doing It* and my favourite hymn *Onward Christian Soldiers*. I
could have gone on playing for I seemed to have an
inexhaustible repertoire, but my mother burst into the

room, listened for a bit and said, "That's good, you won't
need to have lessons." It did not strike her or me as being
in the least surprising that I should be able to sit down and
play without ever having touched a piano before. I had, of
course, seen the one at Sunday School and the one at
Forest Hill, but they were both kept locked when not in
use and up to the moment of the piano's arrival at our
home I had not been interested. Connie was soon on the
scene, placed at the piano and reprimanded for not knowing how it worked. "You'll need lessons," said my mother.
"I'll see Mrs. MacLaren in the morning." This lady was
one of the local music teachers who gave lessons for one
shilling and sixpence an hour on Saturday mornings. So
poor Connie, always the unlucky one, had to give up the
main part of her precious Saturday mornings to learn
about minims, crotchets, semibreves, demi-semi-quavers,
scales and *The Bluebells of Scotland* from a book called
Czerny's. This must have been before the war because I
remember my father coming into the room and playing
some of his favourite songs with thumb and little finger.
He was a great whistler. Perhaps that is why I seemed to
know all those songs in a flash. There had always been
whistling and singing in our house and we were taken to
the local music hall almost as soon as we could walk so we
knew all about songs like *The Sunshine of Your Smile, Thora,
The Volunteer Organist, Just A Song At Twilight, The Holy City,
Nellie Dean, Flora Dora* and *Blue Eyes*. My father also took it
for granted that one of us should be able to play the piano
at first sight. I remember his saying with relief, "I'm glad
it wasn't money wasted, the nipper has got the hang of it."
He usually referred to me as "the nipper".

Some play by ear with disastrous results. They can pick
out a melody on the keys but have no natural sense of
harmonics. The left hand knows not what the right hand
does and the result is discord to any unfortunate listener
with a true ear.

Those who have not been blessed with an ear for music

can go blundering on quite happily, blissfully unaware of the fact that they are inflicting a cruel form of torture upon some members of their audience. An inborn sense of rhythm is an asset if not a necessity to a poet so it was lucky for me that I had this advantage when I first began to write verse.

The arrival of the piano was a milestone in my life. In due course I became the local accompanist and was invited to a great many parties and to what were then known as musical evenings.

Nell, who lived next door and went to London every day as a shorthand typist in the offices of an American publisher in Henrietta Street, was active in the district and well known for her Nigger Minstrel Troupe. She kept me well supplied with books published by her employers. There was one called *Bobtail Linnet*—which inspired me to form a secret society. This, like Constance Camelia, found a place in *Nursery Versery* published over thirty years later.

I was soon writing songs for the troupe. The band consisted of piano, banjo, mandolin and violin. The items that won most applause were *Shine, Shine, Moon, My Little Octoroon*, *The Old Folks at Home* and *Picanniny Lullaby*. We performed for charity in various local halls and were in great demand for Sunday School Christmas parties. After the war Nell went to Australia, ever the pioneer seeking new worlds to conquer.

It is strange that out of all the agony and misery of wars we remember them by their songs. Each generation has its own musical memories to cherish. When Hitler's war followed the Kaiser's there was another set of songs for the world to remember, identifying with places and people.

Songs reflect the times in which they are made. The great war was the golden age of what was known as the concert platform ballad. Even though I was still a small child I can remember the tunes and the words of the songs that were all around us in those days making us laugh and weep. Their very titles pluck at the strings of the music of life. They never die. They will go with us to our graves: *Two Eyes of Grey, When the Great Red Dawn is Shining, God Send You Back To Me, My Little Grey Home in The West, There's A Long, Long Trail Awinding, A Paradise For Two, I Hear You Calling Me, Parted, The End of a Perfect Day, Somewhere A Voice Is Calling, Absent, The Bells of St. Mary's, Until, Because, Mifanwy.* The beads on the rosary of song can never be counted; there is always another lying half forgotten in the casket of memory.

I never cease to wonder how we knew all the songs that everyone seemed to know in that pre-armistice world where there were no radio or television sets to transmit them. I suppose it was just people going to the theatre and hearing the real thing, instead of having it handed to them at home on a plate selected and canned like sardines or dried fruit.

Aunt Ada, my mother's unmarried sister, lived with us during the period that my father was away on active service, so she is well to the fore on the stage of memories spanning that period. She was a character; lively, shrewd, witty and amusing.

By the way, where have all the characters gone? Everyone, in those pre-radio-television days seemed to be a personality, interesting and unique. Now, spoon-fed day and night like pre-digested mental fare, they roll off the assembly lines all very much alike.

Auntie Ada travelled to Tower Bridge by bus every day except Sunday and worked in the office of a friend who had invented a patent medicine. Invariably, by the time she arrived at the bus queue at 8.30 the buses were full and the conductor seemed to delight in calling out, "Full Up Inside. Outside Only."

With what pleasure the conductor used to make this announcement especially when there was a bleak wind blowing, a hailstorm or a downpour of rain for which a mackintosh cover was attached to the seat in front to protect laps. "Outside only." This was usually greeted

with groans of mock misery from the passengers, followed
by gales of laughter and good-humoured raillery. Rough-
ing it was good fun. As each new passenger ascended the
open stairway he would be cheered by the crowd. There
were no long faces. No surly discontented murmurings.
The outside only spirit was the spirit that brought us
through two world wars.

Later, I sometimes joined the "Outside Only" folks
when I had missed my train and had to rely on the buses
which came along every few minutes bound for the City.
You didn't really care whether you were inside or outside
so long as you got to your job on time.

After the Saturday morning stint in the offices of a firm
called Microbe Killer, my Aunt Ada used to meet a friend,
Jinny, in a Lyons teashop where they partook of a frugal
lunch before joining the queue outside one of the West
End theatres, usually for a seat in the pit, or if things
weren't so rosy they would ascend to the gallery. Because
of the regularity of Auntie's habits I came to know about
most of the shows attracting London audiences at that
time: *The Maid of the Mountains, Desert Song, Rose Marie, Chu
Chin Chow, The Co-Optimists, Tonight's The Night.* Sometimes Auntie and Jinny would switch from José Collins,
Harry Lauder, Nellie Wallace, Gertie Gitana, Marie
Lloyd, George Robey etcetera and they would have a run
on straight plays; names like Godfrey Tearle, Gladys
Cooper, Ivor Novello, Owen Nares, Gerald Du Maurier
come to mind.

Another way of keeping up with the latest songs and
singers was through the Sunday newspapers. Words and
music of a song were published weekly. I used to cut them
out and paste them on cardboard.

By the time Hitler's horror had pitched us into another
German war the new type of song had been born.

The concert platform ballad had faded out perhaps
forever. Now it was Vera Lynn and *The White Cliffs of
Dover*, Noel Coward and *I'll See You again*, Ivor Novello

and *We'll Gather Lilacs in the Spring*, Richard Tauber and *You Are My Heart's Delight*.

I came in at the end of the golden era of the concert ballad when ballads were on their way out and dance music was on its way in. Edward Teschemacher was at that time the king of the ballad lyric writers with hundreds of published songs to his credit. I met him for the first time in a little restaurant near the offices of Cary & Co., in Middlesex Street, off Oxford Street. I was very conscious of the honour of being asked to take tea with this famous man. He was dignified, kindly and helpful. He obviously wanted to encourage me. He and Frederick Drummond were great friends as well as collaborators. Since as far back as I could stretch my memory I had admired the Teschemacher songs. They were known in every part of my own little world.

Sunday tea was an institution amongst relatives in those days and most of them arrived clutching music cases, expecting to be asked to sing a song later, and amongst these songs were many the words of which were written by Edward Teschemacher or Edward Lockton, one of his pseudonyms.

He questioned me closely over the scones and cakes on the willow patterned china, and I shall never forget the moment when he put down his tea cup and said, "Little girl, my mantle will fall upon your shoulders one day." Those words showed his generosity of spirit. He was at the top of his own ladder. But it was not to be. We were swimming against the tide. The day of the ballad was basking in the light of its own sunset. The new music was overtaking us. New Bond Street had but a few more years to go before the dust was to settle upon the shelves of the houses of Chappell, Boosey and Cramer. The future was Denmark Street and the Charing Cross Road.

Although I had more than a hundred songs published before I was twenty-one, and although by that time I had already gone with the flow of the tide and was writing lyrics for Lawrence Wright, Jay Whidden, Maude Craske Day and others, it was not to be anything but a period of marking time before I was led onto an entirely different road.

I must go on to tell my adventures in Tin Pan Alley because it is all a part of the serial of my life, but I cannot close this ballad period of my writing life without making an affectionate mention of my friend Maud Craske Day. It was Frederick Drummond, the composer, who had brought us together, since Maud had a house in Devonshire Road, Forest Hill which I had to pass on my Wednesday evening visits to the Drummond home at Dale Lodge. It is not possible to paint an accurate word portrait of Maud Craske Day because her kind are so rare. She was an artist, temperamental, eccentric, vital.

5
NOSE IN A BOOK

*J*IT HAD BEEN my intention to record only that which had a direct bearing on my own story but it is not easy to dissociate personal recollections from the background against which they have been lived out, especially when that background is a global war. I cannot remember which great battle was raging on the western front when my father came home for his first leave, but I do remember having been sent out on that morning to stand for most of the day in a queue for two ounces of butter, the news having gone round the district that a certain shop had had an allocation. The ration card had not yet been introduced and it was then that the queue became part of the national life, a demonstration of the British passion for orderliness and fair treatment.

As the war dragged on towards the end of its fourth year there was talk of the king calling the nation to a day of prayer on the fourth of August 1918, the fourth anniversary of the declaration of war. Special services of intercession were held throughout the country. The king and his ministers and members of both houses of parliament assembled in St. Margaret's, Westminster, calling upon Almighty God to do for them what they were unable to do for themselves. So grievous was our plight after the breakthrough of the Germans at the section of the line held by the fifth army and the morale of the people at such a low ebb that we had come to the point of confrontation with the Eternal, the point at which an individual or a nation turns in its death-agony to keep an appointment with destiny. From that day the tide of battle turned in our favour carrying us on to the victory which culminated with the armistice signed at the eleventh hour of the eleventh day of the eleventh month of the fateful year of 1918.

I remember the air was suddenly filled with the sound of music, maroons and bells. How news travelled in those radio-less days is beyond understanding, but travel it did. Fleet are the feet of those who publish the tidings of peace. All schools were closed. I ran home shouting "It's over," and Margery and her mother were already at the door, mother struggling into a coat. Laughter and tears were on all faces. My small brother, wearing a scarlet coat with brass buttons, waving a Union Jack in one hand and clutching a toy trumpet in the other, was strapped securely into his go-cart. It was over.

Over forever, or so we thought. Our prayer had been answered. Everybody was on the streets, moving like a surging tide towards the town hall, an imposing building with towers and a handsome clock, to be demolished and rebuilt later into a modern functional horror.

Shortly after this came something called demobilisation. The soldiers and sailors came back to what Lloyd George had hoped would be "a land fit for heroes to live in."

A tragic epilogue to this tragic war came in the form of a great plague in which millions went down under the sickle of death which cut through the population of the world at every level, outnumbering the casualties of the war. Walking to school I remember that blinds were down in the windows of half the houses. A number of my schoolfriends lost their mothers; mine caught this so-called Spanish influenza and survived.

After my father returned life started again, but not in the same way. Nothing could ever be the same again. There was a temporary housing shortage. Most houses were privately owned in those days and let to suitable tenants, but there never seemed to be any shortage of accommodation except immediately after the return of the men from the war. We were lucky and within no time moved into a larger house.

Moving was in the blood of the pre-1914 generations. Everybody seemed to have somewhere to live except those who chose to be vagabonds and they had the compensation of being vaguely romantic. Comical Kate was a character who roamed the local streets, picking up waste paper from the gutters and collecting anything she could come by honestly in a sack, retiring at night into the woods, harmless and happy. Then there was Hairy Harry who went about whistling and who, it was suspected, slept in a sort of dug-out in Verdant Lane, but no-one ever saw him come out of it or go into it; he eventually died in it and was carried away by the police, a peaceable, contented happy-go-lucky vagrant.

Moving house was a part of the family philosophy in which it was implicit that you should never allow yourself to fall into a debt or a rut. Cease to plan and you ceased to live. Debts were shackles and grooves were graves. Keep moving.

Connie and I devoured all we could find that interested us in the public library. We loved the silence that lay beyond the ornate entrance. It was rather like entering a church. Although we were not encouraged to stray too far into the Alibaba's cave of fiction during this period, we must have made a few excursions into this enticing realm. I remember that Connie often used to sit up in bed saying, "Is he in heaven or is he in hell, that demned elusive Pimpernel?" So Baroness Orczy had not escaped her questing mind. All was grist to our mill. Literary snobbery was outside our ken. Angela Brazil was of the company that trooped through our processions rubbing shoulders with writers as diverse as George Eliot, Jane Austen, Marie Corelli, Dickens and Thackeray. Our nocturnal

poetry sessions continued until we moved and had separate rooms, but we were great walkers and most of the
time we had our noses in books when seated in the
branches of a tree or on a seat in the park. After the war
Rupert Brooke became our favourite poet, after Kipling
and Tennyson. The world of books became the gateway to
life itself. There would always be a book under the pillow
ready to hand or tucked into the carrier of the bicycle. One
of the things instilled into us by our parents was a reverence for books; they must, they said, never be handled
roughly or defaced in any way. A good book was a friend
for life if treated with respect. Never turn down a page to
mark the place, and never ever put another book on top of
the Bible for this was the book above all books, to be
handled with great care.

The only thing that tempted us away from our books
was the love of walking. The repairing of shoe leather
must have been a considerable item in those days, but
there was a cobbler's last in every home and it was real
leather then, lasting a long time. London did not sprawl
and bulge in that golden age of the suburbs. You went as
far as the tram terminus and there was the country. There
were no ugly excrescences of bungalows and council es-
tates thrusting out to blur the edges of the town and cut
into the natural green belts of farmland. Nothing but
cabbage, turnip and beanfields lay between the London
tram terminus at Southend duck pond and Bromley in
Kent. All along the route across the fields there were
places where you could shed shoes and stockings and
paddle in the Ravensbourne.

I shall never cease to be grateful for my good fortune in
being able to remember the London suburbs in what I like
to think was their prime. I was able to run down the road
in one direction, board a tram or bus for twopence which
would take me to the Old Vic or across the river to the city
which was the heart and nerve centre of the greatest
empire the world had ever known. In the other direction

the road would lead within minutes to where I could walk knee-deep in bluebells or lie and dream my dreams in buttercups and sorrel, larks above and silence all around.

New plans were made for me as soon as my father came back from the war. I knew exactly what I wanted to do so there were no time-wasting discussions exploring possibilities. I was determined to take the quickest route to a London office, preferably to work for some sort of music or book publishing organisation. I had already had several verses accepted by local newspapers and had made enquiries about the costs of taking a secretarial course at one of the commercial colleges that were springing up to meet the demand, so I had a clear cut plan ready to lay before my father when at last he was demobbed.

Things had changed for women. There was a general urge to get into an office. During the war they had been compelled to come out of their domestic shells and serve in shops, factories and offices. The doors of City offices were opened at last. There was a great enthusiasm amongst my friends to become expert in Pitman's Shorthand. Eventually I was enrolled at Cusack's College for a three year course which comprised a training in shorthand, typing, book-keeping and commercial French. I forget what the fees amounted to but I do remember they were payable in advance which was rather a bad bargain from my father's point of view because I raced through the three year course in a year and was all set to launch myself on the world before I was sixteen. I enjoyed every moment of that year. Cusack's was a Georgian house with a lovely walled garden of drunken-looking old pear trees leaning in all directions. Sitting between two boughs in one of those pear trees I used to eat my lunch-time sandwiches and curl up amongst the leaves with a book, usually of poetry. It was all tremendously exciting. There seemed to be no present, only the future, and the confidence that bubbled within us like an underground spring ready to gush out of the earth and spread itself in the sunlight.

6
IN AT THE DEEP END

*M*ANY SERVICEMEN came back from the 14-18 war feeling embittered and frustrated. They had given up a great part of their lives and their homes in defence of their freedom of their country. Life would never restore those lost years and it must have been difficult for them to settle down into the old ways. Their experiences had left them with a deep sense of unrest. Many emigrated to parts of the empire, to South Africa, Canada, Australia, New Zealand and Rhodesia, driven by a desire to send down roots in new soil, still British, therefore still home. But men like my father whose early training had given him a strong sense of responsibility found it hard to tear up his roots again and face the unknown so he settled for resuming the old way of life in the office slot, though I do remember there was a temporary upheaval when his uncle invited him to go to New Zealand where he had established a thriving firm for the marketing of his own inventions. His fire alarm was a great success and he had won the contract for the equipping of the Queen Mary with his fire prevention installation. He had been a major with the Expeditionary forces in Egypt and had given his house in Cairo to be used as a convalescent home for invalid soldiers. I suppose this was why he was awarded an O.B.E. I am glad now that my father abandoned that New Zealand dream. How strange it is to look back and see what hinged upon our decisions.

I am a little hazy about the day to day details of this period caught up as I was in so many streams of thought, but I think this must have been the time at which I started out on a serious search for what I called "reality". Having reached the age of fourteen and coming to the end of attendance at Sunday School I was approached by the pastor about my becoming a member of the Baptist Church. This would entail a rigid adherence to Baptist principles and a ceremony of total immersion. I discussed it with my parents who were nominally Church of England telling them that I wanted to seek for myself before commitment. I felt there was a great secret to be discovered and that being tied to a particular denomination would put oil on my wings, hampering flights of discovery. "Very well," my father said, "If that's what you feel go on seeking until you find something worth finding." He was always ready to encourage us, never saying anything to dampen the ardour of youth, a far-seeing man with a deep, intuitive faith. Freedom of the mind he considered to be the birthright of every creature, freedom to explore wherever the spirit led. So I set out on my journey of discovery through Methodism, Sufism, Buddhism, Zoroastrianism and various other isms. How lucky I was to have that mine of information on my doorstep, the public library.

Many of my friends were being confirmed at this age. I was to arrive at that point twenty-five years later having made a pilgrimage to Canterbury by a circuitous route, learning on the way.

I was now writing poems for various magazines. What scope there was in those days when most of the numerous magazines published verses sandwiched between stories! It was a good gap-filling device for the editor as well as an opening for the would-be writer. *The Novel*, *The Strand Magazine*, *The Windsor*, *The Yellow*, *The Royal*, *Nash's*, *Good Housekeeping*, *Home Chat*, *Home Notes* and many more provided a ready market for verse. Now there is no such encouragement for the aspiring poet and all too often they fall into the trap of the publisher who invites these innocents to submit material for publication to be paid for by the writers, assuring them of a good return on their money when and if the book began to sell. The truth is that in most cases the writer is the loser for such publishers rarely possess the necessary organisation for promoting the sale of a book.

The craze for *vers libre* opened the gates of the literary world to poets with a new approach. In spite of the aura of aestheticism in which the modernists of the twenties circulated in the drawing rooms of Bloomsbury and Chelsea, they were really rebels and cowboys, straining in the straitjacket of tradition, non-conformist, cynical, iconoclastic. Perhaps it was an inevitable reaction against Kiplingism, and against everyone and everything that smacked of the jingoistic patriot. They did not want to take a long look at the facts of recent history. They had had enough of realism. Blood and bone, they had been ground in the mills of history, flung into the giant mincing-machine of the great war and physically as well as mentally they were a lost generation.

Now several wars later, we have turned from what they offered us and once more we feed upon the giants, Tennyson, Keats, Shelley, Kipling, Wordsworth, Milton, Coleridge, wanting to remind ourselves of the great national literary inheritance that we Anglo-Saxons possess. We find in this library of poets a rich compensation for our lost greatness in other fields. Here in the world of the poets we walk amongst the peers of paradise.

The true poet must have a natural ear for music even though incapable of playing an instrument. Anarchy has no place in the workshop of poetry making. Certain rules must be obeyed and wild thoughts tamed under the discipline of what is aesthetically acceptable. The gift of the know-how can never be taught or acquired. Either you were born with this gift or not. A poem should write itself with the minimum of intellectual or artistic midwifery on the part of its creator.

When I am asked to give an opinion on a poem in which I can find little merit, I feel it is kinder in the long run not to say anything that would raise false hopes doomed to disappointment, but I always encourage people to go on writing even if only for their own satisfaction. It is never a waste of time to commit thoughts to paper. It is better to have unsaleable thoughts than no thoughts at all. Time will tell whether or not a thought was worth recording.

I commenced writing magazine verse when I commenced my secretarial training at Cusack's and my first poem to be accepted was published in Nash's magazine for which I received payment of one guinea, which was considered handsome. For the next, in *The Novel*, I received seven shillings and sixpence which was about the average fee.

Events seemingly insignificant in themselves can have dramatic and far reaching consequences. A chance meeting can lead to something that will decide the shape and direction of the future, and it often happens, or so it has worked out in my own experience, that such a happening always brings another in its wake, sometimes immediately. You go for months or years when nothing of significance stirs the uneventful days, but you turn a corner and find you are caught up in the stream of destiny. Before you can get your breath something else comes along, the same sort of thing. Swedenborg wrote of the stream of providence and Emerson of "the current that knows its way". I suppose the current and the stream spring from the same source. It is idle to speculate as to how things happen and why. They happen because they have to happen.

My first experience of being pitchforked into two different situations at the same time came about the day after I had left school and two days before I was to start on my first job. One set of circumstances was to lead me ultimately to a romantic adventure on the island of Anglesey. It was also to lead me to the realisation of my ambition to be a writer. It was as if the details of my personal and my working life were arranged on that Saturday afternoon in February, when I was still only fifteen.

It was an exciting weekend apart from what was to happen, for I had made my escape from Cusack's and was to start work in the office of a firm of Patent Agents in Chancery Lane on the following Monday.

All that Saturday I had felt excited and I put it down to the fact of being at one of the turning-points in life, school days behind and a new kind of life in store. I little knew how near I stood to that new life when I walked out of the white gates of Cusack's for the last time on that Friday.

This is what happened. I had always loved February twilights, especially in towns when the light deepens to blue and there is the feeling that everything is waiting for a signal. February is the only month of the year when you can hold time on a rein. Once the flags of spring can be seen fluttering in the air and green tips come thrusting through the earth the joy of anticipation has all but spent itself.

It was about five o'clock in the afternoon. I was feeling a little guilty at not having offered to help with the tea things, but it was a special day for me and I felt entitled to a little rope.

I decided to work off my excitement on the piano so I went into the front room to play some of the popular tunes of the day: *The Naughty Waltz, Destiny, Pasadena, Coal Black Mammy, Missouri, Nights of Gladness.* Suddenly there was a knock at the door and I rushed to open it. There stood a young man, a stranger. I had never seen him before and would never see him again after that night. I do not think I ever knew his name, but he was to be the link in the chain that led me to the real beginning of my life.

"Good evening," he said, "I apologise for this intrusion but would it be possible for me to speak to whoever it was who was playing the piano." "Oh yes," I responded. "That was me. Why?" He hesitated then went on to explain that he played the piano every Saturday with a small dance band at the Manor Mount Club in Forest Hill. He had had the opportunity of playing in the West End that night and it was a chance which he did not want to miss, but he had been unable to find anyone free to take his place at Manor Mount. His situation was desperate. He could not let the band down, nor could he break his promise to the other people. At this point I asked him to come in. The poor young man seemed distraught. "I suppose you couldn't take on the Manor Mount thing?" he asked suddenly. "All the things you were playing would be fine, there's a saxophone, violin and drums and I'd give you two guineas."

Two guineas, I thought. That's nearly twice what I'm going to get for a whole week's work next week. It was not so much the reward that dazzled me as the excitement of this unexpected opening of a door into my dream world. Anything could come of it. Everything did come from the opening of that door.

"Just a minute," I said, asking him to sit down and wait while I asked my father's permission to go. I ran down the garden path where Dad was pruning roses. "Something wonderful," I said. "May I play with a dance band to-night at the Manor Mount Club at Forest Hill? It's a professional engagement," I said, "and they'll pay me two guineas." Dad caught my mood. Having been trapped himself into a humdrum routine, he was not going to deny his children freedom to try their wings. "It's your life. You know what you want to do and I shall not be the one to stop you, but run down to Ouida's place and ask her to go with you. I'll take you both and I'll call for you at midnight."

I was out of the door like a shot trying not to remember

that Ouida's father was what was known as strict. Fortunately our fathers were friends having once for a year or so shared a house which was divided into two flats. We, Ouida and I, must have been about three at the time. I was relieved when Ouida opened the door and I was able to pour out my story. She almost exploded with excitement at the turn of events in what she had thought was going to be the usual evening programme of Ludo, rummy and cocoa.

"But what about your father?" I asked. "What will he say?" "I shan't tell him," she said, "until I come back. I shall go in my dancing shoes and hide the others behind a bush in the front garden." This sounded rather risky but there was no holding her, so I accepted the situation and we discussed what we would wear, deciding on our white crêpe-de-chine party dresses trimmed with swansdown, our black velvet court shoes fastened by black velvet lacings criss-crossed over our ankles; coral beads and silver bangles. We both had naturally curly hair so we never had any worries on that score. Ouida's hair was coal black, mine was golden. We were both very confident when we set out that night. Ouida met Dad and me at the tram stop. We got out of the tram at Forest Hill Station and walked up the steep incline. Neither of us had ever been in a club before, so we felt we were being very sophisticated. Dad came in with us and introduced himself to the manager saying he would return at midnight.

I was introduced to the members of the band and we made out a list of the numbers to be played. Every now and then I would look up and see Ouida whirling past. It was like some strange dream. Who would have thought that this momentous Saturday would end like this? But a greater surprise was in store.

During the interval Ouida disappeared into the refreshment room with one of her partners and the manager came up to me and said there was a member of the club who was anxious to meet me. His name was Frederick

Drummond, composer of many well known songs. He had just published his latest song *Rosebud*. We were introduced and at once there was an affinity between us. He seemed quite old to me then but actually he would have been no more than thirty-six or seven. He looked the part, with rather longer hair than was customary at that time. His hands were slender and pale. He looked and was artistic, a character, an extraordinary man. I had never seen anyone like him before.

He started at once to tell me about Menai Bridge, the Anglesey village in North Wales where he and his wife Ethelwyn spent the summer months. "You must come and stay with us," he said. "This summer."

I was nervously fingering the poem in my pocket, wondering. Dare I show it? I always carried a selection just in case I ever met anyone who would be grist to my mill. Now it had happened. The impossible had somehow become fact from which endless possibilities opened out.

"Who taught you to play the piano?" he asked. "Nobody," I said, and then on impulse added, "I write song lyrics too."

"Oh do you," said Mr Drummond. "You must let me see something you have written one day," to which I replied, "I can do that now," and out came *To sing awhile*, from the pocket of my dress. I thought it was more casual to take a poem out of a pocket, than to fumble for it in a handbag. As my dresses were made at home or the dressmakers along the road it was an easy matter to arrange to have an inconspicuous pocket in every outer garment. I watched his face as he read the lyric. He then looked up and said, "I could use this one. Come along to my house next Wednesday evening." He gave me his card and shook hands. The boys came back and we started the second half with a Paul Jones. My mind was in a turmoil. There came an awful moment when I thought I was going to be sick but it passed.

Ouida was beginning to look a little less exuberant. I

Myself as a three year
old

Family group taken during the first world
war. My father was absent in Alexandria.
L to r: my brother, mother, myself and sister
Connie.

My father at the outbreak of the first world war.

My maternal
grandfather and step-
grandmother,
Emma.

Aunt Gracie, 'the
serious one'.

Connie, my sister, aged about
six and myself, aged between
two and three.

Aunt Ethel, my
godmother, 'the smiling
one'.

Aunt Florence, on duty as a
postwoman in the first world war.
Still alive in 1981.

felt that with the approach of the midnight hour she was becoming more and more anxious, fearing the wrath to come. Poor Ouida, having a father of whom she was afraid. I was lucky to have parents who were essentially kind and who, I felt, were on my side.

For poor Ouida, with her black curls and her red lips and coral beads, chilling shadows of things to come were cast across that lighted room. The price of this evening's innocent pleasure had to be paid for and an angry parent placated. Poor Ouida, for me that evening had changed my world, but it was to lead to something even more wonderful than could be imagined there and then.

Dad was waiting in the hall for us. We boarded the tram and alighted a few steps from Ouida's house, noting the light in the hall. There was nothing we could do to help so we hurried home while I chattered about the unbelievable turn things had taken and the shimmering vistas which had suddenly opened up on my horizon.

On the Monday I set off on the 8.10 train, crazy with excitement at the thought of my first day in a London office, earning my living and becoming an independent entity.

Office hours were from nine to six and nine to one on Saturdays. I was allowed an hour for lunch, but during that hour I had to go to the bank in Southampton Street, to pay in cheques and to bring back any petty cash needed for day-to-day expenses. On Fridays there was a large sum to be brought back, or it seemed large in those days; for the salaries of the draughtsmen in the drawing office, my own salary of twenty-five shillings a week, ten shillings weekly for the office boy plus the cash required by Mr Garrett, the boss, and his wife and sister, Miss Garrett who ran a separate business from a corner of our tiny office, something to do with wholesale stationery.

Shall I ever forget that first hurried walk from Black-friars station to the Jessell Chambers in Chancery Lane?

IN AT THE DEEP END

There were wings on my feet as I sped across New Bridge street and along that magical strip of history between Thames and Fleet Street where one walks with the ghosts of monks and merchants. The alleyways and narrow streets leading off St. Thomas Street up to Pump Court and King's Bench Walk are saturated with the intoxicating wine of the real London. At Temple Bar I walked under the arch which marks one of the main boundaries of the city. Every time a reigning sovereign wishes to pass this rubicon the royal carriage must be halted and the lord mayor of London gives permission for the king or queen to enter the city before proceeding along Fleet Street and up Ludgate Hill to St. Paul's Cathedral.

We led a busy life in that Patent Agency, but I enjoyed every moment of it. I took dictation from the boss and typed piles of letters during the day. Mrs Garrett taught me how to type the wax sheets which were run out on the Gestetner machine.

Amongst the many jobs I had to do in Chancery Lane the typing of specifications required for the taking out of a patent on an invention were the most interesting, copied from what were invariably manuscripts written in ink. The name Constantinescu comes to mind, very technical and not always easy to decipher, but the wax typescript and close checking with Mrs Garrett added considerably to my vocabulary, not additions which would be of much use so far as some writing went, but there was a certain stark beauty in these technical terms which I found fascinating even though ignorant of their meanings.

Deeper and deeper I fell in love with London. My father had instilled the history and romance of London into me when a child. We used to go up to the city on Sunday mornings when the streets were quiet, except for the clamour of church bells, but here now was another London, between the city and the west end which lay beyond Trafalgar Square. Here was new country to explore, the territory which took in Holborn, Bloomsbury, St. Giles, St. Martin's Lane, the Strand, the Embankment Gardens, Kingsway and Covent Garden when it was still a busy flower, vegetable and fruit market. London, my London. Proud I am to have walked her streets freeborn in the time of her greatness; London, my village, my backyard which covers buried treasure and secrets not yet discovered. It is no wonder that working in London was not only a privilege but a pleasure so intense for me that it has verged upon ecstasy.

I managed to pack a lot into those lunch hours. First I would go into the Lyons tea shop in Chancery Lane and have lunch which consisted of what was described on the menu as a bean lentil cutlet, price twopence halfpenny, and a glass of hot milk for two pence. This was my daily fare for the week and very enjoyable it was. I have never considered food to be of great importance as the buying of it and the cooking of it takes up more time than it is worth, but it must be remembered that food in the twenties was unadulterated, therefore nourishing. That was before people had become vitamin conscious and faddy on the subject of health and weight, before packaged food had become big business. Sheep, horses and cattle seem to develop great strength from a basic diet of grass so perhaps human beings do not really need the vast quantities of meat which they appear to consume. After lunch I would rush round to the bank, then still carrying the paying-in book plus the cash on Fridays, would run at speed down the Lane, into the Strand and up Fleet Street weaving my way through the dense crowds; then over Ludgate Circus past The King Lud and up the hill to the steps of St. Paul's. I had a ritual to perform here. It was rarely that I omitted to keep my daily tryst before Holman Hunt's famous picture, *The Light of the World*, a copy made of the original by the artist himself.

There was a magnetic fascination about this picture for which I could spare only five minutes a day, but it had a tranquillising effect upon my grasshopper mind and there was something about it that fed the underground streams of awareness, enabling me to go back to the turmoil of the physical world in a state of inner quietude, though running through those lunchtime crowds in what must have been the busiest corner of the kingdom.

One afternoon in the autumn of that fateful year Mr. Garrett came out of the inner office to tell me that I was wanted on the telephone, adding that it was not usual for a member of the staff to receive calls, but that he would allow me to take this one this time.

It was Frederick Drummond telling me that he had set to music my lyric *To Sing Awhile* and it had been accepted that morning by Keith Prowse for publication the following spring. I would be receiving a cheque for three guineas for being an outright sale which meant that no royalties would be payable. It is needless to relate how I hurried home that night with my news. The train as usual was crammed with commuters but we didn't call them that in those days; they were merely people going to and from their work.

That night, arriving at the barrier at the last moment I was able to fling myself into the guard's van which was always packed with passengers like vertical sardines in a tin. Physical discomfort was of no consequence. I had not heard of Thomas Browne's *Urn Burial* then, but when I did come to know it, a sentence sprang out of the printed page to grip my imagination forever. It puts into a nutshell the feelings of the young, hungry for life, caring not what came so long as they could seize Time by the forelock and dance on regardless. "Ready to be anything in the ecstasy of being ever."

7
POLITICAL ANIMAL

$\mathcal{I}$ SUPPOSE THAT the discovery of a political animal
growling underneath the strata of one's psychological make-up is part of the growing up process. When
there is a public poll on a particular issue I always feel
sorry for the "don't knows". A blind man lost in a fog is
lost indeed.

In the years that followed the end of the first world war
the young were active idealists, passive pacifists and violent iconoclasts. It was a natural reaction against war and
the economic blizzards that came after. The hungry men
of Jarrow were to march to London when the League of
Nations was lifting its futile banner and the bright young
things were doing the Charleston, playing yo-yo and hop-
ping around on pogo sticks, but it was an exhilarating
point at which to be launching out on the deep.

Our spare time was fully taken up with political meetings, lectures, rallies and dances on Saturday evenings at
the local tennis club. I pull the strings behind the puppets
of memory and see Ramsay MacDonald at the Albert Hall
during the campaign which carried him to No. 10, as the
first Labour Prime Minister with Jenny Lee on the same
platform, youthful and vigorous in kilt and red jumper,
Lloyd George at an open air meeting in the playground of
a school in Bromley and George Lansbury at Speakers'
Corner, Hyde Park. We had lost faith in the old names
and were looking to politicians like Philip Snowden,

45

Clynes, Herbert Morrison, Margaret Bondfield, Susan Lawrence and Sir Stafford Cripps to give us a new lead.

Turning again to my Chancery Lane days, I see myself saying goodbye to Mr and Mrs Garrett on a Saturday morning, a year after my first arrival. I think they regarded anything to do with the music world as suspect and gave me a kindly warning of the many pitfalls that lay in the path of the unwary. It was nice of them to be concerned over my moral welfare, but I assured them that I was not interested in "that sort of thing", wanting only to become a songwriter. We shook hands and on the following Monday I went to Poland Street.

I now had two ballads published by Keith Prowse and had recently met Bobby Sanders, the manager of their professional department. We met at Olympia, where José Lennard and Santos Casani, the famous demonstrators of ballroom dancing, were judging a competition to the tune of *Cheerio* to which I had written words and which had been published that week, my first venture into the world of popular music. Bobby had asked me if I would like to join the Keith Prowse staff; it was an interesting proposition as I felt I needed a change.

There were five of us in the Pro. Department, Bobby, Jock, Tommie Best and Georgina Baker. Bobby was the manager; he coped with most of the singers and artistes who came in for new material. He sang the numbers over to them and Tommie Best or I would accompany him on the piano. He also dictated numerous letters to Georgina and me. Tommie was the orchestral arranger and a brilliant pianist. When he was rushed he would sometimes give me a musical manuscript to copy which I enjoyed doing. I never discovered exactly what Jock was supposed to do but he flitted in and out and was very amusing. Three evenings a week I would go to some music hall or revue on the lookout for a spot in which one of our numbers might be placed. Bobby, a black-haired boy from

Glasgow had had his right arm shattered on the western front, a tragic fate for anyone, but to him who was a trained violinist it must have been a bitter moment when the surgeon told him his arm had been amputated. But always resourceful and a fighter, he had taken singing lessons. Impish and irrepressibly full of life in spite of disabilities, he was independent, needing help only with one thing, the tying of his shoe laces.

Who but Bobby would have had the audacity to submit an expense account which included an item of one shilling and sixpence for a hair cut? He was duly summoned to the office of the general manager, a Mr Van Lear, a dapper little Dutchman and something of a tyrant.

"Vot is zis?" he demanded. "Does you 'ave your 'air cut in the firm's time?" "Certainly, it grows in the firm's time," came the logical reply.

"Zat is not allowed," said Mr. Van Lear drawing his pencil through the item on the expense sheet.

What a happy lot we were in that dingy little office! Hilarity was in the air. Everything seemed to have a comical side. We were always getting a laugh out of something or other.

One day Bobby said to me, "I dare you to go down and ask old Van for a rise." "Right," said I, springing to my feet, "I go with the speed of the arrow from the bow." But I had lost a little of my confidence by the time I found myself being ushered into the thickly carpeted room where little Mr V. sat bolt upright in his chair fixing me with two beady black eyes.

"Vot do you vont?" he asked.

"Well," I said, "I was wondering if I could have my salary raised to thirty shillings a week."

"Vy?" asked Mr V. in icy tones. This threw me off balance. I had expected a plain no or yes, not a question. Frantically but in vain I searched my mind for some legitimate reason for my request. After all, I wasn't starving, homeless or desperate.

"Well," I said lamely, "I make myself generally useful in the Pro. Department."

There was a chilling silence.

"Zat" said Mr V. "is vot you is 'ere for."

"Of course," I agreed, wishing I had a more ready tongue as I crept back to the second floor with my ego somewhat deflated. They were waiting for me all agog, but when I told them what Mr V had said it provided them with a joke that lasted well into the next week. Every time Bobby dictated a letter he would say "And look sharp. There are fifty more to do before the post goes. Zat is vot you is 'ere for."

Thomas Hewitt, the music master for several schools in north London, used to come in regularly, probably it made a vivid break from the tedium of teaching. Was it chance? Here again was something that triggered off a train of circumstances which were to affect the whole course of life for someone I had not yet met. Thomas Hewitt was a composer and had recently set one of my lyrics to music, *Out Where The Big Ships Go*, a meaty item for basses and baritones. Keith Prowse had accepted it and it was already on the stocks. Just before publication date he came in one day with an invitation from his wife for the following weekend, which I accepted.

Over the teacups Mrs Hewitt mentioned that an old friend of theirs might be joining them, Stephen Southwold, a teacher who wrote books and occasional articles for the papers under the name of Neil Bell. "But he's very unpredictable," said Mrs Hewitt. "He comes and goes in a very unconventional manner; a bit of a Bolshie too."

About six o'clock Stephen Southwold appeared, announcing that he would be staying until Monday morning. Conversation had been easy and pleasant up till then, but with the advent of Stephen it became provocative and abrasive. He seemed to be anti-everything, but his harsh views were tempered by a puckish wit which enlivened every subject on which he embarked. He had been through the war and hated every minute of it. He said he regretted not having declared himself a conscientious objector to sit it out behind bars, but as I pointed out, this course would not have been open to him as he was an avowed atheist, or said he was, but the glint in his mischievous grey eyes left one in doubt as to what he really did believe.

He was short in stature, but his was an interesting face, the broad brow furrowed by intense cerebral activity, the marks of which had scored the flesh with deep lines. He would have been about thirty-seven, twenty years my senior, but I felt the fascination of his maturity. I had never felt attracted towards young men. They bored me. I remember the strong feeling that came to me then that if I ever married it would be someone of his age.

The cross-fire continued over the poached eggs at breakfast the following morning. On being asked what I had ever done to bring the brotherhood of man nearer to reality I launched out on a biography of John Wilmot who had been a near neighbour at the time when he was working as a clerk for the Westminster bank and for whom I had worked, voluntarily for a month to help in his campaign to win East Fulham for Labour. He was successful and transferred to the Russian bank of Arcos. I was proud of the small part I had played in his achievement, but somewhat disillusioned when a few years later he became Minister of Supply ending up with a directorship in a big firm, a peerage and an estate in Norfolk. Well, well. So much for all the froth and fury of those anti-capitalist speeches.

Stephen vanished after breakfast and did not return for lunch, but his hostess was unconcerned, and I dismissed him from my thoughts. But I had not seen the last of him. I arrived home from the office on the following day and my mother handed me a letter which had come with the morning post. It was from Stephen. "If you could find it in your sweet young heart to dine with an ancient, meet me next Saturday evening at the Florence Restaurant in Rupert Street at 6.30 and after eating we'll go to a low-brow show of some kind. Roget's *Thesaurus*, Brewer's *Dictionary of Facts and Fables* and Fowler's are in the post, three necessary tools of your trade which I gathered you did not possess."

That first evening with Stephen was a landmark. I had borrowed Connie's blue evening dress. The Florence was just one of many delightful little London restaurants on the edge of Soho where in those days you could dine for a modest sum in a quiet room. Stephen was an accomplished conversationalist, but he was no pedant. There was nothing precious, arty craft or affected about his well turned sentences. He romped verbally into all the corners of life, leaving the listener breathless. It was all harmonious so long as we avoided the subject of religion. His cynical humanism left me unmoved, more convinced than ever that I was right and he was wrong. That was to be the first of many such evenings at the Florence. Several times during the year he invited me to literary dinners at the writers' clubs to which he belonged. I remember well a dinner at the Pen Club given by Mrs Dawson Scott and at which H. G. Wells was the guest of honour. I was introduced to the great man which was thrilling because I was, at that time, heavily under the spell of *Ann Veronica*.

When Stephen wrote his autobiography nearly thirty years later, *My Writing Life*, published by Collins, he mentioned this particular evening and referred to me as being the most fortunate being in the assembly of the famous because I was the youngest. I wore my youth carelessly and casually like a brilliant cloak blowing in the wind. Later in life when we have become aware of the troubles of other people the cloak grows heavy and drags along the pavement. We are only beautiful when we are young because we are self-engrossed, egotistical, therefore lit from within and single-minded in pursuit of our own special star.

POLITICAL ANIMAL

The following summer was the first time it had been possible to accept Frederick Drummond's invitation to go to Menai Bridge. Billy, the faithful boyfriend I had had since my school days was spending this holiday with me. We were good friends and it was nice to have him as a dancing and skating partner, looking after my bike, adjusting brakes and mending punctures. Occasionally we would go to the cinema or a dance or a party together and he always came to my home for Sunday night suppers, usually after a Sunday Night Concert at the New Cross Empire or the Lewisham Hippodrome. The Sunday suppers were an institution. Connie's boyfriend Jo, whom she married eventually, was also a regular and lively member of the company. He could play the violin like an angel and talk brilliantly. All subjects were grist to our mill ranging through religion, philosophy, music, marriage and politics. How arrogant we were, voicing our opinions, all talking at once. My poor father could not get a word in edgeways, and when he was given the opportunity of telling one of his meandering stories about how he found a dead German in a ditch outside Arras, my mother would always interrupt him just as he was warming to the subject and say, "Don't be too ponderous; the time's getting on."

So off I set with Billy for a week in Anglesey. I was staying with the Drummonds and lodgings had been found for Billy in the village. He was a sensitive, gentle boy. He worked at the head office of a bank in the City and was usually immersed in exams. He also wrote poems and would slip his effusions through my letter box at all times of the day or night. As we wandered the fuchsia lined lanes of Anglesey vaguely in love but not wanting to admit it we little dreamed that the following year on that very island something was going to happen which would nip his hopes in the bud, and my destiny was going to come at me like a juggernaut out of control on a steep hill. Nothing could have stopped it.

51

8
A SONG UP MY SLEEVE

F CANNOT REMEMBER A TIME when I was not writing
something or other, song or poem, but it was, I think,
on my fifteenth birthday that this pleasurable form of
self-indulgence resolved itself into the intention to live by
my pen for the rest of my life. I did not then know how it was
all going to happen, but my meeting with Frederick
Drummond opened up a glimpse of what was to become
an unfolding pattern of circumstances leading in a certain
direction. First I had to equip myself to ensure that my
star would never lead me into a situation in which I would
find myself without a song up my sleeve or a poem in my
pocket, like a shopkeeper who has nothing in the window,
on the shelves or in the stockroom. You must be prepared
to work at life if you want it to work for you, doing the
spadework regardless of success or failure, even if you
have enough rejection slips to paper the walls of a room.
But the writing itself must be effortless. Book, song or
poem must write itself.

I have found that most composers prefer to have a
ready-made lyric on which to hang a melody, and the lyric
writer usually likes to work in that way, but I used to like
writing words to a ready-made tune; it is more of a
challenge because you have to wrestle with your words
licking them into the shape of the notes, making them
dance to the piper who has called the tune. When the last

line has fallen felicitously into place you experience the satisfaction of feeling that you have fitted the right keys into the right locks. I felt this particularly when writing the words for *The Haunted Ballroom*, *The Dream of Olwen* and *Jealousy*, which I wrote to order when called to the 'phone late one night.

My mother called upstairs to say that I was wanted on the telephone. It was Lawrence Wright saying, "I'm just back from Paris with the British rights of a marvellous tango by Jacob Gade. It's published as an orchestral over there but it will make a wonderful song and I want you to do the lyric. We shall have to keep their title *Jalousie* or *Jealousy*. Have you pencil and manuscript paper?" Of course, always at the ready; you never knew what might turn up. "Good," said the boss. "Now I'll put on the record so you can get the hang of the tune. Then I'll play the top line and you can take down the notation. Here we go." As I listened to the record the song seemed to write itself, and by the time Lawrie had played the melody over with one finger, the whole thing was as good as done. "I'll ring you again in half an hour," he said, so I rushed to the piano and sat there in my nightgown. Despite the iciness of the room I wrote fast. I was ready for the ring when it came, sitting in the unheated passage by the front door with a fiery glow of enthusiasm pounding through my veins. There is nothing so exhilarating as the knowledge that you have written a good song. The technical exercise of connecting every syllable with a crotchet, quaver, minim or semibreve, balancing every word on the right point in the rhythmic sequences is sheer joy when it all works itself out, like trying on a well-made glove and finding that it fits to perfection. It is more of a craft than an inspirational art, much more satisfying than the writing of a poem because having to conform to the structure of the tune imposes a strict discipline upon runaway words.

It took only fifteen minutes to get Jacob Gade's tango fitted out with words, and while I was sitting by the telephone waiting for the call I memorised the words and music so that I could put down the earpiece and sing into the mouthpiece with hands free for manual demonstration. Though undemonstrative by nature, you have to let your hands talk for you when the communication is telephonic and not face to face and you are bubbling over with satisfaction over something you have just written.

Lawrie, seated at the piano in his Eaton Square flat, was making approving noises when I took up the earpiece on reaching the concluding lines:

> *The heart aches I cost you!*
> *No wonder I lost you,*
> *'Twas all over my jealousy*

"Fine," said Lawrie, "come into the office tomorrow and we'll draw up a contract. Mark my words, this'll be sung all over the world." It was and still is. But it was to be another ten years or so before it was "discovered" by "Hutch" during the second world war and spirited out of the oblivion to which it had been relegated on a dusty shelf amongst the non-starters.

Jealousy was in the hands of the printers within hours of the signing of the contract. As usual I was more interested in the work than in the reward, so was quite happy to assign the sheet music and recording rights for a royalty of one twelfth of a penny. Today, fifty years after, scarcely a day passes when *Jealousy* does not have a public performance in one of the five continents of the world.

Although written at the end of the twenties *Jealousy* really belongs to the war-time hit parade. No one quite knows what triggered off its fantastic career apart from the fact that Hutch must have stumbled upon it in the archives while rummaging for something else, for the boss was up north at the time taking refuge from the London bombs in his famous Blackpool castle, sold later to Epstein, and it was Hutch's recording that lit the fuse that led to its explosive success. Almost overnight it was top of the charts, sung by the stars, and whistled by milkmen, porters, postmen and errand boys hurtling round the streets on their bicycles.

Following on the H.M.V. record made by Hutch came recordings by Gracie Fields, the Boston Promenade Orchestra, Stein's Tango Band, Richard Tauber, Vera Lynn and others. I had often wished to be associated with a successful song but when it came I wasn't really very interested. The sudden coming to life of *Jealousy* was a nine-days' wonder to me but to Lawrence Wright it came as a bombshell. It must have been the only hit song that had come to him instead of his having to go out and make it. So back he came to London unable to resist the limelight that plays around the publisher of the current winner. But, alas, his new triumph was to be short lived. Once back on the Tin Pan Alley treadmill of business and pleasure, under the nightly bombardment of Goering's Luftwaffe, poor Lawrence Wright was felled by a stroke that robbed him of speech and movement. But for his fighting spirit it would have proved fatal. It was the same spirit that had driven him on to walk from Leicester to London, writing and publishing his own songs, packing his own parcels and sleeping under the counter; with that same spirit he fought for his life in the Middlesex Hospital with all hell let loose in the sky above London.

I sometimes think it is more difficult to find such men today in a society which discourages personal ambition and stifles private enterprise under V.A.T. forms, tax demands and tangles of red tape.

But I jump ahead of myself and must go back to the end of the twenties. This was the period when I was doing four jobs a day for six days a week, working a nine to six day as secretary to the bosses behind the Talkie Publicity Company in Regent Street and from 8.00 a.m. to 9.30 a.m. typing the manuscript of Paul Trent's current novel. He was a prolific writer of light romances and had to churn out two or three a year for his publisher from whom he collected a retaining fee which he received in weekly instalments collecting it in person every Friday morning. More and more he came to rely upon me to fill in the dialogue, checking the times at which his fictitious characters were due to keep their appointments; he could never remember where he had left them or what they were supposed to be doing, sipping tea at the Savoy, cocktails at the Mayfair or dining and dancing at Ciro's or the Berkeley. But he himself was always on time in the mornings, eager to pick up the threads from where he thought he had left them on the previous day, but on resuming the following morning I would have to point out to him that Roy and Rosemary or Daphne and Claude could not be bowling smoothly down the Mall in the Daimler because we had left them sitting in the rosy glow of a lamplit table at Murray's. It was all very confusing.

Paul Trent was an elderly gentleman, or seemed to be, so I used to alter the situations, sometimes re-writing the whole chapter and he was none the wiser. This went on for several weeks and when I tentatively suggested that the monthly sum of £5 on which we had agreed for the six daily sessions from 8.00 a.m. to 9.30 a.m. was overdue he pretended not to hear, remarking that his hearing was not so good as it used to be. However, I plodded on, since I could see that he was wholly dependent on the advance royalties which he collected on Friday mornings. Actually, I had never been a natural early riser, but it was summer and I came to enjoy that early morning dash across Trafalgar Square and up Haymarket to Piccadilly Circus.

The mood of London changes with the hour and the light, and walking hurriedly along Regent Street just before 8.00 a.m. was a new and pleasant experience. He never ceased to be grateful, charming and polite, although I never did receive any remuneration for this part of the day I felt vaguely grateful to him because something useful had come out of these morning sessions; I had discovered how easily I could write that sort of thing, so regarded it as another arrow in my quiver. In addition it solved another of T.P.'s many problems. Mr Trent was not so punctual as he had been in delivering the scripts for the advertising films, and as he had told them how helpful I was being with his novels they asked me if I would be able to take on the scripts. "Certainly," I said, "I have a few here. Just in case Mr Trent should at any time be indisposed. I can write them in prose or verse, as you prefer." The six gentlemen who sat round the large mahogany table in the room next to mine were delighted. I don't know how much Mr Trent was paid in his capacity as official script writer and nothing was said regarding an addition to my thirty shillings a week but I did not expect it, being only too glad to gain the experience as it was great fun writing little stories in verse about such things as Ovaltine, furniture polish and face powder, a change from the moonlight-and-roses love songs. There was a very happy and pleasant atmosphere in the place springing from mutual respect and the desire of all to see T.P. succeed at a time of national penury.

I was the only "staff", except for Tom and Stiffy, who had charge of the van. We didn't even have an office boy. The bosses in the big room were not interested in tea drinking and neither was I. It was all very dignified and formal.

Each film ran for about ten minutes and was projected from a van which, when we had sufficient material and orders, would travel the country. A jolly fellow called Tom Barnes was in charge of the van assisted by a younger technician with a wooden leg, who had a Byronic limp and was referred to as Stiffy.

During the lunch hour I put in my daily appearance at the Wright house as I was still under contract with Lawrence Wright. That run along Shaftesbury Avenue to

Charing Cross Road was an enjoyable part of the daily routine. It was quicker to walk than take a bus; the traffic jams in those days were much worse than now as there were few one-way streets and an almost non-stop service of buses on all routes, so traffic was thickly clogged.

When the van had been equipped and they were ready to make the films an advertisement for artistes was put in *The Stage* and other professional papers, and it fell to me to give them an initial screening, in order that no time should be wasted at top level over those who were obviously unsuitable. One applicant remains in my mind and I often think of him. He introduced himself as the ugliest man in the world. It was no exaggeration.

I had been told as a child that it was ill-mannered to stare at anyone, but my eyes were glued to this Goliath who was only just able to squeeze through the door. "Don't be frightened," he said. "I'm used to being stared at; I'm billed at circuses and fairs as the world's ugliest man." It was some minutes before I could regain control of speech and thought. It was a large hard face, swarthy, pitted and scarred. He would have been well cast in the role of an ogre, but I could not think of any of our picturettes into which he could be fitted with any degree of suitability.

My fourth job of the day was at Park Crescent, Regent's Park where John Wilmot, prospective Labour M.P. for East Fulham, had the use of a room in the flat of his friend a Dr Hector Monroe which served as an office and unofficial committee room. Here I typed letters from six to eight for the "cause" voluntarily and for free. To what lengths of folly does idealism lead the young! Fifteen years or so later I was standing in the front line of the V day crowds at the edge of the pavement watching the M.P.'s walk from the House of Commons to St. Margaret's for a service of thanksgiving. They passed within touching distance. Winston Churchill led the procession, tears rolling unashamedly down his chubby cheeks and in due course along came John Wilmot, later to become Lord Wilmot, beaming to the crowds as if he personally as Minister of Supply had stage-managed the whole affair. So much for the anti-capitalist fireworks exploded at so many meetings in his less glorious days when he worked for the Russian Bank of Arcos in the city. There was a time when our gardens had been end to end. We were not friends then as he would have been about ten years my senior but I knew his mother slightly, a nice woman but a little eccentric, who used to go shopping with a cat on a lead. I followed his career with interest.

One of the advantages of being at the T.P. office in Regent Street was the convenience of having one of the beautiful Christian Science Reading Rooms almost opposite, in which I always contrived to have a few minutes of absolute peace each day. It was particularly lovely during August when hundreds of gladioli were reflected in the highly polished oak tables where the Bible and the key to the scriptures lay open ready for the reader.

The T.P. episode came to an abrupt end one morning with the sudden arrival of the bailiffs. I had not known that the firm was in trouble. At first I thought they were actors come to apply for a part in one of our films and welcomed them with the sweetest smile I could muster on a Monday morning. They must have thought I was rather stupid, not being able to grasp the full import of their presence. At twelve they went out for half an hour telling me that under no circumstances must I admit anyone in their absence. Ten minutes later Tom Barnes and Stiffy appeared in their usual cheerful morning mood, but when I told them what was afoot they beat a hasty retreat in the direction of the Euston coach station in which they garaged the van. I never saw them again.

There was an unaccountable absence of the board, and Paul Trent did not put in an appearance at any stage in the proceedings. Just before the return of the bailiffs a young woman from one of the offices on the floor above popped in, ostensibly to say good morning though we had never spoken before, but as she left she whipped up the doormat, so she evidently knew something. Then someone else from another floor stopped for a chat, but I stood with my feet planted firmly on the other mat. I had a sudden feeling of sympathy for my sister Connie slogging away in the clockwork routine of the Press Exchange in the City taking dictation from correct looking bespectacled gentlemen clad in pin-stripe trousers and black coats. Not for her the extravaganza of a life which included such people as the bailiffs, the ugliest man in the world and the young woman who flitted off with the doormat.

The following December I was tempted by a Thomas Cook advertisement for four days in Paris covering the Christmas period for the sum of five pounds inclusive of everything Newhaven – Dieppe by channel ferry and train to Paris; the idea was to take my schoolboy brother who was a born linguist and an ardent Francophile. My parents were a little alarmed at the thought of their two children wandering at Christmastime through the streets of Paris, but they never opposed anything that might broaden our experience and as muggings were then unheard of, off we went. It was a wild night crossing. I cannot remember anything about the rest of the journey but I do remember our arrival at a tall house with wrought iron gates leading into a paved courtyard. We did the usual things: we climbed the Eiffel Tower, spent an afternoon at Napoleon's tomb, sat for a while in Notre Dame, visited Fontainebleau by coach, were duly impressed by the Arc de Triomphe, browsed amongst the bookshops on the left bank and risked a stroll and a glass of wine in a café in Montparnasse, and pretended to be unperturbed when a red devil complete with horns appeared to come up through a trap door in the floor with a bang and a plume of smoke. "Take no notice," my brother said with the sophistication of his fifteen years. "They take us for tourists." How right they were!

I was determined that I should return with something very attractive in the way of a hat which I hoped would be admired by my friends and to which I should be able to say casually, "Yes, it is rather sweet, isn't it? I picked it up in Paris." I wish I could buy a similar creation today, but alas, Paris like London, no longer takes pride in well hatted women.

I cannot close this chapter without a brief description of the hat over which my long suffering brother was called into the shop to describe exactly what I wanted and to haggle over the price. I could manage a straightforward request for a definite object like a book, a croissant or a pot of face cream but the delicate niceties implicit in the description of a *chapeau* was beyond my capabilities to say nothing of the top speed negotiations involved in arriving at a price satisfactory to both parties. The hat in question was made of black felt as soft as velvet and lined with white satin which flared out from the inside like the petals of a flower uncurling around the brim. It was exquisite. What a pity the art of millinery has been stamped out by the mass-produced article and the casual fashion of not wearing a hat at all.

My sister, Connie, was married in the following June. Another relative and I were bridesmaids, clad in lilac *crêpe-de-chine* dresses and carrying dainty baskets of pale mauve sweet peas. The dresses were made by a local dressmaker. Connie wore a dress of white lace, also made locally; her fair hair shone like a gold leaf under the transparent veil. The same bells chimed for them as had chimed for our parents. Joseph Stelling, the bridegroom, lived nearby when we were children, in a large old house which was said to be haunted. You entered the rambling garden by a gate in a wall which completely hid it from the passer by. We had never really believed the stories of the hauntings, but Jo who was psychic, the seventh son of a seventh son proved that it was by various experiments, such as having his hands tied to the bedpost by his mother to prove that it was not he who was responsible for the rearrangement of the furniture which took place at night. He was a very remarkable young man and extremely good looking, versatile, sociable and amusing. He played the violin divinely though untaught, also the banjo and mandolin. It had always been assumed that he and Connie would marry though in many ways they were unsuited. Jo liked company, Connie shared my love of solitude. His chief pleasure was to take a car to pieces and reassemble it. Connie liked to sit alone reading or writing poetry. We sometimes had poems published in the same magazine. Jo loved to get into a fast car and make it move. Connie preferred to walk. Love of walking seemed to run in our family. My father once took part in a walking race from London Bridge to Tonbridge. He didn't win it, but he never ceased to tell us about it and he did finish the course. A walk was the cure for all ills, benison and balm for every trouble.

Jo made the first wireless set we ever possessed, and the recollection brings a pang of regret at the thoughtless and somewhat arrogant way in which I dismissed something that I considered to be of no interest. He had been working at it all the week obviously enjoying himself, completely absorbed. Suddenly there was a burst of music and he sprang to his feet with a whoop of delight. "There you are," he said, offering me the earphones. "I'm not interested," I said. "I'm going for a walk." Connie was upstairs tapping away on her Royal portable typewriter. Looking back I hate myself for being so unkind, but Jo was not in the least aware that his efforts had not been appreciated, so absorbed was he with his new toy which could conjure music out of the air like magic. Though I look back regretfully upon that little incident, it may be that my first reaction sprang from a deep unconscious awareness that here was something that could be misused.

Perhaps my subjective mind was wiser than it knew in its rejection of this strange thing which was going to revolutionise our lives, for I have lived to see it used for the dissemination of much that is bad, vulgar and profane, as well as good, educative and cultural.

That is a thumbnail sketch of Jo; and the following vignette reflects Connie in a way that captures the essential facets of her nature better than a wordy description of her many qualities.

A few weeks before the wedding Mother, Connie and I had spent a day choosing furniture for the Brockley flat to which she would return after the honeymoon in Devon. It was a tall, old-fashioned house divided into four flats which consisted of a spacious kitchen, three large bedrooms, a box room and a lounge. We chose a settee and two armchairs, a dining table and four matching chairs. They could afford only what was basic at this stage. Jo was the manager of a big coach depot at King's Cross and his entire life was wrapped up in this. He had said that he had no idea about furnishings so there was no need to consult him over domestic matters. Mother and I returned home feeling more than satisfied with what had been purchased.

On their return from Devon Connie telephoned asking mother and me to have lunch with her during the following week, so we set forth bearing flowers and wine feeling that this was going to be something in the way of a celebration.

Connie opened the front door in response to our ring and showed us into the lounge which to our surprise was empty except for a table. "But what has happened?" I said. "Didn't they send the things?" "Yes," said Con, "They did, but I sent it all back the next day." I looked round the room for something on which we could sit and recover from the shock. "I'm quite content with this as it is," said Connie. "You see I realised we had made a mistake in buying all that cheap modern stuff. The man at the shop gave me only half what we had paid him for it, but on Monday I went up to town, and spent the morning at Hamptons, resolved to have one good thing rather than a room full of inferior rubbish. I chose this table, not antique, but about fifty years old. Is it not lovely?"

I looked at the honey-coloured oak of the gate-legged table and had to acknowledge that it looked complete in itself, as if wholly satisfied with being what it was and where it was. "And what did Jo say when he came home and found that the furniture had gone?" asked mother. "Nothing," said Con, "He didn't even notice that it had gone. He was too engrossed in telling one of his long stories."

"Well," said mother. "What will his mother say when she sees this room?"

"I don't care," said Con, "I love it. I shall look for a part-time typing job and save up for a divan."

"A divan!" we exclaimed disapprovingly.

"Why not?"

"The word suggests something vaguely immoral," said I. Then we both saw the funny side of it and sat on the floor laughing till we wept. I found mother in the next room sitting on the bed still holding the flowers and a pot of jam, and I realised that I was still clutching the half bottle of Sauterne, over which we felt we had been wildly extravagant.

Gradually in the course of time the room grew, almost secretly. The divan made an unspectacular entrance. It seemed to have stolen in when no one was looking. One day it was not there and another day it was, looking as if it had stood there under the soft golden glow of the lamp on the table for a hundred years or so. It had been a second hand bargain and Connie had had a loose cover made for it in yellow linen. A few weeks later a bookcase slipped in and found its right place between the window and the door. That is the right way to furnish a room. I have always been in too much of a hurry over everything. Let a room furnish itself slowly without fuss. Let the right pieces find their way to where they belong. Connie knew about these things by instinct. Yes, she knew. She was very special, very gentle, yet you had the feeling that underneath there was a desperately passionate soul beating for breath under the external crust of every day living.

She was twenty-five when she married. Four years later she died, or should I say she came alive in a way that would never have been possible had she lived. At the time it seemed cruel that Jo should have lost her before he had ever really found her, but five years after that he too had gone, killed in the first big raid of Hitler's war, the raid that was the curtain-raiser on the battle of Britain, and he was where he would have wished to be, in his beloved coaching station at King's Cross.

9
FAIRY WOOD

*L*OOKING BACK I see that all my roads were leading to a place marked on the local map of Anglesey as Fairy Wood. I do not remember ever hearing a mention of it when I first visited the Menai Bridge the previous year. We were too busy admiring Telford's magnificent bridge across the Straits, exploring Snowdonia, Beaumaris and Conway. It was the first time I had had a holiday anywhere but the south coast and the beauty of north Wales left me breathless, determined to return the next year.

But before that never-to-be-forgotten year, 1926, came round I was destined to make yet another change. Bobby Sanders, who had always deserved a better job than he had with Keith Prowse, suddenly sprang a surprise on everyone with the announcement that he had taken a job with Campbell and Connelly. Jimmy Campbell and Reg Connelly were newcomers to publishing having just set up business under the very nose of Lawrence Wright, uncrowned king of Denmark Street; this they had done on the proceeds of the success of the song they had written together, *Show Me The Way To Go Home*. Bobby with ten years' experience of the business was the very man they needed.

Once in "the business" no-one ever seemed to transfer to any other, so there was a constant movement of staff coming and going between Feldman, Francis Day and

Hunter, Keith Prowse, Lawrence Wright and later, Peter Maurice and Campbell and Connelly all centred on Charing Cross Road and the Tin Pan Alley of Denmark Street with the exception of Keith Prowse.

My next memory is of working for Peter Barnard, whose real name was Pietro Bernardi, born in New York of Italian immigrants. No pen could describe Peter; no words convey any but a pallid impression of that red-haired, flamboyant, rumbustious braggart, but what a character, what a showman, and what a lovable man! Peter's sole claim to fame seemed to be in the fact that he had been the first to bring "ragtime" to England, when he arrived in 1912 with Alexander's Ragtime Band. If that started what now passes for music it is a pity he ever came at all, but if it had not been Peter somebody else would have landed upon these shores with the new syncopated rhythms which had beat their way up from the basements of Haarlem bringing a new sound from the brash new world, a sound as old as Africa.

Peter was larger than life, a strong, self-willed, self-made singer of this new type of song. A puritan in his way, a non-drinker and a non-smoker, dedicated entirely to the propagation of the gospel of self-idolatry, but magnanimous and big-hearted. He invented his own legend living it out to the last superlative. But I saw only the child in Peter, a little boy standing on a table beating loudly on a drum to call attention to himself. I knew nothing of Peter's private life. Probably he was too busy to have one. His personality was like a bonfire that never burnt itself out. I don't think he knew what to make of me, and I certainly did not know what to make of him. When we were first introduced by Bobby, we came upon him talking to himself in a mirror, "I'm big. I'm great. I'm a topliner. I'm big, big, big." He swung round as we entered saying to Bobby, "Ah, you bring me a fairy. Tinkerbell has flown in through the window." His arms went out in a huge gesture of welcome. "You come to join our firm. Not much

doing at the moment but you wait, we're going to be big."
I looked round hopefully for signs of business but Peter
seemed to fill the whole room. "Soon there will be letters
to type. We'll take another floor. We'll end up with the
whole building."

The premises were in New Oxford Street opposite
Glave's. I was introduced to the other members of the
staff, Charlie, the orchestrator: it dawned on me later that
Charlie did outside work for which he paid Peter a small
rent for the desk. Then there was Sonny, the office boy,
who spent most of the day on the piano doing imitations of
Billy Mayerl and Carol Gibbons. A nice boy and always
ready to run an errand or do a job, but the trouble was
there was rarely anything to do or any reason to run. The
manager was Mr Raymond, a charming man, cultivated,
courteous and with a delightful sense of humour.

I deduced that Peter worked in the evenings singing to
raise the rent, at night clubs or suburban and provincial
music halls. The publishing business was a shop window,
an address, a base, a morale-booster. Peter wanted to feel
like a publisher; that was why I was there. He liked to put
up a pretence of dictating letters if a visitor came. I always
knew when things were at a low ebb because Peter and
Mr Raymond would be closeted in Peter's office and Mr
Raymond would emerge looking grave. One day Peter
came up with what he thought was a really bright idea:
that I, his secretary, must also have a secretary. Yes, that
was it. "But there's nothing for me to do as it is," I
protested, but you couldn't argue with Peter. So a girl
called Rene duly appeared and there we sat, wondering.

Sometimes Peter would go on tour in the provinces. I
would inform the music stores of his dates, giving details
of the songs he would be featuring and asking them for a
window display. These tours would mean an absence of a
month or so. While he was away there was no money for
the wages and in our dire extremity Sonny was sent to the
pawnbrokers with the clock. All this was very entertain-

ing, but it wasn't getting me anywhere and I was so sorry for Peter. I think he knew that I saw through the charade.

One morning I arrived at the office to find it full of tiny flakes of paper scattered all over the floor. There had been an invasion of mice in the night and they had consumed almost all the precious stock of notepaper. I looked at it feeling it was symbolic of the whole situation. Peter and I went for a meal that night to a Chinese restaurant and over the chop suey I told him that I felt it was time to part company. "I'll have a comeback," he said. "You'll see. I'll make it. I'm essentially big." And when you were with him you could believe it. His optimism knew no bounds. He had the future in his pocket. Such was the suction power of his spectacular personality that he had us all bobbing along in his wake making frantic attempts to remain above water, believing in the big fairy tale of the Peter Barnard fantasy.

I never was the weepy type but I shed a few tears over Peter that evening going home in the train. It was to be seventeen years before I saw him again. It was in Oswestry during the war. Strange to say I was with a friend and speaking of him, when we almost collided at a street corner. "Tinkerbell," he cried. "My fairy." When asked how he was doing he gave us a glowing account of a successful tour he had just completed in the north west. Whether it was factual or fictional I never knew, but he was bursting with big ideas for the future. I wished him luck and he disappeared into the darkness of the blacked-out street. I hoped he was staying at the Wynstanley but feared it was more likely to be some pro dig in the more dreary part of the town.

After the New Oxford Street episode had come to an end, Bobby changed firms again and went to Peter Maurice, new people just sprung up in Denmark Street who had made him a handsome offer of a job as a general manager. He thought it would be a good idea if I allowed him to arrange for me to go to Campbell and Connelly. I agreed. The finger of fate was at work again. If I had made other plans I should not have been sitting on the top floor of C & C's at the precise moment when Jay came bounding up the stairs. That was a magic moment if ever there was one.

Before starting there I wanted to have my holiday and return to Menai Bridge to which I felt strangely drawn. The puppet strings were jerking me into position. I thought I was in control of my future, making my own decisions and doing my own thing, but really I had no say in the matter. I was going where propelled.

I had a standing invitation to stay at Craig Lodge with the Drummonds, and they suggested that the invitation be extended to my parents and schoolboy brother. This suited me as I had had a difference of opinion with my boyfriend Billy at that time so it all seemed to fit in very well. Stephen was spending the school holiday month in France. My sister always took her holiday later in the year, so unexpectedly I found myself at a loose end, but that is a dangerous place to be for the unseen hand of destiny is always groping around for loose ends to work into its own designs. And it had all started eighteen months previously when Frederick Drummond stepped onto the platform of the Manor Mount Club where I was playing for the mysterious stranger who had knocked on my door earlier that evening.

The stage was set, and never was a romance staged in such a fantastic setting. You would think that some psychic device in the brain or heart would have given some warning of the approach of circumstances which were to change my whole life, present and future, in the twinkling of an eye. But no such warning reached me from outer space or inner depth as our taxi sped across the Telford Bridge which linked Menai with the mainland. Perhaps there was a signal somewhere in the universe, but I was too encased in my own fantasies to be able to pick it up. What was about to happen to me had been scheduled to happen from the beginning of the world; to me, who had always steered clear of whirlpools, content to paddle my own canoe in quiet waters, conscious of the inward joy which lay within myself making me independent of every other creature on earth, hostile towards marriage, unwilling to be bound by any form of emotional attachment. And yet it happened and it happened to me: a miracle, for the inexplicable phenomenon of love at first sight is nothing less than a miracle.

Chance, or what is so called, brings two people hitherto unknown to one another into an instant relationship, an affinity which is permanent and absolute. The moment before meeting they are strangers, but at the moment of meeting they are ready to walk together into the unknown future to share all they have. From the first encounter they know they were meant to meet.

Love at first sight cannot be explained in any terms psychological or spiritual. The chemistry which causes an electric shock of attraction to pass between two people resulting in an affinity which is as compulsive on the mental plane as it is on the physical is something so irresistible as to be beyond analysis. It is better not to attempt an explanation and to accept it as miraculous and therefore inexplicable

Happy is the soul that recognises its mate for in finding the beloved it finds its true home in the flux of circumstances, never more to be adrift in the world. Such souls are anchored and settled. Theirs is the happiness of perpetual romance. Less fortunate mortals must make do with the kind of love that ripens gradually like fruit in the sun. They, no doubt, are compensated in other ways for missing the moment that comes to those who are fated to meet, rushing towards one another like two stars on a collision course.

Undeserved, and unexpected, this wonderful thing came to me when I was standing at a window overlooking a garden which sloped to the water of the Menai Straits with the mountains of Snowdonia spread out along the skyline beyond. It was Regatta week. The yachts were coming from the various clubs along the coast from Conway to the Wirral.

The yachtsmen were making their way in groups up the steep garden at the back of the hotel. They slept aboard their boats, and converged on the Victoria after the day's racing to wash, eat and talk over the events of the day with a final gathering round the piano at night to sing sea shanties.

I was with Chrissie, the daughter of the manageress of the hotel. We were watching the white sails on the water as the boats came in to moor for the night. A rather bedraggled procession was beginning to make its way up through the garden from the pier below. I was not looking with my whole attention as half my mind was on the peaks across the water caught in the noose of the sunset light from the West, when Chrissie said, "Here come the Clytie boys. That's the name of their boat. They come every year." So saying she rushed to welcome them as it was the first day of the Regatta. I remember vaguely seeing three men approaching the outer door, an odd trio, in navy blue jerseys like working fishermen, club blazers slung over shoulders, white topped yachting hats, trousers rolled to the knees, dirty looking rubber shoes and with their faces stained reddish brown by wind, rain, sun and salt spray. I looked but only saw the one in the middle, a thick-set shortish, black haired Celt of a man probably nearing forty, but I was utterly without any curiosity as to his identity, name or age. I knew only one thing: that in that moment I had fallen in love, fathoms deep, that my life had ended and started again and on a new course, all in a flash of recognition. This stranger had stepped out of his boat into my life and I was to love him until he died thirty-nine years later.

I had no wish to meet him immediately. It was enough

to know that such a man was on the same planet, that he existed and was no dream. My instinct was to run away to be alone to savour the marvel of the incredible thing that had happened to me, so I fled to the Fairy Wood, along the narrow road between the Straits and the banks up which the little stone houses climbed to the village. Under the giant stanchions of the bridge I hurried in the gathering twilight. Fairy Wood lay off the road which went on to St. Tyslio church. The wood was a mere cluster of trees and shrubs which followed the bank by the water in a half moon shape, bounded by a stone wall with an opening at each end. The thread of a path curved at the edge where it dipped to the water with overhanging boughs deep in ferns, bracken and ivy. My heart was filled with a happiness so great that I thought it would burst against my ribs, as I knelt amongst the ferns to marvel at what had happened in less than an hour. It was quiet in the wood save for the faint splash of the phosphorescent waves breaking on the rocks below.

The tip of the coracle of a new moon swung between two mountains over on the Caernarvonshire side, silvering the peaks. Everything was magic on that magical night. I wanted the cosmic clock to stand still so that I could feel the enthralment of the moment, but the cosmic clock stops for no-one, not even for a seventeen-year-old girl who walked on stardust, her head in a cloud and her arms outstretched to the mountains.

I had promised to meet Frederick Drummond at eight having offered to play for half an hour to give him a break before supper. When I returned from Fairy Wood Frederick was playing and the room crowded, so I joined those who were seated on the floor. I was facing the piano. There was no sign of the Celt so I presumed he was still in the dining room or with the crowd in the garden holding an inquest on the day's racing.

Presently in response to loud calls for the Clytie boys they appeared and the Celt came over to Frederick whom he apparently knew. They settled for *Paddy McGinty's Goat*, a song which seemed to be a favourite with them all, so thereafter I thought of him as Paddy. A deep, rich, baritone voice came up from that bull neck.

He glanced down and our eyes met from time to time. Whether the transference of thought was mental or psychic I know not, but words were not needed. We had our own secret means of communication; the message was conveyed. After he had sung a few ballads as requested he and Frederick retired to the bar and I took over on the piano, but as soon as Frederick returned I slipped away feeling unable to bear any more for that never-to-be-forgotten night.

I ran back to Fairy Wood. I had had plenty of time to get the details of that happy interesting face as I sat there on the floor and looked up into it. The hair was black and silky, the brown eyes embedded in laughter wrinkles; the ears were small and shapely, folded neatly back against his head. He had small hands and feet and he exuded a glow of inner contentment as he moved slowly through the crowded room. Just to be in the same room with him was restful and satisfying. There was nothing nervy, hungry or tense in him. He was complete within himself, complete and mature. He had arrived at the place where life would have him be, the war years having done their best and their worst for him. There would never be any need for him to move either backward or forward. He had arrived.

The sense of unreality that had come to me that evening was reflected in the peace of the Fairy Wood by moonlight. The papery wisp of moon that had been launched above the mountains now floated white and high over the island. The straits were greenish with a frosty silvery light playing on the surface as light from the passing boats disturbed the water.

I had been so carried away by my own private adventure that I had almost forgotten that my parents and schoolboy brother were at Craig Lodge, so I bade goodnight to the magic of the wood and ran back to our lodgings where they and Mrs Drummond were seated in the front garden facing the water and the mountains. It was strange to find myself saying the conventional things, talking as if the world had not really come to an end at all. They were discussing plans for a trip to the Aber Falls on the following day. Cars had not yet come into their own and we had to order a taxi to take us to the station where we could get a train to Aber. I tried without success to concentrate on the practical details under discussion, but my thoughts were flashing crazily between the moonlit wood and the black-haired Celt who, without speaking a word, had brought down the neat little pile of my carefully planned life in a whirling confusion of unutterable joy. And in my innermost heart I knew that he knew, though we had not yet communicated verbally, only by one or two meaningful glances. We both knew all we needed to know and subconsciously we longed for an extension of the division in a vain attempt to preserve our own identities, playing for time; defending our separateness, though we both knew that the die had been cast. Forces stronger than ourselves had taken over.

The following evening there was an informal Regatta dance at the hotel. Frederick was responsible for the musical arrangements. A violinist was expected from Bangor and I would be relieving Frederick occasionally at the piano. As we were arranging the programme Paddy, the Celt, appeared for the first dance looking as if he had spent some little time on making himself presentable in white flannel trousers, white shirt and blue blazer. He came straight up to Frederick asking to be introduced to me. After the introduction Frederick played the then popular waltz, *Wonderful One*, a perfect choice. Paddy without a word took me into his arms and we began to dance, across the room and out into the future. Nothing was said but as we moved he sang very softly, his powerful though suppressed voice vibrating through his arms and hands.

FAIRY WOOD

"My Wonderful One to my heart I would hold you
Forever and ever to me."

We went round and round the room mesmerised, drugged with our dreams, stupefied by happiness. It all
seemed so right, so natural, there was nothing to be explained. Everything was understood between us. No word
was necessary. After the dance we went into the garden
away from curious eyes, and sat on the wooden seat
overlooking the Straits. Silence lay between us like something palpable warm and expressive with an eloquence
louder than language.

An orange moon came out from behind a cloud, theatri-
cal, almost obtrusive, staring at us with a candour that
was faintly disturbing. I was relieved when it hid its face
once more behind a veil of cloud. We needed no outward
demonstration of affection; it would have seemed out of
place and out of time. We did not break the stillness by
word or movement until as I rose to go back to the hotel
remembering Frederick, he said, "I knew last night when
I first saw you sitting on the floor by the piano," and I
said, "I knew two hours before that."

We walked slowly up through the garden. How lovely it
was to have a silent companion. I had always found
talking exhausting and more often than not, irrelevant
and wearisome. Everything now would be effortless; there
was no tension to be eased, no questions to be answered.
How mature he was, how mellow and controlled. How
easily my life had fitted suddenly into its slot.

10
THE FACTS OF LIFE

*T*HE BUSINESS of looking back surprises the mind with the realisation of how much can be packed into a small space of time. Years pass now, and, apart from disturbances in the outside world, nothing much seems to happen. The time of shocks and upheavals has passed and that is something for which to be thankful. If the days slip by uneventfully, praise God, for when the earth quakes and the foundations tremble then is the time of breaking or making of life.

The discovery that love at first sight does not belong only to the fantasy world of poetry and romantic fiction but is in itself one of the facts of life, is like the discovery of a new continent of consciousness. It is there, like the law of gravity, the courses of the stars in the heavens, the laws of attraction and repulsion and the existence of God; these fundamental verities are facts of life with which we all have to come to terms with at some stage or another.

The phrase "facts of life" has come to be associated with basic matters like economics and sex concerned only with the mechanics of living; both have been exploited and given an unwarranted priority in the order of things.

A new Tower of Babel was set up and the word "permissiveness" slipped out into the world with the result that sexual, industrial and moral lawlessness took over. Man who was destined to occupy a unique position in the universe by reason of the fact that he was made in "the image and likeness" of his Creator sank quickly under the post 1939–45 war lowering of moral standards which synchronised with the world wide extension of communication via the media of radio, journalism, drama and television. The churches caught that fever wanting to be "with it", transferring their allegiance from the gospel of Christianity to the gospel of sociology. This was a catastrophe because the one thing that people wanted most in the flux of those years was something to which they could cling in a crumbling world. They were betrayed by their churches, some of whose leaders were busily engaged hacking away at the doctrinal foundations of their theology, and destroying their redundant buildings.

Dr. Edward Norman, Dean of Peterhouse, Cambridge, in his brilliant Reith Lectures of 1979, gave a timely warning that we were in grave danger of being more concerned with the third world than the next world. Jesus Himself observed that we should always have the poor with us.

In setting out to tell you how Paddy and I faced the facts of life I have been guilty of a circuitous diversion, but on the basis that all is connected and every path leads back to the main road eventually. The first fact of life for us lay in the two hundred of miles of England which stretched between us spatially; the second lay in the twenty years or so difference in our ages, a fact which I dismissed as of no importance but which seemed to have troubled Paddy. Time is of no value when you are a teenager. You can squander it recklessly. That is why I suggested that we did not communicate by telephone or letter until we came back to the island for next year's Regatta. So rich was I, time-wise, that I could toss away a whole year and not miss it. Other vague difficulties haunted that face which had been so creased with the crinkling of laughter, difficulties which brought us up against the stark problem of where to live and on what. It had not occurred to me that we should ever have to descend to considerations of such mundane matters. Paddy had expended five precious years of his working life on the war, and had settled for being a bachelor for the rest of his life; our meeting had posed not a few problems.

Paddy's father, Anglesey born, had spoken no word of English until he first arrived on Merseyside at the age of ten. He soon made his way as a successful master builder. Later he became an alderman on the city council of Liverpool and was an ardent worker in that area for the establishment of the public library service. In middle life he moved to the Wirral and built a splendid house where his family of nine children was brought up, Paddy being the youngest. This house was called *Cartref*, a Welsh word with a spiritual dimension meaning home, and more than home. Having an astute business sense he invested in land on Deeside which consisted largely of sand dunes. Politically he was a liberal with more than one man's share of what was then known as the non-conformist conscience. He looked like Lloyd George with his flowing hair and sounded like him with the musical accent of the Celtic Welshman. As the family dispersed through marriage he built himself a smaller *Cartref* opposite the first one on the road that runs from Birkenhead to Chester. He retired at 55 and lived to be ninety-four always hale and healthy probably due to the frugal but active life he lived mentally and physically, playing golf at the Royal Liverpool with the same single-mindedness that he brought to his Methodism and his Liberalism. All this may seem irrelevant to my story but it was the background which had made Paddy what he was, puritanical morally, yet socially at one with all men at all levels. He must have been born a democrat in that rather class-conscious little pocket of provincial society. On coming back to the old home, to which a widowed sister had returned to keep house for her father, he did not fit easily and submissively into the pattern of a life that he had outgrown, after five years abroad in the army.

Paddy had been born and bred in Liverpool till the family moved to the Wirral when he was seven. Though now almost the whole of the Deeside strip is built up, the Wirral in those days was mostly wild dunes held down against the Atlantic winds by clumps of thrift and sea pinks. To all intents and purposes it was rural open land. He belonged to this peculiarly beautiful peninsula between Dee and Mersey, and in the first ecstatic phase of our relationship I had not given a thought to what it would mean to him to leave it all and settle in London. It had never occurred to either of us that I should leave my world and go to live in his; it was he who must tear up roots and move south. We did not put it into words; it was assumed to be right and we both worked on that assumption without questioning. How self-centred one can be without realising it! Imperious, the young make their royal plans, and expect others to fall in with them, as if mere youthfulness bestows a divine right. But it often happens that what appeared to be a lack of consideration turns out to be for the best and at the end of the day one can say Blessed Culpa. Our wills are subject to the pressures of circumstances and in blindly pursuing our own ends it transpires that we were unconsciously serving the ends of Providence. And so it was in our case. I did not know it, and he knew it only subconsciously, but things at *Cartref* were moving towards change, although everything on the surface seemed to look permanent. The big Depression was on its way. The Liverpool Cotton Exchange was tottering. The mansions along Meols Drive were being taken over by institutions, or divided into flats. The Birkenhead shipyards were losing orders and it was becoming more difficult to build and sell small houses, so the prospect of a new start in new country was not without promise.

Paddy was what is known as a good mixer, widely involved with several amateur operatic and dramatic

societies and the local yacht club, with racing and regattas
in the summer and concerts and shows in the winter. Since
boyhood he had been a member of the St. Luke's
Methodist choir except for the war years. He had old
friends and new in every part of the district in which he
was so popular. That sort of social life was unknown and
unimaginable to one like myself who had always lived in
the unsociable world of the London suburbs, not even
knowing the names of neighbours or being the least interested in them. Every house in the road was a self-
contained unit and apart from that, I was a natural solitary, cosily and dreamily ensconced in my own private
world.

All this was a far cry from the Fairy Wood so we said
goodbye at the end of the week and went our separate
ways. Paddy did break the pact by sending me a Christmas card which I have to this day. I assured him that I
had always earned my own living and would never be a
burden to him in any way, but, unknown to me, as soon as
he returned to Cartref from that fateful week in Anglesey
he took his father into his confidence and the outcome was
that his father offered to advance the sum which would
come to Paddy eventually, a sum which he used to build
an estate of small houses to let, the rents of which would
provide him with a modest income in a world where it was
being said that the generation which had saved us from
the Germans was doomed, too old at forty to start new
careers.

It was three years before the houses were built and let
and during that period Paddy insisted that I should consider myself free and break off our engagement if I so
desired. But we were deeper in love than ever. Once or
twice I was invited to Cartref for a few days, and my father
and I dined with my future father and sister-in-law when
they passed through London, en route for their annual
mid-winter holiday in France.

That year Frederick Drummond died of pneumonia as

many did in those days and I was surprised to learn that he was only forty. He had seemed older. Dear Frederick, the first to give me a helping hand along the road of my song writing career. It was at winter's end and I remember the tablet of white carnations I devised for his burial. The words of the second verse of our first song were picked out in deep purple violets which looked lovely against the snowy purity of the white flowers.

> *To sleep awhile, a dreamless hour*
> *A tear falls on the frozen flower*
> *Those still cold hands no music make,*
> *To sleep awhile and then to wake.*

I can never think of that song without remembering how Frederick, Ethelwyn and I went to a Sunday League concert at the New Cross Empire to hear Guiseppi Ceci give it its first public performance in his extraordinary falsetto voice. We were in one of those cosy little red velvet boxes under the bow of the circle.

His wife, Ruby Sheppard, was on the same programme; she had a deep rich contralto voice. They were a delightful couple, artistic, seriously devoted to music, but always cheerful, always busy, always full of fun. Ceci, of Italian blood, but London born, exuded vitality at every pore. He fizzed like champagne. He was a total abstainer alcoholically, but drank deep of the cup of the joy of life, versatile, vivacious and sparkling. There was no-one quite like him. We remained friends until he died about thirty years after that night at the New Cross Empire. He worked by day in the etchings department of the British Museum and sang by night in clubs, concert halls and Masonics; when he retired he started life anew as an art dealer with two shops on the Pantiles at Tunbridge Wells. In one he sold pictures, in the other china and glass. He was human quicksilver. He ran between those two shops like a streak of disembodied energy, singing as he flashed from A to B.

THE FACTS OF LIFE

He was never anyone else but his own unique self. His friends were legion, but I think his favourite was his former neighbour Cyril Fletcher. Driving, working with his hands in house or garden, or darting to and fro across the Pantiles, Ceci was Ceci. On his retirement he bought a cottage in Horsmonden, Kent, which he attacked with a few tools and bare hands, tearing out fireplaces, ripping off the broken roof and stripping walls down to the beautiful skeletal framework of oak beams. When the restoration of the cottage was worked out of his system he transformed the garden from a backyard to an Eden, then disposed of it and bought a massive early Victorian house at the Southborough end of Tunbridge Wells. This he divided and lived in the ground floor flat for the rest of his life.

Tudor had declined in popularity since Beverley Nichols had put it on the aesthetic map with his book *Up The Garden Path*. Fashion followed Beverley from the Rutland Cottage era to Merry Hall in Leatherhead and that started a vogue for chandeliers, Adam fireplaces, real and fake, ornate and lofty ceilings and Ceci did in a small way in Kent what Beverley Nichols did in Surrey. If I had time I should like to pursue this fascinating line of thought. Does the writer create the trend or does he merely open the gates on trends which are already forming in the public mind waiting for a lead?

As the writing of my wandering chronicle moves on its zig-zag course across the years, it becomes increasingly hard to put out of remembrance names mentioned and scenes evoked. As they come up to take their chronological places in this discursive record of personal encounters and seemingly accidental happenings, I am conscious of a desire to detain them, reluctant to let them slip back into limbo. Having called them up I am left with them, and for the rest of the day must walk in their company, haunted by vague regretful thoughts of words said or not said, and things done or not done when we all communicated on equal terms occupying the same corner of time and space.

But the tide comes in and the tide goes out. Nothing is static. Everything and everyone must move at the pace of time reckoned by the cosmic measurement of sixty minutes to the hour, seven days to the week, and twelve months to the year.

One part of my mind wants to race ahead and the other wants to linger looking back. The past has a magnetic inward pull and we are not always strong enough to resist this subjective tug. We have never really done with the past but it must never be allowed to usurp the present. An obsessive preoccupation with the past leads on a downward slope towards morbidity. The Christian Gospel always pushes and pulls in an upward direction. "Now," said St. Paul, "Is the appointed time." It can never be yesterday, nor is it ever tomorrow. In reality the appointed time is now, the only time over which we have any control.

I have nearly come to the end of my pre-Patience Strong life, but before I start on the new road there are one or two more friends I must salute, and one or two more discoveries to relate because what was discovered then is still part of the life of today, still valid, still unshaken after the holocaust of the intervening years.

11
ENCOUNTER
IN A PEASOUPER

MIDWAY THROUGH the nineteen-twenties I was destined to meet the three men who were each to play a special part in the unfolding story of my life during three consecutive years. Stephen first, Paddy, then Guy. Either you believe that life is chaotic, "a tale by an idiot signifying nothing" as Shakespeare put it, or you believe that there is an intelligent purpose behind all things signifying something, working out towards fulfilment within the time span of the individual. Circumstances and their consequences have forced me to believe that the latter is the true explanation of the mystery of why we come to meet certain people at a certain time and in a certain place, thereby bringing about an instant and dramatic change of direction which affects not only our own lives but the lives of others.

I have already recorded my first encounter with Stephen and my meeting with Paddy, one year later; now I must complete the plaiting of the three-fold chord and relate my meeting the following year with Guy, which so far as the actual meeting was concerned was perhaps the strangest of all strange stories, because it seemed to hang upon such a slender thread of chance. Or so it appeared at the time but these threads of chance are more like wires which connect with an operational centre somewhere at the hub of events.

It was a night such as we never have now. London lay under a thick blanket of fog known then as a peasouper. We scraped the green soupy slime off eyebrows and lashes. Anytime in winter fogs were likely to descend on the capital and its suburbs, a nightmare for drivers of trains and buses and the people who were dependent on them for transport to and from their places of work, especially after dark. There were no motorways in those days, only ordinary roads, and few possessed cars.

I left the office at six and groped my way through the crowds to Charing Cross. There was something eerie about those London fogs. They muffled sound, creating a sinister atmosphere of stealth and secrecy. The trains, of course, were late, but the marvel was how they ever managed to work the system at all. Every platform was jammed with people waiting for their trains with patient British resignation, their faces spectral in the yellowish glare of the station lights. At last I reached home having felt my way by clutching at the railings. The street lamps were scarcely visible, a mere blur seen through the smoky greenish curtain of the fog.

My mother had a hot meal ready for me and a coal fire blazing cosily in the hearth. "Thank goodness you're in," she said. "But I have to go out again," I said. "You'll do no such thing," she said sternly. "Oh yes," said I. "Saklatvala is going to speak at Ennersdale Road School on the Saccho and Vanzetti case." She knew it would be of no use to plead with me, seeing that my mind was fully made up.

In a house about a mile away, unknown to me then, a similar scene was being enacted and a similar conversation taking place. A lean young man of twenty-seven or so had made his way home from the city and his mother was saying almost the same thing as mine had said to me. "You're not going out again tonight." "Oh yes," said the lean young man. "I must. I'm determined to go to hear that Indian chap talk on the Saccho and Vanzetti affair."

ENCOUNTER IN A PEASOUPER

The matter of the two Italians under sentence of death in America was a thorny topic of current discussion, so the prospects of seeing and hearing the elusive Saklatvala, a political figure who had captured the public interest by reason of his frequent disappearances into prison, was not without attraction.

The wires that connect one life with another must have been humming that night at the cosmic telephone exchange somewhere out there on the sky side of the fog. Two lines of communication were about to be brought into contact. Two roads were about to converge. A man and a girl, strangers hitherto, were walking towards one another through the fog unaware that they were moving into an experience the consequences of which would not only change the course of their own lives but the lives of many with whom they were associated. The shape of things to come was hammered out that night on the unseen anvils of Providence, creating something larger than the personal concerns of those who were implicated, something that was destined to light a small lamp of comfort for millions of people throughout the world at a time of great darkness in the terrible years that lay ahead, years that were hidden from us then by a fog of Divine mercy.

When I eventually arrived at the school it was past the time when the talk was billed to commence. The hall was full and an usher showed me to a vacant chair by the centre gangway. I looked round feeling a little uneasy. Some of Saklatvala's pro-left friends had obviously mustered, and a few of the usual toughs who were to be found at any political meeting promising to be lively. A murmur of impatience seemed to be rumbling round the assembly and presently a man wearing a huge red rosette on his lapel appeared on the platform with the announcement that Mr Saklatvala had sent his apologies. He had been unable to travel owing to the fog. Another speaker came to the platform and as he was being introduced by the chairman, the man seated on my right got up to go. I had noticed the knife-edge crease in his trousers which was vaguely comforting as I thought there was an atmosphere of subdued truculence about this meeting, but had not dared to look at the face of the one next to whom I had been placed. I began to wish I had taken the opportunity to slip out before the speaker had settled into his subject. An hour wore on and at last I plucked up courage to make a move. To my amazement there outside the door stood the one who had occupied the next chair and who had left the hall over an hour ago. His tall slim figure was outlined in the fog. He came forward and, raising his hat, asked if he could see me safely home as it was such a bad night. My parents had instilled into me that I must not speak to anyone to whom I had not been introduced, so I thanked him and then went off in what I thought was the direction of the gate assuring him that I knew the way and needed no escort. In the slight confusion of the moment I must have lost my bearings and what I imagined to be an open gate was a very solid wall into which I walked at a smart pace. Immediately he was at my side. "You see," he said, "You do need an escort." After this humiliating incident I was only too pleased to allow him to guide me by the elbow as the fog closed round obliterating all landmarks and the world disappeared without trace.

Here was a political animal if ever there was one. All the way home he talked non-stop about Baldwin, MacDonald, Lloyd George, Beaverbrook and Sir Oswald Moseley and the new party. I gathered that he was a keen supporter of the Daily Express so presumed him to be a Conservative. With such a passionate singleness of mind I felt he ought to have been a professional politician or a parson, so was surprised to learn that he was in the wholesale drapery business.

I learned later that Guy's parents had owned a drapery, millinery and general outfitters' shop in the High Street of

Hythe in Kent where he was born, and when they decided
to move to Quendon deep in the Essex countryside they
were advised by representatives of various wholesale firms
with whom they had business connections that it would be
a wise move to let the boys learn every branch of the
business, which would mean two years "living in" at the
London hostel of whichever firm they wished to join.

Guy, the eldest, was as old as the century, so the fateful
autumn of 1918 found him at the age of eighteen in a
training camp at Crowborough in Sussex. This must have
grieved his mother for to the end of her days she was a
militant pacifist, a contradiction in terms, but the two
points of view seemed to come together in that fiery little
person and to make sense.

I cannot bear to think of how much she must have felt
when the news reached Quendon that her eldest son had
been wounded in France, within a few days of his arrival
and sent back to England to have a bullet removed from
his wrist in Leicester hospital. When he was ready for
action once again the news broke that the armistice had
been signed. He was told that he need not report back to
his regiment but go straight home that day. As the crowds
were moving "up west" to celebrate, Guy was on a push-
bike pedalling his way back through Epping Forest towards the quiet Essex village where his parents were
waiting for news.

On the day after the armistice was signed Guy pedalled
the thirty odd miles back to London to see the manager of
the firm in which he had served his "apprenticeship" to
ask if he could have his old job back, as travelling rep-
resentative or office clerk and was offered a job at seven
shillings a week. Those were the conditions which fed the
early fires of the Trade Union Movement. But he was no
troublemaker; he was one of the "peaceable multitude",
having done his duty in France wanting only now to
resume the business of earning a living, using the experience he had gained during those two hard years at the

hostel. All four boys eventually achieved success in other spheres, but in those grim days a man was thankful to get any sort of job. The war had to be paid for and freedom was costly. It still is.

But I have digressed and must drag my wandering thoughts back to the night when he was guiding me home through the fog.

When I could deflect his interest from political matters, his mother took first place in the conversation. He told me how when he had been sent to the training camp at Crowborough she had forbidden him to submit to vaccination. This infuriated the M.O. and he had him locked up for a spell in the glasshouse, until the situation could be clarified. A week later they had to release him for duty, he being the only one in camp who had not gone down with measles!

I said, "Your mother seems to be something of a rebel. What other orthodox measures does she oppose?" By this time we had arrived at my front gate. "Almost everything you say," he said, "makes me wish that you two could meet. I wonder if you would come and have tea with us next Sunday?" I thanked him and explained that I could not come then because there was a very special meeting at the Aeolian Hall, something I did not wish to miss, but I gave him my telephone number and said I should very much like to meet his mother if he would ring later in the week to make another date. It seemed as if I already knew her, and when I eventually met her she was exactly as I had imagined.

A week passed, and another, and another, and I felt strangely disappointed. A month later came a letter to say that he had been ill with pneumonia since the night in the fog. Pneumonia was a killer in those days. Few survived the crisis which took three weeks to develop. I was told later that the doctor had held out little hope of recovery. I wrote a letter of sympathy expressing the hope that he would soon recover and just before Christmas he wrote again renewing the invitation for me to go to Wellmeadow and meet his mother.

It was not until I was gathering these old memories together that I realised that Guy might have contracted pneumonia through waiting outside the school that night in the cruel cold of that penetrating fog.

On that first meeting with Guy's mother, as I stood at the door looking across the room to where she sat by the window, I knew before she spoke that I had found a friend for life.

We exchanged conventional words of greeting but we knew that the moment was fraught with meaning for us both. Some signal of recognition passed between us in a flash. There was a feeling of suppressed excitement in the air. Guy's two brothers were present. It all seemed unreal like the rehearsal of a play. There she was, a fierce little lady with very decided views on every subject which was raised. It was not a question of liking, loving or disliking her; either you were on the same wave length or not. Affection did not enter into the finely woven web of thought in which we were caught. It was not something to be wondered at or talked about; it was a fact of life to be accepted. Within a few minutes I felt we had known each other for years instead of minutes, just as I had realised my affinity with Paddy at our first meeting in the previous year.

During the past week I had been reading Mary Borden's new book *Flamingo*, and I was still moving under its spell, mesmerised by people who had stepped out of their place in a book of fiction and become real flesh and blood characters. This is the magic of the Mary Borden touch. She has the power to create people who remain with you long after the book itself has fallen apart in your hands, literally worn out with being read, and long after the title has faded from the publisher's catalogue. It is seldom that I pass a weatherboarded house without thinking of the old white house in Campbelltown to which

Amanda Campbell had come as a bride and in which years later her son Peter was to meet Frederika Joyce. These people are more alive to me than some people I have known all my life, that is why at my first meeting with Guy's mother I immediately thought of her as Amanda and not as Ellena which was her real name. She was Amanda Campbell, the personification of Mary Borden's imaginary woman from the pages of *Flamingo*. Tawaska the Finn also keeps me company when alone. He steals silently out from between the covers of *A Woman With White Eyes*. Sometimes I ride with Marion Dawnay and Major Waring when the upper half of a horsewoman moves along the top of my hedge out in the lane, for I am back in the country of *Three Pilgrims and a Tinker* and when walking past the Old Rectory on a Friday evening as the bell ringers are practising I am back in Mary Borden's *Jericho Sands* with Simon and Priscilla Birch.

I once had an overwhelming desire to write to Mary Borden telling her all this and to thank her for all the pleasure her books had given me since first reading *Flamingo*. It was the only fan letter I had ever written. She was giving a lecture at Bromley and I handed in the letter to someone at the door as I went in with Amanda. I can hardly recall the subject but I do remember she related a visit she once paid to a young relative at Oxford. Tea was set in his rooms. Deep windows overlooked the quad below. He was telling her how everything of cultural and aesthetic value would soon be destroyed in the coming overthrow of the accepted order of things. "I looked at the old books," she said, "their gold lettering glowed in the firelight against the sixteenth-century walls. I looked at the elegantly set tray with its Georgian silver tea pot and the Rockingham china teacups and milk jug, then I crossed the beamed room to the mullion window and looking down upon the green velvet of the lawns I said, 'Well, well, well'."

That little vignette was typical of Mary Borden who

had a genius for economy of language. Her style was casually sophisticated. With the flick of a sentence she could convey a vivid impression, capturing atmosphere, and stripping a character down to the bare bones of the psychological skeleton. It isn't to be wondered at that she could get inside the skin of a woman like Frederika Joyce. I sometimes think that Frederika Joyce might have been a self-portrait, but it is unwise to speculate.

At the conclusion, the chairman requested that the writer of the note to Mary Borden would kindly see Miss Borden when the meeting was over. My note had been intentionally anonymous not wishing to involve her in the bore of an acknowledgment. The thought of meeting Mary Borden personally was something I had not envisaged. My first reaction was to run away but Amanda who was with me would hear of no such thing as a retreat so she pushed me forward towards the door at the rear of the platform saying "I'll see you outside."

And so, there I was, face to face with Mary Borden who had given me so many invisible yet real friends. My heart thumped with excitement but my tongue was tied. She tried to help me out but she too was under some kind of strain. We stared at one another in confused silence. She, who had a magical command of words, had nothing to say. She must have sensed my embarrassment because very gently she took my hand and said "Come and have tea with me one day." I stumbled out dazed with the realisation that I had actually spoken with Mary Borden, whom I had idolised ever since Ethelwyn Drummond had first put *Flamingo* into my hands.

A few months later she sent a letter inviting me to tea at her house in Westminster and it was arranged that I should go the following month, but we missed one another. The Munich crisis was upon us so the date was postponed; and when at last it seemed to be possible Hitler was on the march. Mary Borden, as Lady Spears whose husband had a constituency to nurse, was very much at the hub of things. We never met again. I read in the paper that she died in 1968.

It is a reflection upon the reading public of those days that this brilliant American writer was not fully appreciated in her country of adoption. She was never in the best seller bracket but that perhaps is an oblique compliment. It may have been that her portraits came too near the real thing to ensure acceptance in her own world where she was the wife of the member of Parliament for Carlisle, later to become Sir Edward Spears. Her busy life with the social obligations of her Westminster house and the demands of a constituency hundreds of miles from London would have left her little time for writing; but the wonder is how did she manage to write the dozen or so novels that she produced for Heinemann's prior to the outbreak of the second world war? In that war she equipped a nursing unit for the Free French with which she worked for the duration; but when General de Gaulle held his spectacular victory march through Paris no invitation was extended to Sir Edward and Lady Spears who had served the French Cause so loyally and given so generously. The General did not want to see any English participation in his parade. It was too sharp a reminder that it was the British who had delivered France from the Germans; they did not want even a silent reminder of this stark but incontrovertible fact. No one reading *Jane Our Stranger* could doubt Mary Borden's capacity to throw a loving light on Paris in its cultural, artistic and historic setting of old mansions with high shuttered windows towering above little secret iron-gated courtyards, cool in shadow, discreetly exclusive.

I am so fascinated by Mary Borden that I am loath to drag my thoughts away from her and the people she sent rushing wildly through the pages of her books; some on horseback thudding over the muddy fields of the English shires and some playing political chess over the candlelit dining tables of crumbling old country houses or smart restaurants in Paris, London or New York. I must leave them here because the only excuse for allowing them to obtrude on my story is on meeting Guy's mother I immediately identified her with the mother of Peter Campbell and, as Amanda, she became almost a dual person.

I suppose there would have been about three decades between our ages but that was irrelevant; we walked in step together physically and spiritually through all the vicissitudes of thirty years. Our meeting was a landmark. We were in perfect harmony except on the issue of pacifism. We laughed at the same things, believed in the same things; she herself had three sons, but she was all too aware of the burdens life would lay upon them and any joy she had in them was tempered with the pain of this foreknowledge born of a deep compassion for the poor scraps of humanity brought into the world, in many cases, by beings unfitted for the responsibility of caring for children.

Two or three evenings a week we walked together, heedless of time and heedless of where we were going. Best of all we loved walking in the dark under the stars, engrossed in abstract or metaphysical lines of thought on whatever was in tune with the mood of the moment. Rarely did we touch on family matters or personal concerns. Time together was so precious and Bromley had so much to offer then in the way of lectures on comparative religions, literary, historical and ecological subjects, that we fed on rich fare. We once got involved with the Sufis who held a meeting every Sunday morning in a hall near the Market Place. The ministrants stood at a wide oak table placed before the assembly on which were set seven gold candlesticks, and a candle was lit for each of the seven great religions of the world, Christianity, Buddhism, Mohammedanism, Judaism, Zoroastrianism, Sufism and Hinduism. We attended for a few months after which I was asked to play the harmonium for the morning service which I was told would necessitate my participation in an initiatory service to be held at a house in London. This I declined to do and was secretly glad of the opportunity this gave me of breaking away. Amanda confessed that she also had begun to feel a shudder of shame when the Christ candle had been lit, the sacred name which was above every name in heaven or earth was not to be numbered amongst these others who, though leaders of world wide religions, were mere mortals. Amanda had been brought up on a Yorkshire farm steeped in a tradition of nonconformity later joining the Church of England to satisfy the desires for greater freedom of doctrinal manoeuvre.

She told me of how one of the rectors of the Essex parish where they resided had been eager to have Guy trained for the ministry. He had evidently seen the good material behind the pale ascetic face and restless mind always searching about for some new facet of truth.

About that time I joined the City Literary Institute known affectionately as the Cit.Lit. where I spent so many afternoons and evenings enthralled at lectures on architecture and mysticism. It was at a series of lectures on this latter subject that I came to know Miss Sandbach-Marshall; she initiated me into the inner world of such mystics as Blake, Plotinus, John of the Cross, Ruysbroeck, Julian of Norwich, *The Cloud of Unknowing* and on to the treasure islands of Evelyn Underhill's books. It was at the dear old Cit.Lit. that I first saw films of Lincoln, York Minster, Winchester and Salisbury Cathedrals. It was to be some years before I should see them in stone, but I shall always be grateful for those wonderful Cit.Lit lectures which I shall never forget.

I was still in touch with Stephen. We used to meet for an evening meal once a week, and a wide net we cast over the political and literary pools. I used to produce snapshots of Paddy to prop against the sauce bottles, mustard jar and salt and pepper pots on the table, a silent reminder that he was still very much in the picture. One evening when the flashing flow of Stephen's wit and raillery were in full spate he put down knife and fork and emitted a ferocious howl with the imprecation "A murrain on all Liverpudlians." I realised that some sort of a gauntlet had been flung down but I could not work out the implications. The incident had a comic ending; which proved to be the ending not only of that evening's dialogue but of our strange uneasy friendship. He had come to Charing Cross station with me and when the train drew up at the platform he followed me into the carriage and a few minutes before the guard blew the whistle for departure he hesitated before stepping out of the carriage, bent over and kissed me with a violence that left me stupefied. When I recovered from the shock I got to my feet hurriedly and the bowler hat was knocked from his hand and fell into the space between the edge of the platform and the step. I sank back into my seat and realised that the door had not been properly closed and was swinging as we rattled across the bridge over the Thames. Poor Stephen had to deal with an irate porter at Charing Cross station who had witnessed his unceremonious jump from the carriage and for leaving the door open while the train was in motion he was fined £5. I think he must have related this little episode in his book *My Writing Life* because it was referred to in an article in the Daily Express written by the late Nancy Spain.

It was about a week later that I received a letter from him postmarked Cornwall in which he told me he was shaving one morning a few days after that fateful evening and he suddenly made up his mind to give up schoolmastering, find a cottage in Cornwall and write a best seller or bust.

> *"If you can make one heap of all your*
> *winnings*
> *And risk them on one turn of pitch*
> *and toss and lose,*
> *And start again . . ."*

This had meant giving up security, pension rights and a regular if small income, but he was driven by circumstances. Perhaps he would have come to the same decision even if things had worked out otherwise for us. But it was not to be. So off he went that very morning, took a tumbledown cottage in Portscatho for a few smillings a week and settled in to make a new life for himself earning a living by his pen. He started at once on a novel which he wrote at breakneck speed when he was hungry and desperate and on which he spent literally his last shilling when posting the manuscript to his agent in London. This was a book called *The Seventh Bowl* which was to be first of fifty or so novels published under the name of Neil Bell.

We did not meet again until half way through Hitler's war when Paddy and I were staying in Devon for a few days. I telephoned him and he invited us to Brixham where he lived in a stone coastguard cottage with wife and family. He kept office hours and wrote all his books in longhand at a small table in his bedroom overlooking Torbay.

He achieved success in his profession, but he was at war with his world, a clever, gifted man who never quite came to terms with himself. When he had written all he wanted to write he took his car up to Berry Head and took an overdose of some kind of killer drug. It was his last gesture of non-co-operation. Stephen was his unique self to the end and the end was of his choosing.

12
TWO CRAZY PEOPLE

*T*HE FIVE YEARS of separation which Paddy and I had imposed upon ourselves after that first meeting in Anglesey was drawing to an end. It was a decision which had been forced upon us partly by circumstances. We had to submit to being borne along not on a foaming wave of emotion but by the Emersonian current that knew its way moving inevitably towards the haven where our hearts would be. I had been fully occupied with my work and he with the task of winding up the business of his old life and making practical arrangements for the future. Paddy used to say that the indefinite postponement of our marriage by mutual agreement served a double purpose; it gave him ample time to make the break with his bachelor life of sailing, singing and building which must have been a somewhat painful experience in a closely knit social community where all friends were old friends. Moreover, he had confessed to a fear that for me the fairytale romance would vanish like a dream, quickly or gradually, once back in London three hundred miles or so from the spell of Fairy Wood and the magic of the mountains. Not so; and he came at last to accept my assurance that it was no passing fantasy, but a true dream. When he finally came to realise this we were so sure of our feelings and so sure of each other that we could afford to wait five years or ten years or forever. The miracle lay in the fact of having met;

the surprise of it left us breathless with a delight that seemed to detach us from the austerities of time. The future was irrelevant, too far away to contemplate.

We did not allow ourselves the luxury of letters or of conversations on the telephone; it was sufficient to know that we were both in the same world, sharing the same vision. But the separation was not absolute. Every year there was a brief meeting, apart from the annual rendezvous on the Island. One summer I spent a few days at Cartref to meet Paddy's family and the following year he came south to meet mine. Once we paid a fleeting visit to Menai Bridge by the *St. Tudno*, a boat which made daily sailings in the season between Liverpool and Anglesey. This gave us two hours in which to make our way to the little island of St. Tsyilio and here we stood together before the Celtic altar, renewing in silence the vows made at our first visit there together when we thanked God for the miracle that had brought us together in that wonderful place. Then, stepping out of the ancient silence, we hurried back along the stony causeway connecting it with the road by the shore. Though pressed for time, we could not pass that way without taking the loop which enclosed our crescent-shaped wood, secret and mysterious, threaded with a narrow path winding between the road and the Straits. We hurried under the arches of the trees, hand in hand, singing what we called our theme song:

> *"In our mountain greenery*
> *Where God paints the scenery,*
> *Just two crazy people together"*

for that's what we were, just two crazy people in love with life and with each other, a little mad, seeing the world for the first time through the rosy prism of pure joy.

With ten minutes in which to catch the boat we ran under the bridge and on to the pier. The stentorian voice of *Tudno* was hooting its warning signal of imminent departure as we reached the gangway. Once aboard we went to the upper deck to lean on the rail watching our enchanted island drift away as *Tudno* headed towards Bangor. A silence fell between us. There was nothing to be said. How eloquent a silence can be when the heart is full and the mind content. Many of life's most precious moments are shattered like crystal vases because somebody speaks an unnecessary word bringing everything down to the lowest point of social intercourse. Wisely wrote the author of the book of Ecclesiastes, "there is a time to keep silence and there is a time to speak."

Paddy was by nature reticent, reserved and sagacious, using speech with the utmost economy. Never did he make idle conversation to fill a gap. He exuded a quietness around himself and was content to rest in it. They were easy, deep, companionable silences. That was his strength and he knew how to conserve it.

Sometimes it seems a pity that we cannot embalm memories as we can keep photographs, slides and snapshots. Perhaps it is as well. A photograph can be flung away or accidentally destroyed, but anything stored in the wells of the subconscious can be summoned at will. It is only a thought away for it can never be lost or stolen. That memory of our day trip on the *St. Tudno* hangs in my picture gallery amongst the immortals; at any time and in any place I can surround myself with the old stone walls of that tiny island church on a lozenge of holy land set apart by nature from the Island, hemmed in by water except for the finger of the causeway that disappears with the tide. I can see Conway Castle and dim ranges of mountains aflush with the sunset. We have been granted the freedom of the city of our minds.

I was returning to London the following morning. We reached Lime Street station half an hour before the Euston train was due to depart and Paddy said "Let's go along to Wolfe's and look at engagement rings." That brought me down to earth with a thud. I had never connected our romance with anything so conventional as an engagement ring, but Paddy had an almost psychic gift for striking the right note at the right moment. With his usual sagacity he knew that people and especially mothers set great store by the formalities, so off we went to buy the dainty hoop of diamonds that I wear to this day and which is glinting at me now from the hand resting on the paper.

In the following February Paddy came to stay for a few days, and after my father had given his formal approval of our plans we set out on a hectic home-hunting expedition. There was no shortage of flats, houses or rooms to be let at the beginning of the thirties. I had leanings towards the Hampstead area, being a keen Keatsian but in almost all the flats and rooms we inspected in the vicinity of Hampstead Heath we were taken to the window and told that from that point the Crystal Palace could be seen. As I had never at any time lived very far away from the Crystal Palace I did not particularly want to see it, but it was obvious that a sight of this celebrated and unusual Palace was looked upon as an asset to the property.

Paddy must have been not a little bewildered at finding himself in search of a home in London of all places, having regarded the metropolis with suspicion if not dislike for the greater part of his adult life. Accustomed as he was to breathing air freshened by the winds that blew across the Wirral peninsula from three directions, the estuaries of Dee and Mersey and the point at which Hoylake thrust towards the Atlantic, he doubtless was already feeling deprived of air.

Eventually we decided upon two large rooms in West Kensington a few yards from Olympia at which preparations for the Daily Mail Ideal Home Exhibition at that time were in full cry. The house in Avonmore Road was owned by a charming spinster to whom we took an instant liking. Miss Capes was not only human but humorous and from the first moment of our meeting took a lively interest in our affairs; particularly when we announced that we were within a week of being married and would be moving in on the first day of May after a month's honeymoon in Paris. The liking for her was evidently mutual as she readily agreed to our putting in a few possessions, mostly wedding presents although strictly speaking the rooms were to be let fully furnished. The bedroom suite given by my parents would be arriving from Barkers the next week and the grand piano, Paddy's gift to me, would be coming from Whiteley's. Miss Capes agreed without demur. In fact she seemed to be in the mood to say yes to anything we asked. It must have been Paddy's engaging personality which made it all so easy. I cannot think what she made of me, especially when I said she need not bother to show me the kitchen as I had never had the slightest interest in domestic matters, whereupon she offered to provide us with breakfast and evening meal. Nothing could have suited me better, and Paddy was obviously relieved because a sigh came out of his deep barrel chest as he sank into a nearby armchair in what was to be our sitting room. There was a small walled garden beyond the glass door and a huge sycamore tree, which though blotting out the sun was a comfort, seeming to stand for a symbol of permanence. This must have been reassuring to Paddy after a morning in which he had been whisked to various points on Hampstead Heath to inspect high flats perched amongst the sparrows and low ones at traffic level in sepulchral basements. To have come upon the maternal Miss Capes who obviously regarded us both as rather odd but amusing was a blessing indeed, but when we realised that here in this solid looking red brick house we should be provided not only with shelter but food, our cup was full. So ended the search for our first abode, little dreaming that it would be the first of sixteen homes which we were to occupy in the years that lay ahead.

We were married a week later. After the ceremony we went with my parents and brother to the Trocadero in Piccadilly Circus for luncheon with our guests, and a mixed bag we were. Jay Whidden, Harry and Bobbie Isaac, Connie and Jo, Aunt Ada, Paddy's brother from Manchester and his sister Edith from Cheshire, thirteen in all, and I was wearing a green dress and hat. Unlucky? Nothing is unlucky or lucky. Our lives are ruled not by a fictitious phantom known as Lady Luck, but by a beneficent Providence which works for us and not against us if so we believe. Every time Our Lord and His company of disciples sat down to a meal there would have been thirteen at table, so how did the silly superstition ever arise? As for my green hat and dress, it was natural that I should be married in what had always been my favourite colour.

Later in the afternoon we were seen off on the four o'clock train from Victoria to Dover, from whence we sailed for Calais and on to Paris by train. Midnight found us seated outside the Café de la Paix having ordered omelettes des champignons and there we sat, wondering why we hadn't gone to Brighton.

Paddy who had served in France during the war remembered how some of the French peasants had charged the Tommies for cups of cold and dirty water. He looked at me over our cointreau and I knew from the lost look in his eye that he thirsted after a tankard of English beer. I experienced then the melancholy that was to descend on me like a black cloak whenever I found myself on the wrong side of the white cliffs of Dover. Before the month was out we were both eagerly waiting for the beginning of our new life in Kensington. Apart from the annual visit to Brighton as a child, I have never been keen on holidays. I like routine. When persuaded to take a holiday I have always longed to be home after the third day. We were, however, to take several trips abroad but there was always a special reason for each venture; it was never for relaxation. Daily life was exciting enough for us, for we never seemed to remain static for very long and our sojourn in Avonmore Road was short lived; I cannot remember very much about it but I do recall a few things; the old Irish

maidservant, Molly O'Reilly, who brought in the meals
had a brogue that was so fascinating we used to invent
reasons for detaining her. Whenever we said "Thank
you," she would say "You're welcome," but she used to
end all conversations with this pleasantry. Miss Capes
proved to be very kind and all that her first appearance on
the scene had led us to suppose. Without complaint she
agreed to my writing a song in the middle of the night if I
was so inclined. She said she liked hearing the piano at
any time as it brought a "bit of life" into the house. Every
Sunday we would go for the day to Lee, to which my
parents had moved, and I kept in constant touch with
Amanda. I would go out to Grove Park and we would
have long walks strengthening the ties of attraction between us at every meeting. We both walked on air, with
winged feet and winged thoughts flashing between us.
Guy had gone to America. Wellmeadow, Amanda's
house, had been sold and she was now enjoying the delici-
ous fruits of freedom for the first time in her busy life which
had been lived in the service of others. Her bedsitter in a
Victorian house looked on to a garden of lovely old trees
and shrubs. She had given me as a wedding gift a beautiful
green glass bowl with a nymph in the centre. It stands on
the window sill where I can see it today as I sit writing
nearly half a century later. Today the nymph looks at me
thigh deep in primroses from the Kent woods. Throughout the year she has some living thing at her feet; winter
violets, aconites, sprigs of heather, forget-me-nots, summer roses and autumn leaves so that she celebrates with
me the perennial memory of one in whom the beat of the
music of life synchronised with my own for close on thirty
years of friendship, walking together merrily through the
good times and in the deep shadows of shared sorrows. It
speaks for the depth and maturity of Paddy's nature that
he raised no objections to my nocturnal wanderings with
Amanda. A younger man would have voiced complaints
and put in a claim on my company, as I had usually been

out all day on some business in Denmark Street or
closeted with the typewriter behind a closed door. But
Paddy knew how much Amanda meant to me and how
much I meant to her. She always called him Paddy
Perfectus. She was big enough not to have any lingering
regrets that I had not married her son Guy and she shared
with me the treasure that was Paddy. Ours was truly a
marriage made in heaven or wherever it is that the files on
all human beings are kept and their steps directed to the
one person on earth for whom they are suited. As I have
observed in another chapter, love at first sight is nothing
less than a miracle.

It has been said that the happy countries have no
history. Perhaps that is why that first year in Avonmore
Road seems to have been uneventful. How thankful we
should always be for uneventful days when nothing seems
to happen. Things are, of course, happening all the time
but we tend to remember only the peaks of drama, happiness and tragedy thrusting through the mists of recollection. Blessed are the unremembered days, days that leave
us tranquillised, with nothing to record and nothing to
regret.

The following year brought disturbances in the outside
world that rocked our little boat of contentment. It was
something to do with Stanley Baldwin and Ramsay
MacDonald, and there was talk of our going off the gold
standard. I began to notice that Paddy was not his usual
merry self and that letters from his bank manager were
becoming more frequent. A few of the houses which provided his income carried a mortgage and this meant that it
was affected by the change in the bank rate. I always
believed in facing facts, so one morning after Mrs.
O'Reilly had brought in the post and breakfast and retired, assuring us that we were welcome, a thought struck
me like a bolt from the blue, "Can we afford to live here?"
I asked. "Not really," was the reply. "Not with this new
bank rate," he added. "Then we must go at once," I said.

Living beyond one's means was something I had always been taught must be avoided as it led to certain disaster.

I went to the telephone and spoke to my sister who had a large flat in Tressillian Road, Brockley where my grand-parents had lived. There were two rooms which had not been furnished as they were not needed. I asked her if we could come there as paying guests until we could find other accommodation. Connie readily agreed. Poor Con, she always seemed to drop in for other people's troubles, a selfless soul, but I realised later what a sacrifice of her freedom this must have meant, and what an intrusion upon her privacy. She was a loner, a reader and a dreamer. Jo was infatuated with his work and rarely came home before eleven. He was the manager in charge of a large coach station at King's Cross and so much did he love the place that he hated leaving it for a moment. Connie's evenings were spent telephoning his office en-quiring as to what time he hoped to arrive home. She used to keep him informed as to the progress of the meal which she had cooked and was contriving to keep hot in the oven. When it was foggy he used to sleep in the office in the hope that one of his coaches would be ditched on the Great North Road and he being a live wire would leap at the opportunity of taking his car out in the fog and lending a hand in getting the coach out of the ditch. That to him was the supreme joy in life, to be on the job, leaving nothing to others. He kept a violin and a mandolin at his office to keep himself from falling asleep.

We duly arrived at Tressillian Road complete with grand piano, the bedroom suite, piles of books and a gramophone. Immediately the quiet of Connie's flat was shattered and the even tenor of her life disturbed. Jo was delighted at our being there; he even tore himself away from his precious coaches earlier than usual so that we could have musical evenings, I at the piano, Jo playing his violin and Paddy singing. The trouble with Jo was that he never knew when to call it a day. He would be fiddling in a frenzy of excitement long after midnight with my long suffering sister wearily pretending to enjoy the music. Paddy, too, was one who could sing on into the night provided that there was no shortage of liquid refreshment. Sometimes my parents would appear for one of these strenuous but enjoyable evenings and mother would take on the cooking of the evening meal which must have been a partial relief of Connie, especially as mother refused all offers of assistance in clearing and washing the dishes. One evening the gentleman from the flat above appeared at the front door with a request that he might join us with his wife and flute. I could hear a suppressed but anguished moan from the direction of Connie's chair. As was usual, they had never met their neighbours in the two years they had been there. This addition to the trio went to Jo's head and we had to go through all our favourites again.

Soon after we settled at the flat Jo asked Paddy if he would take over the keeping of the books at the coaching station, as he had expressed his disappointment at not being able to find some occupation. At this time the slump had really set in and a man over forty was not likely to get any sort of a job. So off they went in the mornings together. Another of Jo's musical friends worked in his office; he also had a private income and a great sense of fun, and they made a merry trio.

After a few months I realised that our coming to the flat had disrupted Connie's inner life. She was too sweet to voice a complaint but it was slowly borne in upon me that all was not well there. She and Jo scarcely had any time together. Paddy usually returned by train not wishing to keep Jo's erratic hours, though I was usually out. One night Connie was on the telephone to Jo at the coach station and as I crossed the hall I heard her issuing an ultimatum that unless he returned within the hour she would be taking his meal from the oven and placing it on the window sill to cool. He returned within the hour but had taken the precaution of having a double portion of sausages and chips on the way home at one of his favourite eating places. He bounded up the stairs like a boy with a new toy, a dart board under his arm. The next morning there was the usual hilarious departure and the customary promise to be home early.

We sat down to breakfast after our husbands had gone, Connie fully dressed and I in a dressing gown. The birds were singing and on an impulse Connie rose to open the window. I noticed a certain wildness in her eyes. Usually gentle in her movements she rushed to the window struggling with the sash in a way that caused the frame to shudder and calling out "Come in and bless me, thou spirit of the morning." At the same time there was the sound of shattering glass as Jo's forgotten pie in its earthenware dish fell from the sill, disappearing into what we thought was a greenhouse below.

Connie tossed her shapely head with a scornful gesture. "Of no consequence," she said. "I shall go down at once and tell the owner that I shall have it repaired without delay." But events overtook intentions bringing a loud and sustained ring at the front door. There stood the tenant of the lower flat, steaming with indignation.

"I'm so sorry," Connie said. "I put the dish out last night to cool and in the dark unwittingly must have placed it a little too near the edge. I do apologise and will telephone at once for someone to come today and repair it. I do trust that none of your plants have been damaged."

"Plants!" The word was spat out with a venomous hiss. "Do you not realise that we have had our conservatory converted into a bathroom and that my son was about to perform his ablutions. By a stroke of Providence, the dish with its revolting contents came through the roof a split second before Algernon opened the door."

"That indeed was merciful," said Connie endeavouring to straighten her face. "I will go at once and telephone."

The door closed upon the mother of the unfortunate Algernon but immediately she rang again as if struck by another thought. "My son is here on a visit," she said, "and I would have you know that he is a Roman Catholic priest."

Connie hastened to repeat her apologies then hesitated as if undecided as to whether the disclosure of this latest piece of information made the situation worse or better.

When the worst was over and a local builder had promised to spring into immediate action we collapsed into armchairs to have our laugh out in comfort. Suddenly, Connie's laughter was silenced and she said rather sadly, "Oh dear, I do love you, my little sister, but life seems to have changed since you came here. I used to know where I was and what I was supposed to be doing but now . . . everything has suddenly become so volcanic, unpredictable and sort of Bohemian, if you know what I mean." I did. "I'm not getting any work done," she went on, "reading, writing, walking—it's all gone like a balloon in a whirlwind."

I reminded her that yesterday we had had a lovely walk through the cemetery. "But I hate the cemetery" she said, rising from the chair and pacing the room. "When I'm alone I always cross the road to avoid passing the gates."

That touched me on a raw nerve. Since we were children we had always shared an obsessive fascination with the idea of death. The mystery of mortality had kept us talking through many a long night.

I knew then that our sojourn at Brockley had come to an end. The carnival was over. There was an urgency in Connie's manner that prompted me to say, "You're right. Come on, let's find somewhere. There are hundreds of rooms and flats advertised." And so it was in those days. There was never any difficulty in finding reasonable accommodation. Most people who owned large houses and whose family had dwindled were only too pleased to let furnished or unfurnished rooms.

We soon found two large rooms in a quiet district off the Bromley Road. Both windows looked into a belt of cherry trees which were in their full white bloom when we arrived in April.

Our removal seemed to precipitate a general post. Connie and Jo tore up their roots and moved to the other side of London, renting a small house in the new Hampstead Garden suburb. My parents bought a chalet-bungalow in Grove Park near Amanda for which they had been saving all their married lives. My brother, having won several exhibitions, would be going to Oriel College, Oxford in the autumn. It was as if the stage of our lives was being re-set in readiness for the dramatic happenings which were soon to come.

I have lingered longer than intended over the Brockley interlude and am still reluctant to take a last look at that flat in Tressillian Road where we spent those six hilarious months. It was like taking a holiday from reality. An outsider, looking in on us as a stranger would have been deceived into thinking that it was a normal household, newly wed sisters living an ordinary domestic life. We all knew how to play up to what people expected of us, making the conventional responses. But underneath, all four of us were simmering. The pot of life was on the boil. We had been flung together by circumstances and each was dancing to a different tune.

A tingling excitement was generated whenever the four of us were together. Not that there was anything special about the actual place; the exhilaration was in the atmosphere created by the interplay of our personalities. There we were, disparate but intensely aware of one another.

There was Paddy, a little light-headed with finding himself free for the first time in his life, after five years in the army then living under the eye of a father who, though delightful as an individual, was a disciplinarian and an autocrat. Even at the age of forty, still burying the memories of Galipoli, Palestine and the Western Front, Paddy had had to abide by the Cartref rules and not only be home by ten o'clock, but have a good reason for being out at all.

There was Connie, lost in her own private dream, writing and reading poetry, a solitary and an aesthete, ever conscious of the tear at the heart of things, one on whose shoulder the finger of fate had been laid.

Then there was Jo, restless, erratic, wildly energetic, with an instinctive knowledge of the workings of cars, coaches and violins, but not of anything appertaining to the domestic world, a born entertainer, at his best in company, living on his nerves, a flash of human quicksilver.

And there was I, still fathoms deep in love with Paddy, in love with life itself, permanently inebriated with the wine of the wonder of the world.

We were all given to declamatory speeches and sudden upsurgings of a desire to recite, act or soliloquise. What was said was irrelevant, apropos of nothing and not being connected with any perceptible line of thought, no response was made by the others, nor was it required. Connie, who disliked kitchen sinks as much as I did, would often wring her hands under the running tap and cry out "All the perfumes of Arabia will not sweeten this little hand." We took no notice. There were times when it pleased her to be Lady Macbeth. And Jo would burst suddenly into a room and say fiercely "Now would I drink hot blood." No comment from anyone, nothing had to be explained. And I would wander in and out of the rooms with a large vase on my shoulder pretending to be Keats' Isabella, brooding over her pot of basil. There were no emotional undertones to Paddy's spontaneous solos which were mostly Gilbertian. I would come upon him in the box room, seated on a stool amongst the empty bottles crooning softly to himself,

"A wandring minstrel I
A thing of shred and patches

TWO CRAZY PEOPLE

Of ballads songs and snatches
And dreamy lullaby."

"Sing on wand'ring minstrel" I would say kissing him lightly on the forehead threading my way between old shoes and empty bottles. "But don't wander too far away." I was usually on my way out for a five mile walk with Amanda.

Jo also liked to make sudden appearances in inconvenient moments, usually as breakfast was being prepared. Just as Connie was juggling with the eggs he would spring into the kitchen wrapped in a white sheet, head covered by what was supposed to look like a burnous. "Lawrence of Arabia" he would announce, and Connie would say, "Your egg is as hard as a stone." With this he would re-appear in her Japanese kimono announcing himself as Chu Chin Chow. He had a gift for pantomime even at 8.00 a.m.

Probably it all looks rather silly in print but it was lovely to live life just as it came, to let one's thoughts flow out into verbal expressions knowing that it didn't have to relate to anything. Spontaneity was the thing. We were insulated there in the crazy little world we had made for ourselves, and perhaps our foolish posturings were a kind of reckless defiance of the evil thing that had recently reared its head in the papers connected in some vague way with the burning of the Reichstag.

Perhaps that is why we were so very merry. Perhaps Paddy and I did feel the earth quaking under our feet as we sang and danced our way through the beautiful careless days. And Connie and Jo? Did they know by some unacknowledged psychic faculty that for them there would be no season of ripening and no future.

13
BYWAYS AND
CROSSROADS

F RETURN NOW to some memories of my work at the
office of Campbell and Connelly's which I shared
with Miss Young, Mr Connelly's secretary. Our room
was at the top of the rickety old building in Denmark
Street opposite the Wright house where Lawrence Wright
reigned like a king in his castle. Reg Connelly's and
Jimmy Campbell's combined room was lavishly carpeted
and equipped with concert grand and the latest thing in
the way of an H.M.V. gramophone. There was much
voyaging across the Atlantic in those early days in luxury
ships. Big changes were afoot which resulted in the
Americanisation of the British song world as we knew it.
They bought up several American catalogues and we song
writers did not like the trend. With the coming of the
talkies the revolution was completed. The flood gates were
opened when *Sonny Boy* made its first triumphant appearance in Britain at the Marble Arch Cinema. A new
era had commenced.

One day when alone in my top floor eerie, the bosses
and Miss Young being at lunch, I indulged in the luxury
of a few tears. The next Regatta seemed a long way off in
time. My usual *joie de vivre* was suddenly assailed by the
demon of melancholy, and I was reaching for a hand-
kerchief to dab my eyes when I heard a sound of the
approach of someone in a great hurry, taking the steep old

stairs in leaps and bounds and before I could compose myself the most handsome man I had ever seen in my life burst into the room. He was the personification of Long-fellow's Hiawatha, tall, athletic yet muscular with broad shoulders. The cheek bones were high, the eyes alight with the candle of life. His face was a reddish brown, the hair ink black, and when he spoke it was obvious that he was an American with a strong hint of Red Indian ancestry.

"Hullo, lil gel," he said brightly. "Why the tears?" This was not one with whom you could dissemble. His direct gaze deserved a direct answer and a true one.

"I'm hopelessly in love," I said, "And shan't be seeing him for a whole year."

"Lil gel, I can change all that for you. From now on your life can be all joy. Come with me tonight to the testimony meeting at the Christian Science Church in Curzon Street." I pricked up my ears at that, always ready to spring out and explore anything in the nature of a new exercise in religion.

"I will," I said. "Thank you."

"Quarter to seven in the vestibule," he said. As he reached the door he turned and said, "You know who I am, don't you?" "No," I said, "I'm afraid I don't." He smiled, and what a smile it was! The dingy room was flooded with light and happiness. "I'm Jay Whidden," he said. "I broadcast several times a week with my band, the Midnight Follies at the Carlton Hotel. I'm conductor and first violin. We're on tonight at 11.30." "How wonderful," I said. "Of course I have heard of you and shall certainly be listening tonight. Oh, by the way, I write songs." With this I reached for the ever present poem in my pocket. "Here's my latest lyric," I said, producing *Ninette*, one of my first attempts at popular song writing, ballads having almost gone out completely. He took it. "This is great," he said. "Keep it," I said, trying to appear casual. "Thanks a lot. See you later." With this, Hiawatha went flying off down the stairs, leaving me feeling a little delirious, with the prospects of a new religion plus Jay Whidden. All this and heaven too!

At half past six I walked along Piccadilly in the soft air of a September twilight, feeling that I was on the very edge of a new adventure. My feet seemed to skim along the pavement. What, I wondered, would be waiting for me in this grand church within a stone's throw of the Ritz?

I entered its impressive portal and there was Hiawatha and his wife Maud to whom I was introduced. I was relieved as half my mind was beginning to wonder whether it had all been some crazy dream, out of which I would awaken at any moment. But I was reassured when my empty pocket confirmed that *Ninette* had gone so it was true.

I do not remember very much about that important evening in my life; I knew only that I had come to an end which was also a beginning. The beautiful church with its atmosphere of reverent silence made a profound impression which deepened as the testimonies of physical and spiritual healing were given spontaneously. The huge church was packed with people, but they were not the sort of people I was accustomed to meeting in churches and chapels. These people knew something, something wonderful, something potentially dynamic and held within secretly " a pearl of great price". They were quiet people, happy people, people who were anchored in deep water.

I have often felt incomplete when anything controversially political was introduced into a sermon. It struck a jarring note which was out of tune for those who came to religion in search of truth and peace, and who believe that everything violent and evil in the world would fall away if the mind could be concentrated wholly on the basic principles of Christianity as presented in the New Testament and adumbrated in the Old. The whole peaceful assembly was pervaded by a sense of inward and outward calm. I had had my fill of non-conformist militancy and long sermons about social injustice; the restfulness of this place met my deepest need at that particular time; that is how God always comes to meet us, at the point of our desperate personal need. What I liked about it most was that these people seemed to be de-personalised, immersed in their common consciousness of an all powerful spirit of which they were individual reflections. Poverty, discord, disease and death were unreal because they did not reflect the goodness of God. Only that which expresses the Divine perfection was valid. Confronted with this, affirmation of all that was negative seemed to vanish, having no real existence.

On the wall at one side of the reading desk facing the congregation were engraved the words:

> *"Divine Love always has met and always*
> *will meet every human need."*

On the other side of the readers' desks was a quotation from the Authorised version of the Bible.

There is no pulpit in a Christian Science Church because no sermon is preached. The Bible only is read, with its spiritual interpretation from *Science and Health With Key to the Scriptures* by Mary Baker Eddy, founder of the world wide church of Christian Science.

As the crowd moved out of the church, through the vestibule and into the street the silence observed in the church was maintained. There was no chattering, no introductions, no social intercourse of any kind. I liked that. It left one free to hold what one had taken in without reducing the Bread of Life to crumbs of triviality. One left the church with a feeling of wholeness. All too soon it was fragmented in the machinery of the outside world, but to hold it intact until you were on the outer steps of the church was a good custom and helpful.

Jay's Rolls-Royce was parked in Curzon Street and the chauffeur was instructed to drop him at the Carlton, take me on to Charing Cross station, then drive Mrs Whidden to Hendon where they lived, next door neighbours to Jimmy Campbell and his mother. I should have preferred to have walked to the station on that lovely September night, but it would have seemed ungracious of me to unmake plans which had been so thoughtfully made for our convenience. I should have liked to have been alone to savour the past hour, living every moment of it over and over again as a connoisseur loves to let wine linger on the tongue.

I was very conscious of the fact that this had been a day of destiny for me and as I wanted to prolong it I went home through the park, extending the walk from the station by half a mile. I resolved to find a Christian Science Church for the next Sunday. On reaching home, my mother was anxious to know why I had not come home by the usual train. I told her that after supper we would go for a walk as I had something wonderful to tell her. I should have something even more wonderful to tell her the next day, but this great day had not yet been lived out. There was another surprise to come.

I kissed my parents goodnight and ran upstairs eager to get into bed and fix my earphones. We were still in the age of crystal sets. This was one of the nights when I missed Connie, who had bought herself a typewriter and went to Blackheath three evenings a week to deal with the correspondence of an eccentric but very busy old lady. We all seemed to be gluttons for work in those days. Connie had already done eight hours in a City office plus two hours travelling, but as previously mentioned, she was to be married the following year and was busy in the evenings earning some extra money. I heard her come in just after eleven but she went straight to her room and I settled down to the pleasure of hearing Hiawatha's Midnight Follies.

At 11.30 Jay and his band came on the air. After a few minutes of agitated excitement while I adjusted the cat's whiskers on the crystal, I heard him say, "Hullo folks. I'm gonna open our performance tonight with a lovely lil number called *Ninette* written by a lil gel who gave me the lyric only this afternoon, and I figured out the melody for it on my way home. The band soon picked it up—so come on boys, let's go."

Shall I ever forget the moment when that smooth little waltz tune came through the earphones wedded to my words?

> *Moonlight is gleaming, Ninette,*
> *My heart is dreaming, Ninette,*
> *I hear the sound of an old melody*
> *Weaving the threads of a sweet memory,*
> *How shall I ever forget,*
> *That lovely night when we met?*
> *But with the dawn*
> *Like a dream you had gone,*
> *Where are you now, Ninette?*

Next morning I hurried to the office sure that Hiawatha would come bounding up those stairs, and come he did when the others were at lunch. "Hullo lil gel," he said. "Good nooze, Lawrie Wright's just taken our song. One hundred pounds in advance, split even—and here's your share." With this he placed a cheque for fifty pounds on my desk, signed Lawrence Wright. "Contract to follow, 10% royalty between us. Are you a member of the Performing Rights Society?" he asked. "Oh yes," I said. "I've had several ballads accepted for which I receive performing fees but *Ninette* is the first one on which I've ever had a sheet royalty. Oh Mr Whidden, I'm so thrilled. I don't know how to thank you." "Just call me Jay," he said, "and start right away on some more lyrics. We're going to be a great team. Now I'm off to make a record of *Ninette* for Imperial. I'll put it over again tomorrow night. Had lots of requests. The boys love it. So long, lil gel."

And there I was, left with a lump in my throat and a cheque for £50 on my desk. That evening I went rushing home with a huge bunch of red roses for mother, a box of cigars for Dad, a book for Connie and a new cricket bat for Boy. My parents were astonished at my good fortune and gave me some good advice which I have never forgotten. Always save at least a quarter of what you earn. Put five shillings into your Post Office account for every pound you spend. Thrift and work. That was the two-edged sword with which to fight the battle of life. That evening we all went to the local Italian restaurant Comminetti's to celebrate. Here you could get a good four course dinner for three shillings and sixpence, plus half a crown for a bottle of wine.

Dad suddenly said, "You must have been born under a lucky star." "Oh no," I said, "I don't believe in luck. I believe in Providence." "Quite right," he said. I cannot catch the exact words as they cross over the chasm of time between this day and that evening but he told me never to forget that I had been christened by a bishop, the Suffragen Bishop of Woolwich, and my infant brow having been crossed by the episcopal finger, I would, he supposed, be the recipient of some special blessing. If the bishop had known that the female scrap receiving the Sacrament of baptism at his hand would live to write a counterblast to a blasphemous book to be published by a future Bishop of Woolwich fifty-five years later, he would have dropped me in the font. On second thoughts perhaps not, as he, unlike John Robinson, would probably have been an orthodox Christian and could he have had preknowledge of the Robinson frolic he might even have sprinkled me with a few extra drops of holy water.

Things began to move fast after the momentous happenings of the day of the fifty pounds. Hiawatha's lunchtime visits became a daily occurrence and more exciting as time went on. At the end of another week two more of our songs had been accepted by Lawrence

cle Ben, a gunner during the
st world war. He was gassed
d deafened but lived happily
into his eighties.

Uncle Percy, on the right of the
picture, mounted on a camel in
front of a pyramid close to the
Sphinx.

ABOVE: Uncle Percy again,
cutting a loaf. He was present
at the fall of Jerusalem in 1917.

LEFT: Uncle Ernie, who served
in the West Kent regiment.

My husband, Paddy, during the first world war.

Connie about 1933.

Joe, my sister Connie's husband, killed in the blitz of 1940 on London.

Frederick
Drummond, as
he was when I
first met him.

Jay Whidden,
conductor of the
Midnight Follies
band, 'the most
handsome man I had
ever seen in my life'.

In Laurence Wright's office on the hot line to Blackpool discussing my latest song with the boss.

Signing books in Selfridges accompanied by Frederick Muller, the founder of the firm which has published most of my books.

Miss Patience Strong.

The writer of the "Quiet Corner" in the *Daily Mirror*. She will attend the Book Exhibition next week and autograph copies of her books.

Nearly Fifty Years of Loyal Service to the Trade—"The Newsagent-Bookseller's Review."

NEWS
Reviewed
IN
PICTURES

Nov 6th 1937.

Mr. Warwick Deeping.

Universally known as the author of "Sorrel and Son." His new book, "The Woman at the Door," is one of the outstanding novels of the season.

"Grey Owl."

The North American Indian who is now lecturing throughout this country before large audiences. All his books are in good demand.

Lord Southwood of Fernhurst,

Head of Odhams Press Ltd., succeeds Sir Josiah Stamp as President of the Advertising Association.

"Sapper."

The creator of "Bull Dog Drummond," Lt.-Col. H. C. McNeile, whose estate has been declared at £26,166.

(Elliott & Fry.

Rudyard Kipling.

An anonymous donor has agreed to subscribe two-thirds of the cost of Kipling Tors at Westward Ho. This is where Kipling went to school and has immortalised in "Stalkey and Co."

Mr. H. G. Wells.

His book "Brynhild" created a stir in the trade last month. Another new book has appeared this week which accuses Oxford and Cambridge Universities of legend building.

From the Illustrated London News. I was extremely flattered by the company.

Amanda, Guy's
mother, my senior by 30
years but my very dear
friend.

Vera, for whom I wrote the
line 'When we went laughing
up and down – the magic
streets of Shrewsbury town'.

On the upper prom at Brighton, where I love to be.

Coincidence. The writing on the photograph reads: 'Here I first met Paddy'. How strange that it should have been selected as the subject for my Patience Strong calendar for September 1965. He died on the 10th. The calendar was prepared two years before, when he was well. Illustrations were chosen by the publishers.

THE BRIDGE OF MEMORY

Come, my love, and stroll with me — across the bridge of memory — there to seek and find anew — the dreams we dreamed, the bliss we knew..... Why cross the bridge of memory — in search of what can never be? Down long-forgotten paths why stray? The best of all is ours today.

Patience Strong

SUN	MON	TUES	WED	THUR	FRI	SAT
-	-	-	1	2	3	4
5	6	7	8	9	(10)	11
12	13	14	15	16	17	18
19	20	21	22	23	24	25
27	28	29	30		-	-

Paddy, at the time of our marriage.

Woodmans, near Battle, Sussex.

Sitting by the well at Woodmans.

Wright, *Alma Mia* and *An Old English Lane*.

Next day up the stairs he leapt with the news that he and I were to write the songs for the first British talkie film, *Woman to Woman*, featuring Betty Compson. Edison Bell issued records of the three songs from this film, and miraculously they survived my many moves: *Parisienne Doll, Sunshine of My Heart,* and *To You*. We also wrote a song which Carl Brisson sang in the film, *Song of Soho, There's Something About You That's Different,* which was recorded for His Master's Voice and Columbia. These also have been rescued from the litter bin of the past and added to my treasured collection of old scratchy 78's.

When new writers began to glitter on the horizon, lyricists or composers, Lawrence Wright would soon pin them down with a contract in the hope that they would someday write something sensational, or to make sure that no other publisher should have a hold on them. So the royal summons soon came. Jay and I were to lunch with Lawrence Wright at Frascati's, then a popular and pleasant restaurant. Genarro's, a small Italian restaurant in Charing Cross Road, was also a great favourite with people connected with music and stage. Roses and carnations were flown daily from Signor Genarro's garden on the Italian Riviera and on leaving the restaurant ladies would receive a posy from the hand of Genarro himself, bidding effusive farewells with elaborate bowings and kissing of hands. I would eat there occasionally with Peter Barnard who blossomed in this artificial but delightful atmosphere, like a full blown poinsietta in an overheated pot. Frascati's was more famous for its luncheons. It stood near the junction of Oxford Street and Tottenham Court Road, next or near to the spot where the old Oxford Music Hall once stood and was conveniently situated for Denmark Street. The monstrosity of Centre Point now looks across towards Foyle's uglifying that once fascinating corner of old London.

Lawrence Wright loved sitting in a conspicuous position in Frascati's dispensing hospitality in the grand manner with stars of screen, stage and the new dimension of wireless, stopping for a chat with the man behind the largest and most powerful entertainment organisation this side of the Atlantic. He did not know it then but the Wright Empire had reached its peak. So let me take a last look at the Lawrence Wright I knew. There he sits, having walked to London from Leicester to establish himself in the city where the streets were paved with gold for anyone willing to get out and dig for it, that is anyone with a special gift. It would be hard to say what Lawrence Wright's gift was; he wrote songs that could catch at the heart but was no musician. He had vision and a good team of workers to translate his dreams into reality. He owned most of the centres of holiday entertainment in Blackpool and Douglas, Isle of Man; piers, theatres, hotels, shops, arcades and he had a genius for knowing where and how to display his wares. The story of his life was written in his face which coarsened with the years. Increasing prosperity built up his business but ruined his life. I never liked him personally, but maintained loyalty to him in the face of adverse criticism. If anyone has been personally or instrumentally helpful to you in your career he has a right to your gratitude and your loyalty. "Praise where you can," my father used to say. "If you can't praise, keep silence."

On the day of my first meeting with Lawrie, a few weeks after he had accepted *Ninette*, Jay and I were at the famous Frascati table and Lawrie was aflush with his latest gimmick. The previous day he had flown round the Blackpool tower with Jack Hylton and his band to publicise the opening night of *On With The Show*, a production which he put on every summer in Douglas and Blackpool.

"Come back to the office and we'll talk business," said Lawrence Wright to me as Jay dashed off to a recording session. The opulence of the Wright House smothered the visitor like a warm blanket. I was never particularly interested in the business side of writing; not that I did not need to be, but because I always felt that the main thing was the work itself; and when Jay introduced me to Christian Science I found confirmation of much that had sometimes puzzled me in Biblical statements on the question of money.

"I shall not want" sang David in the Psalm that has comforted untold millions for thirty centuries. "Seek ye first the kingdom of God and His righteousness; and all these things shall be added unto you" promised Christ on the mountain. "God shall supply all your needs" wrote Paul to the Philippians. I believe this is to be something more than vague affirmation of a pious faith in the bounty of Providence. It goes much deeper than that for it is founded on a law of the mind which draws to itself that which it needs. Think poverty and you attract conditions of lack, not necessarily lack of money, it applies also to lack of health, lack of friends, lack of wholeness. Think always in terms of universal sufficiency, trusting in the power that comes to meet you at every point of need. The more you turn away from the belief in spiritual and material poverty the more readily will you gain access to the source of all good. It is not outside circumstances that create lack of affluence, it is the quality of mind and the daily conditioning of thought that moves in the direction of poverty or prosperity.

The upshot of my talk with Lawrence Wright was a contract giving him exclusive rights in all song lyrics written by me for a period of three years from that date. For this he would pay £150 a year, payable monthly, and a royalty on all titles published. I was told later that this was minimal, and I could have pressed for more but I was more than content; I was grateful. It was exactly the sum I needed to cover expenses and leave myself free for other activities if the necessity arose. It was a scientific demonstration of the fact proclaimed in all Christian Science churches that Divine love meets every human need.

There was a pattern emerging in my life. At first I feared it would be a digression but as it unfolded it proved to be confirmatory of the metaphysical truths discovered and declared by Mary Baker Eddy in 1890.

One dreary November Sunday as I was walking down New Bond Street, I passed the Aeolian Hall and saw the announcement of a lecture to be given there that afternoon by a Dr Charles Wase, President of the British School of Practical Psychology. The lecture was entitled *The Re-education of the Subconscious Mind*. People were already beginning to go in and I joined them unable to resist the temptation to explore yet another path into unknown country. This proved to be an adventure of the mind which I would not have missed for worlds. It was one of these landmarks to which I am sure I was led by unseen hands. There must have been about forty people present. A Christian Science silence prevailed which added to the impressiveness of Dr Wase's entrance. He was a shortish thick-set man with dark hair and the most piercing luminous eyes I had ever seen. Before commencing the lecture he ran those eyes along each row, the concentrated gaze resting for a moment on each person before passing on to the next. I gathered the School of Practical Psychology had been formed to provide its students with a meeting place, an address for correspondence and accommodation for a library from which books on the subject could be borrowed.

The lecturer had an easy simple approach to metaphysics which he explained in a manner that made this subject relevant to everyday living. He drew much upon the writers who had laid the foundations of the school of thought at the end of the last century and the early part of the present one. Emerson, Ralph Waldo Trine, Mary Baker Eddy and Prentice Mulford, to name a few of the Americans. He quoted often, too, from the *Edinburgh Lectures on Mental Science* by Thomas Troward. Religion was not mentioned but one felt that a very deep

stream of spiritual experience flowed behind the tech-
nicalities of the subject as he presented it. It was pro-
foundly interesting. The basic idea was that the difficulties of life could be eased and eventually overcome by
the re-education of the subconscious mind and in a short
space of time reform the whole personality. It could also
be directed for purposes of physical and mental healing,
and circumstances could be controlled by the subjective
powers of the mind. This was challenging, exciting my
curiosity to know more. I resolved to go to next Sunday's
lecture at the Aeolian Hall and to the weekly one given
every Thursday evening at the Caxton Hall, Westminster.
I also made my way to the school and enrolled as a student
during the following week which entitled me to borrow the
books and use the Quiet Room for study and meditation.

Meditation as it was practised then was on a higher
level than that which has been popularised in recent years
by the much advertised non-Christian Indian school
under the somewhat ambiguous name of Transcendental
Meditation. Dr Wase's system was based on the life-
giving words to be found in the forty-sixth psalm: "Be Still
and Know That I Am God." Repeated affirmations of
fundamental truths will in time obliterate the old tracks of
negative thoughts which have cut deeply into the all too
receptive subjective mind. We are what the subconscious
makes us in its own image of wrongly directed thoughts, or
positive thinking. I cannot allow myself to take this any
further from this point, but I have gone into it more fully
in a book I wrote some years ago called *Life Is For Living*,
published by Frederick Muller and dedicated to the memory of Dr Charles Wase; a truly remarkable man whose
work helped many people for so many years. His was a life
lived at the full stretch of his power to help and heal. In the
richness of his intellectual and spiritual maturity he died
where he had worked so hard for others, at his desk, "in
contemplation of the bliss absolute," to use the words of
his biographer.

BYWAYS AND CROSSROADS

It was shortly after I had signed my contract with Lawrence Wright that I was asked to write a lyric to be set to music by Richard Crean, musical director of the Palladium to commemorate the sixth birthday of the Princess Elizabeth, elder daughter of the Duke and Duchess of York. Words and music were quickly completed, copies rushed out and a record of it made on His Master's Voice by Webster Booth as soloist with the Palladium orchestra. It was to have its first performance at the next Royal Command Performance in the presence of their Majesties King George and Queen Mary. A special copy of the song printed on white vellum was to be presented to their Majesties during the interval. It was all perfectly planned, but in the event, it did not get the publicity Lawrence Wright had hoped for owing to the fact that it had been arranged that a quartette should perform in the interval and interest was divided. I was not in the least concerned: I was content to know that I had done my part of the job to everybody's satisfaction. However, there was an amusing sequel which might be worth recording.

The following day I had lunch with Lawrence Wright at Frascati's and we were joined by several who had been at the Palladium on the previous night. We were discussing the notices in the papers and Lawrie was displeased with Hannen Swaffer for ignoring our song and making mention in the Express of the American number which had been performed in the interval. Suddenly he said to me, "I dare you to go along to Fleet Street and raise hell with old Swaff. Tell him he ought to be boosting British songs." I doubted whether I should be able to beard this particular lion in a den which would be well guarded against intruders, but I agreed to go, and set out for Fleet Street with the Express and some sheet music packed into a solid roll. At the enquiry desk I was given a form on which to state my business and I wrote "matter of great urgency and of vital importance to the British Empire."

Five minutes or so elapsed and a young man appeared

and asked me to follow him. After I was shown in Hannen Swaffer rose to shake hands with me and I decided to employ shock tactics wasting no time in apologies and explanations but plunging aggressively straight to the heart of the matter, "What is the meaning of this?" I demanded banging on his desk with the roll of music. "You call yourself a patriot," I said, "I call you a traitor. You have betrayed the song writers of this country. Here was a wonderful opportunity to boost Britain and what did you do? You devoted a whole column in praise of that American drivel. Now go to it and make what amends you can. Good-day to you Mr Swaffer." So saying I withdrew leaving him limp with astonishment and as I made for the door I heard a faint gasp of relief; his eye had been fixed on the roll as I brandished it and I think he had feared lest the situation should develop into a personal assault. Poor man; he little realised what that display of mock violence had cost me, but I too was astonished when opening the next Sunday Express I saw that he had given the song *Princess Elizabeth* a very good write-up with a vivid description of how an angry young woman had burst into his office demanding that he make reparation for the unpatriotic mistake he had made in praising the Americans and ignoring the British. An evening paper took it up so my effort with Swaffer had paid dividends.

But life is unpredictable and the song did not become popular because suddenly someone called Amy Johnson had decided to fly solo to Australia, a remarkable feat which had never been attempted before. So Lawrence Wright was off on a new track, he and Joe Gilbert wrote *Amy Wonderful Amy* and had it printed and distributed within a matter of days. *Princess Elizabeth* was dropped and *Amy Wonderful Amy* won the success it deserved. But I still have the *Princess Elizabeth* recording which has survived many moves and which I once included in a televised programme.

I cannot drop the curtain on my song writing career

without mentioning *The Dream of Olwen* which was the one I liked best of the songs I wrote for films. Although ballads had all but faded out by this time, I had a few published in the twilight of the ballad which I like to remember: *Rise Up and Reach The Stars*, music by Eric Coates, *Spring Is A Lovely Lady*, music by Montague Phillip and about twenty with Maude Craske Day some of these being published under one of her pseudonyms, Laurel Blane. Maude Craske Day was an artist, an eccentric, a true musician and a very old friend of mine. She owned a house in Devonshire Road, Forest Hill, which I used to pass on my way to see Frederick Drummond. Frederick asked me to call on her and that is how our friendship started. She composed music for many of the Teschemacher lyrics, and of these her most famous was *Arise O Sun*, known, I suppose, wherever English songs were sung. The music was so perfectly wedded to the words that it well earned its place in the repertoires of amateur and professional singers. I often play it and it never fails to thrill me with its triumphant melody inspiring the listener with a new measure of strength and faith, so much needed in the dark winters of the second world war.

> *Show us the way and faithful we will run*
> *Arise O Sun.*
> *The long march ended*
> *And the battle won,*
> *Arise O Sun.*

The last time I saw her was during the London blitz when she lay ill and crippled in a dark room of a shabby old house in the Lee High Road. The room was blacked out according to war time restrictions but no gleam of sun ever found its way into that lofty cold room by day, for none could reach up to those high windows to draw aside the blackout screens. She was one of my kindred spirits; so deeply did we understand one another that we could talk naturally of God, aware of His presence, the unseen third never separated from His creatures, omnipresent, immanent and transcendent. I have never forgotten the horrors of that room, mice scuttered across the uncarpeted floor, books, music and instruments of every kind lay about amongst unwashed plates and saucepans. She was helpless. I was the only friend she had left in the world, but could do nothing to help in a practical way. She refused to go into hospital. I was there one day when the doctor came. "An ambulance will be sent for you tomorrow. If you still refuse to be helped you will die," he said angrily, but it was the doctor who died that night, not Maude Craske Day. He was killed in that night's air raid.

She did not lack money, her publisher saw to that. Royalties still poured in but life ebbed out. There she lay, helpless, but not hopeless for she was animated by a tremendous faith which never failed her. It was paradoxical that she should die in the dark, she who had bidden the sun to rise, and had run so faithfully in the steps of the Him who was and is the Light of the World.

14
WITHOUT MY CLOAK

$\mathcal{D}$URING 1933 Amanda and I discovered and joined the Swedenborgian Society, concerned with the philosopher Emanuel Swedenborg born in 1688. His exploration into the reality of other worlds was neither a psychic nor a metaphysical penetration into explored dimensions of time and space. It was a unique revelation and Amanda and I were intoxicated with our discovery of this new continent.

We were too near the unrolling scroll of the thirties to realise the full significance of what was taking place in Munich. That decade, which had been heralded by the Wall Street crash on the other side of the Atlantic, and brought to its birth here at a time of financial turmoil was to be fraught with difficulties not only for England but for the world. We thought we had finished with discord and strife. This was to be the epoch of peace, reconciliation and orderly reconstruction. Germany had, we hoped, learned her lesson. War was uncivilised, a barbarous obscenity. Nationalism, militarism and dreams of world conquest were out. Or so we thought, and when we were told that a few madmen in a Munich beer cellar were airing their grievances in bellicose terms and goose stepping all over the place we ignored them. No one thought it conceivable that they meant business; but they did, and their business was nothing less than ruthless enslavement of their own nation and ultimately the whole world. That was the size of the dream that inflamed the imagination of this rabble of ignorant louts calling themselves Nazis. Even when we heard of the Night of The Long Knives the truth did not dawn. It was too fantastic to contemplate. By the time we had taken a full look at the worst we realised that this was something more than a mob of troublemakers. We were witnessing the opening of the gates of Gehenna, spewing out vicious demons which had given up any right to call themselves human. Satan was back. Actually he had never gone away. He had always been lurking somewhere since taking the shape of a snake persuading our Edenic ancestors to abandon their state of perfection and eat of the tree of the knowledge of good and evil. Thus was duality introduced into the divine scheme of things. We were dealing not with something that had come out of a beer cellar, but out of the mouth of hell itself, something elemental and fundamentally evil.

This horror had been brewing since Versailles but it was the burning of the old Reichstag that rekindled the fires of 1914 sending sparks of unease blowing around Europe. The League of Nations was as incapable of holding back Hitler as the United Nations is impotent today in the path of the Russian juggernaut. No world organisation is ever of any practical use. It breaks apart at the centre with the dead weight of its own fractured limbs.

When I think of what lay before us as we stood tip toe at the edge of our great time of tribulation, it seems incredible that some sort of psychic early warning system did not quicken our awareness of what was in the wind. And what was in the wind? Enough to fill a library of volumes plus a world war. Was ever such a congestion of history packed into such a ten year span?

This book is not intended to be a diary of wartime and international events but how can one alive at such a time, chronicle an account of mere personal happenings without becoming inextricably entangled with the threads of the web of fate in which the world revolved? One cannot think of that decade without the year 1933 flashing up from the pit of memory. 1933: the year when Adolf Hitler came to power in Germany. In February 1935 the first Essex Regiment and the Royal Corps of Signals were pictured in the papers arriving home from the Continent at the end of their service in the Saar. On May 6th, 1935 King George and Queen Mary drove from Buckingham Palace to St. Paul's to a thanksgiving service on the occasion of their Silver Jubilee. In the evening the King, George V, broadcast to his people and I cannot resist recording a few extracts from this speech, not only because of the poignant relevance they bear to our own times, but because they throw a light on the thought of what the world might have been today if the ties of Empire had been strengthened instead of broken.

"I look back on the past with thankfulness to God" said the King Emperor. "My people and I have come through great trials and difficulties together. They are not over. In the midst of this day's rejoicing I grieve to think of the numbers of my people who are still without work. I hope that during this Jubilee Year all who can will do their utmost to find them work and bring them hope . . . To the children I would like to send a special message. I ask you to remember that in days to come you will be the citizens of a great Empire. As you grow up always keep this thought before you: and when the time comes, be ready and proud to give to your country the service of your work, your mind and your heart."

In the following July the King and the Prince of Wales reviewed the Royal Navy at Spithead. In less than six months the King lay on his death bed. With his dying breath he asked if all was well with the Empire. Some unutterable fear must have lain heavily upon his heart. Perhaps he had seen the announcement in a Berlin paper early that January that the conscription of children from the age of 10 for enrolment in the Hitler Youth organisations was about to be introduced.

On the 22nd day of January 1936, the Prince of Wales was proclaimed King. Seven days later on the 29th the late King Emperor was laid to rest in the vaults of Royal Windsor. On the 10th day of December of the same year came the drama of the Abdication of Edward the Eighth. In May of the following year the Duke and Duchess of York were crowned in the Abbey King George Sixth and his Queen, their elder daughter the Princess Elizabeth, was the ten-year-old heir to the Throne. In the eighth year of this epoch-making decade came the run up to Munich.

By March of the 9th year Hitler had hoisted his flag in Prague and the little yellow men from Japan were on the march across Asia. By June the British Concession in Tientsin was under blockade by the Japanese forces invading China.

After the agonising suspense of this trail of crises across Europe it was almost a relief when Neville Chamberlain came to the microphone on September 3rd 1939 to announce that we were at war with Germany, an announcement followed by the first air raid warning which proved to be a false alarm.

Before I jump the barrier between the third and fourth decades of the century, I must resist the suction power drawing me into the tumultuous years of the war. Remembering the reason for this recollection of personal memories I must go back to what was happening in my own little world.

Back I must go to that fifth year of the thirties. My mother had had a stroke. Connie had given up the house in the Hampstead Garden Suburb and moved to Forest Hill so that she could be nearer to Grove Park. It was typical of Connie to be the one to take on these duties.

Doctors had time to be human in those days. Mother

had a lady doctor who was particularly kind, but none of us understood about illness. I remember opening the door to her on one occasion and saying, "We are keeping your patient entertained." "Oh," she said, "That's the very thing you must not do. You must realise that she has very high blood pressure and must be kept as quiet as possible." This invalidism must have been torture for my mother to endure as she was very active and could not bear to lie still. However, her faith and her will to live pulled her through and in a few months she was better and went with my father for a holiday in Herne Bay. She wrote saying how much they were enjoying the fresh air from the North Pole and what a joy it was to be on the old road again around the coast, and walking the length of the long pier.

That autumn Connie mentioned that she had a "bit of a pain" in her side. Mother and I, it must be confessed, were not very sympathetic and advised her to forget it, so I take comfort in remembering that she had established the habit of visiting our favourite Auntie, every Friday evening. Connie was her special treasure. Aunt Ada was unmarried, being of the generation who lost their sweethearts in the holocaust of the Great War and my mother was her only sister. She was a character, astringently philosophical, no sentimentalist, but between her and Connie there was a deep bond. She had a crisp wit combined with a gift for analysing and seeing to the heart of a situation in a flash of insight. She worked in an office on the eastern approach to Tower Bridge. In the basement of the old building the boss, who with his wife were also old friends, made a week's supply of microbe killer every Friday which was sold for medicinal purposes, and according to the label, which bore the illustration of a skeleton, it was a cure for every ailment afflicting mankind. The formula was secret. The mysterious tank in the basement was within a stone's throw of that most intriguing of all bridges spanning the Thames from Bermondsey on the south bank, the water gateway to the City. The secret formula, the picture of the skeleton and the proximity to the bridge which was opening and closing all day long surrounded Aunt Ada with an aura of lively interest as she darted in and out of our lives. So it was to her that my sister turned in this crisis. It never occurred to me, my parents or her husband that this was anything serious. But looking back I do remember an afternoon of that autumn when we were visiting another aunt who lived in Dulwich. It was a rich October afternoon all gold and copper, Dulwich Village being deeply embowered in old trees which were then in the full blaze of their autumn glory.

We were on the top of the bus and the leafy branches seemed to part like waves before the prow of a ship. Connie said, "Is it not a desolating thought that however long we live we have only a certain number of autumns before us." A shadow seemed to fall momentarily on the tossing boughs of the burnished birches, lowering the temperature. For Connie this was to be the last autumn. But I thrust these thoughts from my mind, thoughts which seemed to be far away when we were together. Sometimes at the very peak of a joyous experience we would suddenly stop laughing as if at the same moment we both heard the same far faint bell with its reminder of the transience of all things lovely.

There was the afternoon a few weeks later when we all went to grandmother's funeral. After the service Connie and I escaped to a strip of woodland bordering the road by the cemetery. Every tree was familiar to us; we took off our gloves and affectionately touched the trunks in passing as if greeting old friends. For Connie it was a gesture of farewell for she never walked that way again. Perhaps she knew. We stood by a magnificent beech whose bough structure was hidden under a strangling network of ivy, and laid our bare hands on the cool grey bark. But the trees had withdrawn into their own secret world, excluding us from their company, leaving us to go home uncomforted.

A few weeks later my sister was operated upon in Kings College Hospital, Denmark Hill. Jo came about nine in the evening, an hour after the surgeon had told him that Connie had about three weeks to live. It was a case of incurable cancer. Fortunately my mother disbelieved the surgeon's diagnosis. That was a mercy. Always optimistic she clung to her faith, affirming the supreme power of good over evil. I, too stunned, refused to accept the facts as presented. They had made a mistake. Even if it were so, surely there was a cure. We had heard so much about advances in medical science but what did it all amount to if Connie was being sent home to die. It is a merciful thing that the mind is incapable of taking in at once a truth that is too terrible to be tolerated. The mind has the right to reject what it does not wish to believe. That is not ostrichism. It is one of God's ways of conserving our strength for future battles.

A fortnight later Connie was sent back to my parent's home in Grove Park. Fortunately, I had left our apartment amongst the cherry trees in Canadian Avenue and had moved into a small house on a new estate on the outskirts of Bromley, twenty minutes walk from Grove Park. In view of the difficulties of home buying or renting today, it is interesting here to note that we rented this five roomed newly built house, for twenty-three shillings and sixpence a week, payable monthly, on a three year lease.

So I was able to be with Connie all day. My father came home every evening at six looking weary and grave. We all felt a sense of helplessness. I know now that there might have been avenues we could have explored outside the scope of medical orthodoxy. To have to accept a sentence of death without putting up a fight was unthinkable. I did not know anything about the grape cure at that time, nor I suppose, did anybody else. A woman doctor in South

Africa was to experiment along these lines and cure herself permanently of a malignant growth. A German dietician whose name was Gerson was to do much good work and cure many so called incurables by a scientifically balanced diet of raw vegetables. Interesting and successful experiments have been made in the homeopathic field by the use of Iscador in the treatment of cancer. Observations on the subject, reprinted from the British Homoeopathic Journal by W. Thomson Walker, confirm many cases which have been helped by this means, and for those who refuse to take no for an answer many other homoeopathic remedies lie open for investigation. Spiritual healing also offers hope to the hopeless, not without foundation. Christian Science has its own methods of non-medical therapy, backed by a world wide organisation and the numerous testimonies of its adherents. Psychological cures, though on a different plane of consciousness, also produce notable results based on the re-education of the subjective processes by which thought determines the body tone and is eventually externalised as organic ease or disease, according to the quality of mental action and reaction.

But what of the well equipped Lincoln's Inn Fields Laboratories paid for by public subscription and maintained by the Imperial Cancer Research Fund? What would become of all this expensive equipment if somebody somewhere suddenly found a simple cure for cancer in a wild flower or plant, in a particular kind of thinking or way of life. If this happened perhaps the professionals would kill it before it got off the ground.

Radiology has had a limited success but it is admitted that healthy tissue is destroyed with the diseased. Vincent Nesfield, F.R.C.S., of Harley Street was on to something with his Bychresyl but he was born too soon. When he died in 1972 at the age of 94, still practising, that extraordinary brain of his was worn out with the long battle against professional bigotry.

One cannot embark upon anything honestly autobiographical and hope to by-pass the cubicle of the confessional. Sins of omission protrude like bones under the X-ray of introspection and retrospection. I see now that I should have spent more of that period in trying to strengthen my mother, not that she appeared to need it then. She too was insulated from the reality of the situation. Every minute away from the sickroom was spent with Amanda who was at my side through this "dark night of the soul". We would walk in the blue twilights of February, the lengthening days of March and deep into the starry nights of April. She buoyed me up because she shared my rejection of the facts, denying the thing that was happening to us.

Mother and I were hopeless as nurses and Connie must have realised our incompetence for there came a day in January about a month after she had been sent home from the hospital when she said "I know you do your best and I'm sorry to be giving all this trouble, but there are times when I miss the swishing sound of crisp linen." It was a pathetic appeal for professional attention, following a very bad night. The next day my father and Jo arranged for her to go into a private nursing home, in Canadian Avenue, the road from which we had just moved, about four miles from Grove Park. We visited the home every day and Jo and my father went in the evenings.

Our good friend Dr Reuben was in attendance several times a day and morphia was given. This was before the pain killer drugs were in use.

It had been December when the surgeon made his prognosis and we were told that Connie had about three weeks to live, but she lived for another four months and died in the April at Eastertide. Spiritual healing was sought and many prayers offered for the saving of her life, but it was not to be. There was a sickness in her body beyond the power of any human agency to heal. Somehow Amanda and I had to sublimate this experience or it would have destroyed us.

It was only in the long shadows of memory that I realised what this must have meant to my parents. She was their first born child, greatly beloved and dearly cherished. As for poor Aunt Ada, she withdrew into her sorrow. I had Paddy and my friend Amanda, Mother and Dad had each other but for Auntie Ada there was only a wound that never ceased to throb. She was too gallant a soul not to put on a brave face before the world. Not for her the outward showing of the inward grief. She went on with the little round of her life as she found it, going to Clacton every year for a week's holiday, to a West End theatre every Saturday afternoon and to the office on Tower Bridge from 8.30 to 6 o'clock 5½ days a week taking her part in the battle against the microbes. She had never had a cold since she entered the firm at the age of sixteen, maintaining that the sulphur in the "Mikes" disinfected the whole system.

Jo had the bitter companionship of a thousand regrets for the hours he had given to the coach station when he might have been with Connie, but it was only a five year penance. When the first daylight raid broke over London one Saturday afternoon, he was killed by the blast from a bomb, where he loved to be, amongst his coaches, at work, on duty.

We should not allow the acid of regrets to eat into our minds and bodies. We do what the spirit moves us to do. If Jo preferred work to the domestic evening it fitted in with Connie's love of solitude in which to read, write, think and walk alone. We do what we are impelled to do and if the heart is right then all is right in the end.

Connie died on the Wednesday after Easter and up till the Saturday my mother maintained her optimistic view that she would recover. It was good that this was so. When on that Easter Saturday evening the realisation of the truth touched a nerve something broke in her. She was dazed, surprised and bewildered at what had happened. She had been cheated of the ripeness of the future, misled by her belief in the inherent goodness at the core of everything.

Shakespeare in his 34th sonnet echoes the cry of all who have felt to be betrayed by their own faith in the ultimate felicity of life, tempted by the sun of an inward happiness to venture out in the flimsy covering of an inadequate philosophy.

> *"Why didst thou promise such a beauteous day,*
> *And make me travel forth without my cloak?"*

But she had her reward and her comforting. She who knew nothing of the jargon of the seance room and less than nothing about psychic phenomena, etheric bodies or extra-sensory perception was to have a brief glimpse of her lost daughter in a moment of extreme need, some months later. Truly, it is with the simple-hearted that the angels are most at home, but this wonderful thing experienced by my mother belongs to the next part of my story.

I wrote a last minute fare-you-well message which was interred with what remained of my sister's body after the devilish cancer had done its worst, and it lies with her up there under the wild grasses which I know she would prefer to a neatly tended grave.

LOVE LAUGHS AT DEATH

> *Go now, sweet spirit, lovely and beloved,*
> *Wing from your cage and take the sky in flight,*
> *Freed from the prison of the body's pain*
> *Soar out, released, into the infinite.*
>
> *In the confinement of your human flesh*
> *It was not meant that you should beat your wings,*
> *You were called out to wider ways of life*
> *Destined for greater and diviner things.*

WITHOUT MY CLOAK

Love is enough. We do not ask to hear
The well-loved voice, nor do we seek to see
The angel form; sufficient for the heart,
Peace—and the faith that heals its agony.

Love waits unchanged, through all the changing years,
Fed by the streams of living memory.
Love laughs at death, for death is but a dream
From which we wake to immortality.

1935

15
THE TELEPATHIC MESSAGE

*E*ARLY IN THE MAY of that year Paddy's father and
sister invited me to join them for a holiday in Yorkshire where they had planned to spend a golfing week in
Ilkley. It was, as they intended it should be, a change for
me after the grinding anxiety of the past few months, but I
felt guilty at welcoming this temporary release from mental pressure and about leaving my poor little mother in the
emptiness in which she now seemed to exist. She had the
comfort of my father's nearness but he had suddenly aged,
though still in his early fifties, retreating into the seclusion
of his own grief.

I suppose that subconsciously youth puts up a resist-
ance against anything that impedes the full flow of its
natural joy in life. I used to find myself walking quickly
with the old jaunty step, then memory would tug at my
sleeve until I slackened pace. But life will not allow you to
stand still for very long. It pushes at you from the back and
beckons you forward from the future. It is in God's providence for us that this should be so, and paradoxically, in
thrusting forward I have moved along the curving course
which has led back to the past. I feel closer to my sister
now when I keep my daily morning rendezvous with her
photograph than when we walked together on the physical plane of existence.

There was a bitter spell of weather that May and one of

my memories of Ilkley was of the sheep and the bluebells both with their heads peeping out of the snow; a strange sight, the deep blue patches on the whiteness and the half submerged flock immobilised in the drifts, waiting to be rescued by the farmer.

It was sheer ecstasy to walk the moors alone while the others were playing golf on the rugged course. One of the holes was called the Khyber Pass. This memory sprang out at me the other day when listening to news of the invasion of Afghanistan by the Soviets.

One day Lily drove us over to Haworth. The engine overheated panting up the steep hill to the old parsonage and I thought of those Brontë sisters in the bitter winters dying one by one of the consumption which was the scourge of the times, yet working indefatigably on at their novels, poems and letters, leaving to English literature the legacy of some of its greatest treasures; Anne, Emily, Charlotte: immortal names surviving those brief mortal lives lived out within sight of the bleak moors, incarcerated in the cold, draughty parsonage of Haworth.

Two months after I had returned I began to revise the three books which I had written during the previous two years. Connie had kindly offered to do a set of extra copies from my typescripts. Leonard Moore of Christy and Moore, whose advice I had sought, gave a very encouraging report on them, expressing the opinion that they reached a high literary standard and he hoped to find a publisher for them without too much delay. One was a satire in humorous vein dealing with the arty crafty dilettante entitled *What is a Girl to Do?* Another, a novel with a Welsh background and the other, I confess was blatantly reminiscent of the style of my idol, Mary Borden. In spite of the agent's glowing praise I knew they were not as good as they might have been had I persevered. But it was not to be. Fate had other plans for me.

Something happened which set me off on an entirely different course. News came of the death of Wilhelmina

Stitch, who for years had written a feature for the Daily Sketch called "The Fragrant Minute". I had noticed a note of ennui had crept into her recent work. When she died I was told that she had had a long illness and much unhappiness. After her last Fragrant Minute verse had appeared a poem was published in the Daily Sketch which was something quite different from her usual style; I think it must have been written with the intention that it should be published at the time of her death. It expressed a weariness of life that made a deep impression on me. I did take a copy of it but it must have been lost in one of my moves. I wish I could find it. It was something on these lines; I have had to substitute a few words where memory has faltered, but I think I have captured the essential meaning that Wilhelmina Stitch was trying to convey.

> *Tired of the way the buttons go.*
> *Tired of the tulips in a row,*
> *Tired of the tea in its morning cup.*
> *Tired when a voice says Drink it up.*
> *Too tired to listen when blackbirds sing*
> *Tired to the bone of everything.*

I am almost certain that the first line was what Wilhelmina Stitch wrote. I am not sure of the rest, but it was the gist and the drift of it. I pondered on this cry of weariness and felt glad that a woman so weary should now be free of her burden. Then followed the thought that I could take up what she had laid down.

I did not wish to tread directly in her steps by approaching the Daily Sketch. Somehow that would not have been cricket. I would try my luck with the Daily Mirror, naming my feature The Quiet Corner. So off I set next morning with a hope in my heart and a poem in my pocket.

It was a perfect summer's day towards the end of July. My brother was home from Oriel and walked with me to the station.

"I'm not too happy about it," he said. "If you get caught on this sort of treadmill you may never write any really good stuff again. You'll be stuck in your corner, like a pigeon in its hole."

"I don't care," I replied. "The other would be mere literary self-indulgence but this would be a job and I want to do it." So off I went to Fleet Street sending out a signal for the future to begin.

My feet hardly touched the ground as I hurried through the Embankment Gardens, under the Temple Bar arch and out into Fleet Street. I knew in my bones that I was on the brink of a new kind of life and a new kind of work. That was forty-five years ago and here I am still on the same treadmill, as my brother had envisaged.

The stream of life goes flowing on, come day, go day, year in, year out, war or no war, the sails of the mill of The Quiet Corner keep turning. I certainly started something on that morning in 1935 when, still in my twenties, I ran up the slope at Waterloo station confident that I should be able to produce a rhymed message for the Daily Mirror readers six days a week for as many years as I might be required to do so.

I went to see Mr Nicholson who was then Features Editor of the Daily Mirror. He seemed interested in my proposition and I showed him the verse I had written on the previous night.

He said to me abruptly—"Go home and bring me another eighteen verses tomorrow." I suppose he was testing me to see if I could stay the course. "I like the Quiet Corner idea," he said, "as the title of the feature, but we must think up another name for yourself— something with impact—and bring it with you tomorrow."

So far, so good. I went home and tapped out the eighteen verses on what had been Connie's typewriter, the much prized Royal portable which she had asked me to take care of for her when she was sent to the nursing home.

I still have it and still use it every day. That too has had a strange history which I will relate in another chapter.

I was pleased with the verses. That was before the war time paper shortage reduced them in size, but those first ones were 100-130 words in length. This was no problem. The problem was thinking of a name which would be exactly right. Strange to say, nothing came to mind. Even Paddy's fertile brain could not think of anything suitable. That was because the name was destined to come through a different channel.

It was not part of my job to find it which is why it did not come to me direct, but through Amanda. Life for me has been one strange thing after another. One strange thing might be coincidence, but two, three or four strange things add up to something that becomes more than flimsy chance, forming itself into a pattern and a purpose.

That night in 1927, when I had walked into a stranger in the fog, was a part of the story of the finding of the name. If I had not crossed paths with Guy that night I should never have met his mother and my search for a name would have led into a vacuum, for without the name of Patience Strong I doubt if the Quiet Corner would have lasted into the war. Names are important. There is a mystique about a name that cannot be defined or put under a microscope for analysis. Either it conveys something or nothing; if something then it must be harnessed to the right kind of horse. It is no good having the right name for unsuitable work or doing the right work under the wrong name. Before I tell you about the finding of the right name I must make it clear that Amanda did not know of my dilemma. I had not seen her for a few days and had thought of the Quiet Corner idea only the day before. I had just resolved to go for a walk, hoping an inspiration would come before darkness fell, when there was a ring at the front door. I opened it and there was Amanda in her customary neat black clothes, obviously in a hurry.

She was holding a book which she held out to me. "I

shall not come in," she said, "I want to get back to the play I was listening to on the wireless but felt impelled to go to my bookcase to look for this book and bring it to you. I cannot understand why there should be such a sense of urgency about it—but it has been disturbing me all evening, so here it is. It was given to me by my brother-in-law in 1896 as you will see by the inscription."

I looked at the book with its red binding and gold lettering. It was called *Patience Strong*, published by Routledge and Bell, probably issued by their American house. The name of the author was Mrs A. D. T. Whitney.

I looked up but Amanda was already at the front gate. I called after her "I'll come down tomorrow evening. I shall have something wonderful to tell you."

"Everything is wonderful," she called back. "I shall count the moments until you come."

"This is it," I said to Paddy. "I wonder how Amanda knew I should be wanting this particular book at this particular moment and she has had it for all those years?"

I was so enthralled by the name that it was sometime before I looked into the book itself. I opened it at random and these words stared up at me.

"I knew that the world was built by correspondencies before I ever heard of Swedenborg; that there were meanings in things, and that things had to be made for the giving of the meanings."

Amanda and I were deeply involved with the Swedenborgian Society. How odd to open this fateful book and find that Mrs Whitney's Patience Strong had also been out on this great spiritual adventure. Those words sharpened my interest. "Things had to be made for the giving of the meanings."

So the next morning I set off again for Fleet Street. Mr Nicholson was pleased with the verses and overjoyed when I introduced myself by the new name. "Perfect," he said. "Exactly right. Now I suggest we give this feature a month's trial, for which we will pay you four pounds a week." I was more than delighted.

There was a sequel to this little episode. I opened the book after Amanda had gone intending only to read the list of chapters, but I read it all from cover to cover. No words can describe what it did for me. It is just a simple book written in the first person by the spinster of thirty-six who shares the old New England home with her widowed mother. It is a fin-de-siècle chronicle of homely events in an American setting but it is more than a little story about little people. It is something greater than a cameo of country characters in the New England of the last century before the new world had lost the dignity of its essential goodness; before films, television and 'the new freedom' had begun to sap the moral qualities of the American people. The canvas of the story is small, though stretched out on the framework of big thoughts. The main character, the fictitious Patience Strong, moves through the book with a simplicity that only partially hides a philosophy that is as practical as it is profound.

I had found more than a pseudonym. I had turned a corner and found, by chance, my true vocation, the work that I have now been doing without a break for nearly fifty years.

The charm and the power of that book, *Patience Strong*, is something I cannot define. It would be like pulling the petals of a flower apart in an attempt to discover the secret of its beauty. I place it reverently on a pedestal alongside Mrs. Gaskell's *Cranford*, Jane Austen's *Emma* and *Our Village* by Nancy Russell Mitford.

In finding Patience Strong I was doubly enriched because it took me back to the verities of the Sunday School theology after my feeble attempts to sift truth through the sieve of adolescent questionings. And the extra blessing bestowed was that in coming back to a basic fundamentalism I found that grief for my sister vanished under a towering wave of happiness for her because I knew that with her all was well. She had gone only a few steps ahead along the road that all must travel.

If Amanda had not picked up the telepathic message out of the ether that evening, the Quiet Corner might have caved in with the war because if I had never come to know the first Patience Strong, how could I have kept it going month after month through the grinding years of the war, turning out the messages that so many people were waiting for day by day? How could I, without Paddy's help, have carried that large postbag on my back replying to each personally, never wanting for inspiration or having to hesitate for a title? I sometimes wonder if the first Patience Strong was not harnessed to the second in that uphill struggle though she was only a wraith conjured from the imaginings of her creator, A. D. Whitney.

The first Quiet Corner verses were written according to the requirements of the Features Editor. He wanted something which would appeal to his women readers on subjects like homes, gardens, friendships, happiness, trouble, all the things that go into the bundle of life.

I used to keep office hours posting six verses every Monday morning. The trial period seemed to go on indefinitely, and it was soon obvious that the trial had hardened into a fixture.

As the political situation grew worse the Quiet Corner lost some of its domestic flavour. Patriotic subjects crept in, and by the time the Munich crisis had burst on the European scene there was a marked change in its tone, though the old favourites were still in demand. Bereavement, love, engagement, marriage, holidays, nature, the country, anniversaries and birthdays. Occasionally a reader would ask me to write something about a special day, cat or pet, but I did this only when a verse was specially requested as I cannot write sincerely if it is on a subject about which I find it impossible to work up any personal feeling. Never having had pets of any kind I cannot write with any degree of sincerity about them.

A few months after joining the Daily Mirror I was asked to write a weekly poem for the Woman's Illustrated. This continued for two or three years until in 1939 I was asked to write a weekly verse for Woman's Own and this I still do.

The size of the panels for the Daily Mirror feature were seven inches by five which included the space taken up by an illustration. Quiet Corner brought in a steady stream of letters which I dealt with personally day by day. I have never at any time entertained the idea of having a secretary. Knowing myself so well, I can write only if alone, whether engaged on correspondence or creative work.

This would, I think, be the right moment to insert the story of the Royal servant for it spans at least fifty years of our lives from the time Connie bought it in 1930 up to the present day when it is still in daily use.

I have already told how my sister had the sudden urge to own her own typewriter and the pride with which she introduced it to the family. Mother and I expressed the opinion that it was rather a waste of money, but my father commended the purchase as being an act of faith, and so it proved.

I already possessed an old Oliver. The keys were blunted, it was constantly in for repairs and frequently let me down when I was engaged in an important piece of work. When Connie's Royal portable came into my possession, I gave the Oliver to one of my old song writing friends, Eileen Price Evans of Tunbridge Wells, who collaborated with my friend Frederick Drummond. She was the youngest of a family of ten and her father was a dentist in Church Road, Tunbridge Wells. As a teenager I used often to go to lunch there on Sundays and enjoy a long ramble on the Common with Eileen in the afternoon; an interesting family, all characters, all artistic in some way or another. That old house in Church Road is now converted into business premises. It is a pity that this has to happen, especially in Tunbridge Wells, where it is still possible to close your eyes and imagine you see sedan chairs in the Pantiles and hear the sound of music coming from the Pump Room.

From Royal Tunbridge Wells I must return to the Royal blue typewriter which, through my sister, was destined to play such a busy part in my life. This my Royal servant served me well until the sad day when the mechanic told me it was obsolete, and so it was put away for ten years. But it had a miraculous comeback which I will relate in due course.

After ten years writing my daily feature for the Mirror under the editorship of first Mr Nicholson and then Hugh Cudlipp, later to become Lord Cudlipp, I left the Daily Mirror. About this time I met Rupert Crew. My brother who had had some short stories published in Picture Post mentioned my name to Rupert Crew who offered to help me in any way possible. I had had an agent at one time but when I met Rupert Crew I knew I had found a friend. The office was in a mews with a red door. Charming. The firm was called The Author's Advisory Service. At the beginning of 1946 Rupert placed my Quiet Corner with the Sunday Pictorial which was later to be changed to the Sunday Mirror.

My association with Woman's Own is now in its 45th year. I have recently joined the Christian Herald for which I write a weekly poem and which has had a revival under new management.

Another of my regular contributions is to This England, a beautifully produced quarterly edited by Roy Faiers in Cheltenham. I must pause here to relate the strange circumstances which landed me with an illustrated feature which occupies the whole of the back page of this magazine which, like Puck, puts a girdle round the earth, strengthening the ties of the Anglo-Saxon world.

It came about in this way. Doreen Montgomery, who

has now taken over the Rupert Crew organisation, telephoned me one morning to say that This England had printed my well known poem *If You Stand Very Still* under somebody else's name. "What fun," I said. "They are bound to publish an apology. Good publicity." But Mr Faiers had not imagined I would be satisfied with a mere apology. On enquiring it transpired that a lady who had lost her husband had found this poem in his wallet written in his own handwriting and had genuinely believed that he had written it.

"I believe her," I said. "It could easily happen." So relieved was the editor that there was not going to be any unpleasantness that he was on the telephone to Doreen Montgomery next morning. "If only Patience Strong can do it in time for the Christmas number which goes all round the world, I'll give her a two page spread for an article and a photograph and sufficient space to set the poem out in full."

I set to work at once and the finished article was in that day's post. But it was strange that it should have been that particular one because that too has a history and I was able to tell it to the readers of This England.

During the war it had been sent on a Christmas card from London to Ireland and redirected to Texas. The Texan, with whom I had a lively correspondence throughout the war, was taken with this verse and sent it to the Cliftons in Los Angeles. They ran a chain of restaurants in the city. Each was called The Cafe of the Golden Rule. You had a good meal and paid only if you felt you wanted to, and could afford to do so. Or alternatively you could leave a donation for the refugees. This card arrived as they were completing a chapel of meditation in the redwoods. The building was finished but they were looking for a verse suitable to record and use in the chapel to be heard at the press of a button. They seized on this and with the addition of a few lines from another poem it made the perfect background piece with the melodies of *O Sweet*

Mystery of Life, and *Trees*, played on an organ. They sent me the record but it is a 78 so not now very clearly audible.

This verse had been published originally in the Daily Mirror and reproduced in one of the Quiet Corner books but somebody in search of a suitable verse to paste onto a Christmas card had posted it to a relation in Ireland. From there it had gone on its travels to Texas. This brought me in touch with Winifred Shultz, a Texan cattle farmer, with whom I kept up a lively war-long correspondence. She must have been a Boadicea, riding the range from horizon to horizon, but her ranch was burnt to the ground with its livestock and what she described as "the ingathering of the years". After that this giant of a woman was silenced. I never knew the end of her story, but before she went she passed on to the Cliftons of Los Angeles the verse that had drawn us together across the Atlantic.

If you stand very still in the heart of a wood
You will hear many wonderful things,
The snap of a twig and the wind in the trees
And the whirr of invisible wings.
If you stand very still in the turmoil of life
And you wait for the voice from within
You'll be led down the quiet ways of wisdom and peace
In a mad world of chaos and din.
If you stand very still and you hold to your faith
You will get all the help that you ask.
You will draw from the silence the things that you need
Hope and courage and strength for your task

Now learn a parable from the redwood trees
They were centuries old in Abraham's day
Their lives were half lived when
The star of Bethlehem led the Wise Men
To the infant Saviour.

In 1948 Clifford Clinton and his wife went on a world tour distributing their meals for millions, the concentrated food which they had devised for the multitudes starving in the wake of the war. They came to see us as they passed through England. We had just moved from Battle to Winchelsea and we were very grateful for the big supply of Meals for Millions Mixture which they left for us as we were still short of food.

They could not believe Winchelsea when they saw it. They kept rubbing their eyes and taking a second look before making a comment.

We took them to the look-out, a parapet on the old wall, overlooking the marsh, by Ellen Terry's house. A man is still paid to go there daily and scan the horizon for marauding French.

There is something unreal about Winchelsea. You feel that it would float away if you blew on it. Names like Maritau, Peritau, Flambou, Three Kings, Cordwainers, light the imagination as you wander round the marshbound plateau that looks across to Rye. The houses rise sheer from the streets, crowding around the church. Only the chancel is left, but the ruins arrange themselves round the walls as if they had been worked into the original design. When we told the Clintons that New York had been laid out as a copy of Winchelsea they were even more astonished. It was Winchelsea that had given someone the idea of laying out a town like a noughts and crosses board. Of its 39 squares only one now remains. New York increased and Winchelsea dwindled to a huddle of beautiful old houses clustered closely but elegantly round its old church. I moved to Winchelsea from Battle after the war, and by so doing, became interested in the efforts the local builder was making to preserve this unique locality from any development that would detract from its character. The outcome of our combined effort was that the house on the corner by the church was transformed into ten separate houses under the original roof all the lovely features being restored. Whenever I am passing that way, I stop to reflect upon what it might have been if left to chance. I take special pleasure in the thought that a cluster of ordinary bungalows or houses might have stood where now stands a block of Regency style flats, screened by trees and built around a garden court. Thus, at least one of the charming old Winchelsea mansions has been rescued for posterity. This rescue operation took place at the time of the Berlin air lift so there was an element of risk in the whole enterprise. Not only did it provide at least twenty homes for people in that historical setting but it ensured that Winchelsea would always retain its character.

16
THE YEARS BETWEEN

Q UICKLY WAS the reel of destiny unwound before us
during the fateful decade of the thirties. It was as if
the operator of a projector had touched a switch which set
the filmstrip unrolling at three times its normal speed.
The years between the tragic Easter of 1935 and the first
year of the new decade were so packed with drama,
personal and national, that in looking back upon that
period it is hard to get it into focus.

The Christmas of 1935, the first Christmas without
Connie, was one that we were all dreading for our own
private reasons, for to each it was going to bring back its
own special memory. But it was for my mother that I was
chiefly concerned. The doctor had warned us that she
could have another stroke at any time as she had high
blood pressure due to organic causes.

At the time we were living at the Grove Park end of
Bromley within twenty minutes walk of the house where
my parents lived in Burnt Ash Lane, and having something to tell which I thought would please my mother I
hurried there immediately after lunch on Christmas Eve.
It had been a night of keen frost and the sloping path to the
front door was still patched with a thin crust of ice. I
remarked on the dangerous condition of the path and my
mother, always quick to take immediate action, rushed
back indoors for a shovel and before I realised what she

intended to do she had fallen and broken her arm. I saw the bone protruding through the flesh as she lay on the path. It seemed like a cruel blow at the least deserving of all God's creatures. After the injury had been attended to in Lewisham Hospital she was able to go home. I blamed myself for yielding to the impulse to run down and tell her something that I thought would give her pleasure. If only I had not gone; but I clung to my belief that there is a guiding hand in all things leading to ultimate blessing for all who believe in the goodness of the Almighty and it came to me about a week or so later that there was perhaps a reason why it had to happen. All through that black Christmas my mother lay in bed, bruised and bewildered, and we all agreed that it would be better for her and for my father if she were moved to our place. My father had to go to London every day and if she were with me there would always be someone on call.

A few days later, when the whole country was under a pall of sadness because the king's life was moving to its close, I went in to my mother's room with a cup of morning tea. She stared at me helplessly unable to speak. Her foot seemed to be wedged between the wall and the bed. She was unable to take the cup from my hand and I realised that the dreadful thing had happened; she had had a second stroke. My first feeling was one of thankfulness that she was not alone. Had it not been for the accident she would probably have been alone as my father left for the station just after eight.

A week later she was moved to Lewisham Hospital where she remained for six months. She had belonged to some organisation which provided hospital accommodation and treatment for its members, and the cost was a matter of a few pence a week. She had the best possible care, and it was only at her own request, six months later that she left the hospital, even though two specialists begged her to remain for a few more months.

There were stairs at the Grove Park place so while

mother was in hospital my father sold the house and took a lease on a bungalow in Sidcup. At this time our three years' lease had expired and we moved into a flat in Farningham. It had once been a public house called The Bricklayers' Arms, and it was situated at the end of Sparepenny Lane. There was a Green Line bus service hourly so it was easy enough to get to Sidcup. Sparepenny Lane wandered off to Eynsford following the course of the little river Darent. We were there for one year. Two memories of our year in this strange old place stand out in my mind: a Victoria plum tree in the garden so heavily fruited that it bent to the ground under the weight of its branches and I shall never forget how a nightingale sang from the honeysuckle hedge from dusk to dawn on the night before we left. I had never really heard a nightingale before, although I knew Keats' Ode by heart which was almost as good as the real thing. And I do not think I have heard one since. Nightingales like skylarks seem to have vanished with the mechanisation and chemicalisation of farming, so perhaps that nightingale had made a special effort to sing angel music for me that night.

Before my mother left hospital something occurred which I feel I must relate. Being something very personal therefore sacred, I would prefer to keep silence over it, but because the little incident might be of some comfort to someone I will put it on record.

Amanda and I used to have lunch together every Sunday at a Lyons in Lewisham before going to the hospital. I went in alone. Mother had partially recovered the power of speech. It was pitiful to hear her trying to tell me something, but fortunately her sense of humour had not been in any way impaired. And efforts to make herself understood always ended in hilarious laughter. And what a gift is laughter! As it says in the Bible, "A merry heart doeth good like a medicine".

Mother seemed to be under some cloud that Sunday. There was something that was worrying her and I could not find out what it was, so when visiting time was over I asked one of the nurses. "I think I know what it is" she said, "tomorrow we are getting her out of bed and giving her a walking lesson." So that was it.

On the following Wednesday afternoon Mother looked radiantly happy, but made no reference to the walking lesson so I did not ask any questions. When an hour had elapsed and there was still no mention of it I made an excuse to see the nurse. "How did the walking lesson go?" I asked. "Splendid," said nurse. "She was very nervous at first but suddenly she gained confidence and seemed to enjoy it."

On returning I said, "I hear they have been teaching you to walk." Immediately she seemed to withdraw into herself as though I had touched upon something she did not wish to discuss.

"Were you nervous?" I asked.

"No" she said, and she smiled as if she had some secret joke that she had no intention of sharing.

"Tell me what happened." I said.

She hesitated then said, "Connie came."

"You mean, you were thinking of her," I said, determined to get to the bottom of the mystery.

"No, no," she persisted. "I wasn't. She came."

"Beside you?" I questioned.

"In front," she said, pointing forward with her good hand.

"You mean you saw her ghost," more than ever determined to get at what had really happened.

With this she made one of her old gestures of impatience.

"Ghost," she said with a sigh of exasperation. "Connie. As she was. Connie. She walked in front of me—down the ward."

It was obvious to me that she had had a genuine psychic experience. For the simple-hearted it is permitted that the veil be drawn aside at times of extreme need. It was not for me to ask any more questions. I was only groping, for knowledge, but she knew without the knowledge.

After she left hospital she was unable to walk but we took her out in a wheelchair. There was never any atmosphere of invalidism in the place. Although communication was sometimes difficult it was with the same humour that had always bubbled through our family conversations.

Paddy and I decided that the time had come to have yet another move and we bought a house in Sidcup about a mile from my parents. It was a newly built double fronted affair, nothing very special about the house itself, but its chief attraction was a most fantastic silver birch tree which when in leaf, hung a green curtain across the window, which was always fluttering in the wind.

The tree itself was taller than the house, but I had made up my mind not to stop there while sitting on the doorstep waiting for the moving van to arrive. Paddy had to go in with the furniture because they had packed his shoes and it was too late to retrieve them.

So we remained there only three months after which we let it on a three year lease to one of the local bank managers and we moved into the bungalow that my parents had vacated. They had decided to buy a house in Eltham as it was conveniently near the station for my father.

After a few months we sub-let the bungalow and bought a house in Eltham within a short walking distance from my parents.

It was about this time that my Quiet Corner verses were published in book form by Simpkin Marshall and I was beginning to work out plans for publishing a calendar. At that time most calendars consisted of a single picture on cardboard with a paper calendar hanging from it.

I selected twelve suitable verses, one for each month, attaching an appropriate illustration. I felt rather pleased with the idea as this, in those days, was a novelty. In fact, I think I am right in saying that my

Quiet Corner calendar was the first of its kind. I had to fight hard to get it on the market and at last the Daily Mirror arranged to take it on, provided I paid any losses that might be incurred. I readily agreed to this being confident that it would be popular. The Mirror advertised it in the Quiet Corner panel. It was not then in the shops but obtainable from the Daily Mirror for one shilling; I think it was post free. So they set aside an office and were surprised at finding themselves inundated with postal orders for the Quiet Corner calendar.

It involved so much work for them that they had to look around for a publisher to handle it for the next Christmas. Photochrome of Tunbridge Wells took it on; they also did a series of my Christmas cards. Photochrome carried on with this until they went out of business during the war. It was then that Delgado came on the scene. It was a family business managed by a Mr. Finzi. Some years ago they were taken over by Fine Art Development, a large concern. The first Delgado Quiet Corner calendars were fifty pages, consisting of a weekly verse, my photograph on the cover page and a ribbon tie. The Quiet Corner calendar has gone through many metamorphoses. There have been changes in size, changes in the quality of the paper used, changes in format. The most dramatic change of all was when colour printing was introduced. This meant a rise in cost of production but illustration in colour was very much more attractive and they found that though the price increased the sales kept pace.

Delgado now do a large size $9'' \times 10''$ with twelve monthly verses illustrated in colour, a small size $9'' \times 4\frac{1}{2}''$ with twelve monthly verses, and an engagement diary with colour floral illustration. There is also a long narrow one with space for notes suitable for hanging in the kitchen.

After a visit to South Africa where the stand-up type of calendar is favoured, I resolved to do one of these portables and Henry Walter Ltd of Worthing published it.

Personally, I prefer it, as the hang-on-the-wall type is not always convenient to position, and in some places one is not allowed to put hooks in walls. I find this is more intimate as you can carry it from room to room if you so wish. I sometimes feel a calendar needs company and must sometimes feel out in the cold if hung in a room not often used.

This calendar business tends to make time fly even quicker than it does. I have already done my calendar verses for 1983 and always seem to be living a few years ahead of myself.

As we approached the closing years of the decade of the thirties the shadows lengthened over Europe. By the time that Munich was upon us we decided that we ought to get mother out of the London area as in the event of war my father would have to be on fire-watching duty at the office and if raids were too bad would be unable to travel home, so we all set out on yet another move.

This time it was Orpington, only a few miles away but it seemed the right thing to do, though its proximity to Biggin Hill placed it in the line of fire so far as air raids were concerned. My father found a flat within walking distance of the station and we bought a house nearby.

In 1939 I joined Woman's Own for which I still write weekly, but with the outbreak of war the character of the verses changed. Not that I made any conscious effort to make them different. It was almost as if someone else had taken control and I worked merely as an amanuensis. The domestic theme was no longer appropriate with homes being broken up all over the country, children being sent off to strangers as evacuees, husbands going off to serve, sons and daughters leaving home. Patriotism too was an old fashioned thing that was suddenly not only relevant but popular. The countryside also took on a new meaning. Not only were we going to have to rely on it for much of our food, but the beauty of it was going to be remembered by many a Briton in the years to come, remembered with a tear when thinking of home on faraway battlefields.

Before the war had entered its first month I was having letters from people whose lives had been changed by it. The Quiet Corner was to play its small part in one of the great dramas of all time, the drama of Great Britain standing alone against the might of Germany.

The first few months of the war have been described as phoney. Nothing appeared to be happening. The war itself seemed to be marking time.

Paddy became an air raid warden and my father was enlised into the fire fighters of the City.

It was merciful that my mother died before the bombs started to fall. It was in the February of 1940. She had become very weak and lost the use of her limbs. She was 59.

On a quiet evening in February as the gold light of the evening stole across the yellow wall of her room, she said to me, "So tired," and slipped away. A few days later she was buried in Orpington churchyard. The snow drifted softly over the coffin and I remembered the saying, "Blessed are the dead upon whom the snow falls".

17
BETTER THAN LIGHT

ON THE FIRST Christmas Day of the war, King George VI, father of our present Queen, broadcast a message to the Empire from Sandringham. At the conclusion he said, "A new year is at hand. We cannot tell what it will bring. If it brings peace how thankful we shall all be. If it brings us continued struggle we shall remain undaunted. In the meantime I feel that we may all find a message of encouragement in the lines which in my closing words I would like to say to you: 'I said to the man who stood at the gate of the year, Give me a light that I may tread safely into the unknown. And he replied, Go out into the darkness and put your hand into the Hand of God. That shall be to you better than light and safer than a known way.'"

We could not have had wiser words spoken to us as we stood at the gate of that year. This great Christian king who had had kingship thrust upon him at a most crucial time in the history of the Empire did well to remind his people of the Hand that would be to them better than light and safer than a known way. That Hand was surely stretched above these islands for from the military viewpoint we had few defences, no hope of survival against the oncoming hordes of German tanks, German guns and planes going through Europe like a knife through butter. France's much vaunted Maginot Line collapsed like a pack of cards. In April Norway and Denmark had been invaded. On May 10th the news broke that Holland, Belgium and Luxemburg had fallen to the Nazis. Brussels had been bombed.

The French to whose rescue we had gone left her allies to get back as best they could. Both the French and the Germans had short memories. They had forgotten that Britain had a guardian. They had forgotten the Hand of which the King had spoken. They had forgotten the Angels of Mons and the miracle of the White Cavalry.

Earlier in April Winston Churchill had been appointed war leader in the new Cabinet. The miraculous deliverance of a great part of our army from the Dunkirk beaches by the spontaneous inspiration of so many of the boat owners in the kingdom to put out to sea and save our men was something that will be remembered for as long as we are a nation. I remember seeing them pass through the station at Orpington. Weary, some wounded, but unbeaten.

One year after the beginning of the war Hitler started his aerial attack on London in earnest. The fires at the docks reddened the sky with a glow that could be seen for miles. Wave after wave, the bombers came in and the wonderful words rang round the world, "London can take it." And she did. I was never more proud of being a Londoner than I was during that first onslaught. The good humour of the people in the shelters was something Hitler could neither destroy nor understand. No wonder the RAF boys in their frail little Spitfires fought and flew like supermen. A great wave of confidence seemed to surge over the whole nation. The Battle of Britain boys knew that the people underneath their wings were worth fighting for; and dying for. The war from beginning to end was a series of miracles. It was as if our king had given us the watchword in that Christmas message as we plunged into the dark years holding on to something that was better than light.

It was to be seen wherever the British were operating, as

service men and women in uniform or doing ordinary jobs in homes, factories, offices, transport or on farms.

During that first year of the war I think the Daily Mirror must have been a firm favourite with the forces, for each day brought in a pile of letters from readers with various requests. Many of them were from serving soldiers, airmen, sailors who had cut out a particular verse which had appealed to them and which they wished me to send on to wife, mother or sweetheart. From the women came similar requests to send certain verses on to their absent menfolk. These items were of a personal nature so that started something which kept me at the typewriter almost non-stop.

Soon after the beginning of the real fighting came letters from those who had been bereaved; I was constantly being told that wallets had been returned containing one of my verses which, by its tattered state, had been carried around for some time. To the end of this, my own story, I will append a small collection of these poems from Quiet Corner which were much in demand at that time. From my point of view it was now no longer a job, but a mission, my war work, my own small niche in the war machine. Small it certainly was, but from letters received I had reason to believe that for many it was lighting a candle of faith in a dark world.

When the time came for me to be conscripted into some sort of military service I went for the interview, explaining what my occupation was; the interviewer absented himself for some hours, then reappeared saying that he had had consultations by telephone with various people and it had been decided that for the moment I could not be better employed. I was much relieved as having no knowledge of practical matters, I am sure that had I been put into a factory, I should have blown it up by mistake, or held up operations by having to have everything explained at great length. Also, without any undue pride on my part, I knew that what I was doing in giving a little daily message to hundreds of thousands who were over-wrought, homesick, unhappy and afraid, was helpful and valuable.

I made the discovery that most people are sentimenta-lists at heart even though they would deny the mere suggestion of anything that smacked of such weakness. We are all weak when it comes to something, all vulner-able, all children, lost in the dark.

Patriotism, sentiment, loyalty, faithfulness, religion; these were subjects which never failed to pull at the heart. It was a pity that it took a world war to re-establish these virtues, and a greater pity that when the war was over people so easily forgot and lapsed into the old negative life under which there were no foundations.

War, like adversity, brings out what is highest in human nature drawing the best from the worst. I suppose that is because in war time we walk in the shadow of death. Life is not something to be taken for granted. You never knew whether you would live to hear the next all clear, or worse, if you would live to become blinded, maimed, or disabled.

All London office buildings had their basements which were converted into air-raid shelters with sleeping accom-modation, so my father decided to stay in town as trains during raids and even on a short journey to Orpington, were likely to have hours of delay.

Paddy joined the A.R.P. We had an Anderson shelter in the garden and sometimes the candle went out as there was no oxygen getting into it. After a while, we, like many others, abandoned the shelter and took a chance on stay-ing in the house, though Paddy was out on patrol most nights.

It was at this time that I met Clare Kipps. It was upon her doorstep that Clarence the sparrow arrived one night denuded of its feathers through the blast of a bomb. When she came in off duty she discovered the pathetic object and placed it in her airing cupboard in a saucer. She was surprised a few hours later to hear faint squeaks coming from the cupboard and to find that it was still alive. She gave it warm milk and made a nest for it in an old fur glove. Within a few weeks it had grown a new coat of feathers and Clare was giving it singing lessons. Living alone and with death and danger all around she clung to that bird and grew to love it dearly, christening it Clarence. Clarence responded in an almost supernatural way. Warmed by being cherished it developed an ear for music, and instead of running true to form and emitting the chirp which was all one might expect from a Cockney sparrow, it developed the voice of a nightingale. Delighted at this, Clare included Clarence at the wardens' concert, had him on a length of cotton and when he heard the introductory notes which she had trained him to follow, he obliged with a nightingale song which would have charmed the heart of Keats.

After the war Clare said to me, "I must make some money." She was over-generous to too many people and suddenly found her income drastically depleted. We were seated on Charing Cross Station late one night waiting for a train. "I think I'll write my life story," she said. Clare had gone three times round the world as a concert pianist and had had many adventures. "That would involve a vast amount of work," I said. "Lots of people have played themselves round the world but you are the only person who has ever trained a London sparrow to sing like a nightingale. There's your subject."

She cogitated, then broke into a sparkling smile. "Of course. But I must have an arresting title."

I said "You must call it *Sold For A Farthing*, Matthew 10, verse 29."

She did. It was duly written and it had a fabulous success not only here but in many parts of the world. I am glad to be able to say that not only had I known the famous Clarence, but had heard him sing.

A few months after the Christmas following the Battle

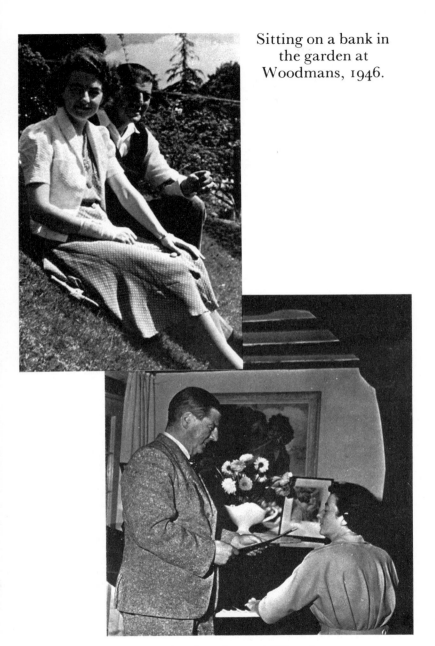

Sitting on a bank in
the garden at
Woodmans, 1946.

At the piano at Woodmans.

Dr. Vincent Nesfield.

My father in the garden at Orpington, Kent, 1940.

A commemorative photograph taken in 1960.

One of the treasures of Avalon.

Myself in 1971 at Meadow Cottage beside one of Henry
James' bookshelves which I had been lucky enough to
buy at an auction at Lamb House, Rye.

Myself, with my faithful Royal typewriter, in 1951.

Myself, thirty years later, with the same Royal typewriter.

of Britain, the warden rang the bell to tell us that the road had to be evacuated. This was a short cul-de-sac of about a dozen houses most of which were unoccupied, their owners having fled to the West Country, though from then on they started to dribble back. Not that the raids had abated, but the misery of living in the houses of strangers, however kind, was weighed in the balance against the magnetic pull of home.

Some sort of unexploded bomb had fallen amongst the trees by the roadside and they had to make sure everyone had been evacuated before taking any chances with it. They wanted us to be gone by next morning. So I took a train to Sydenham where Aunt Ada was living, thinking she would be delighted to be taken out of it all for a few days, but she stoutly refused to go away. She was a typical Londoner. "I'm having the time of my life," she said. "I've never met any of my neighbours before. Now we all go down into the public shelter every night and thoroughly enjoy ourselves."

I found it hard to imagine anything more ghastly, but there is no accounting for tastes and that, after all, was the foundation of the spirit that won the war; Londoners taking it.

We were just wondering where to go realising that the whole countryside was swarming with evacuees, when a telephone call came from another aunt who was staying with relatives in Shropshire. She said she had been trying to get me for days to beg me to go and spend a few days with her. She had reserved a room for us at a farm outside Oswestry. How strange that it should have come just at this time. Some instinct told me to take my typewriter. I was afraid that it would be bombed and it, to me, was no ordinary typewriter, but something very special, having once belonged to my sister.

There was a raid on while we were waiting in Paddington station so the train was delayed for many hours. At last after a wearisome journey we arrived at Gobowen.

Opposite the station there was an inn called The Hart and Trumpet. After the turmoil and the ruinous desolation of London this looked too good to be true. So in we went for a meal and there we sat stunned by the silence. You could almost reach out and touch it. I thought of my father, away up there in the hell of London, wishing that he too was going to have a few peaceful days. After the meal we telephoned the place where my aunt was staying with her in-laws, and within minutes they arrived in a car to take us to the farm. But first we called in at Hengoed where the mother-in-law lived. I shall never forget the first sight of that old cottage. There was a fire burning in the black-leaded grate on which sang an enormous copper kettle. The room was lit by an oil lamp hanging from the low ceiling. A wall clock struck the hour. Old Mrs Hughes was sitting in the chimney corner in a Windsor chair. The whole scene was one of homeliness and wholesomeness. The smell of freshly baked bread hung in the air.

We received a warm welcome. I had stepped into another world. Outside the window there was a view of blue hills flowing away into the sunset. I not only stepped into a new world but I was within minutes of making a new friend, for the door opened suddenly and in burst an excited schoolgirl, satchel on back and eyes like stars. It was Vera, the fourteen-year-old daughter of my aunt's sister-in-law. It was like my meeting with Amanda. An electric shock of recognition ran between us. We were friends for life.

We went to the farm in the van, up the Bath Banks, a slope that was almost perpendicular. I looked out of the rear window and to my astonishment there was Vera, running behind the van, black hair blowing in the wind, merry, happy, beautiful Vera.

When we arrived at the farm she said "I couldn't bear to see you go—oh when can we have a walk together. I could come up for you after I've done my homework tomorrow." So it was settled.

The farmyard was busy with ducks, cats and chickens and at last we picked our way to the front door. It had been a busy day and we were thankful to collapse into the deep goose feathered bed.

I woke to the sound of cocks crowing, sheep bleating, a stream babbling and birds singing. It was like waking up in wonderland. My first glimpse of real country, with the exception of our night at The Pink and Lily.

When Monday morning came I felt reluctant to go. Paddy went to the call box and telephoned to my father's office. Yes, he was all right but he sent me a message. If you like it there, why not stay for a week or two. Paddy was all for it. I had my typewriter with me. Having met Vera the temptation was irresistible. Paddy had to return but I promised to telephone every evening if it was possible to get through.

I rigged up an office in the bedroom from which I had tranquillising views of the gentle Shropshire hills from one window and an inspiring sight of the mountains from another where, a few yards up the Bath Banks, England disappeared into Wales, near Offa's Dyke. Paddy did not have much difficulty in persuading me to stay for at least a fortnight, a request which was backed and urged in a letter from father.

I should like to launch into a description of the amusing things that happened during my stay at the farm, but I must press on and content myself with an inadequate description of my evening walks with Vera. She used to run up the Bath Banks and arrive on the doorstep all breathless and eager to go "over the tops", as they used to say when passing the "First In and the Last Out" by the church; this was a delightful little pub-cum-farm run by two people known generally as Uncle Oliver and Auntie Meg. This was the first inn in England if you were coming along the road from the Offa's Dyke direction, also the last out of Wales.

It was a low ceilinged building with sloping floors and

huge stone fireplaces. At that time of the year the hearth was usually strewn with newly born lambs which had been brought in from the cold mountain pastures. You had to step over the lambs to sit down. On Sundays the verger would bring the collection in from the church to be stacked in piles of coins on the bar counter and duly checked by the Vicar's warden. Strictly speaking the Welsh part of the house was closed on Sundays but nobody seemed to know exactly where the boundary lay.

The receipt of letters was a somewhat dicey affair, as Old Dick the postman had to take his mail bag "over the tops" and as the wind reached hurricane force sometimes up there in the winter many a letter was blown far from its destination, but seemed to turn up eventually. Nobody bothered. Life revolved round cows, sheep, harvest, church and chapel. It was no good trying to envisage what was going on in Europe. Hitler was a myth, although the papers told us he had just made the biggest mistake of his life, imagining that he could leave Britain unbeaten, turn his back on her at a time when she was within reach, and march east to attack Russia.

My father wrote saying he was due for a week's leave of absence and he proposed to come up with Paddy when he returned, the following week. The room at the farm had been taken for only a long weekend so I was moved up to The First And Last, and here in my little room under the beams I was able to work all day at verses and correspondence sent on from Orpington.

All too soon we were on our way back, but Vera and I remained friends and had several short holidays together even before the war ended. I wrote about our excursions into Shrewsbury in my Quiet Corner:

> *"When we went laughing up and down*
> *The magpie streets of Shrewsbury town."*

Over thirty years later, still haunted by that smile, I used it as the subject of one of my Woman's Own verses.

On arriving back in Orpington I had an experience which changed the whole course of my thinking and of my life. After travelling all day I was longing for a breath of air so decided to walk up the High Street as far as the pond. The air raid siren sounded; I had almost forgotten what it meant; things started to happen at once so I thought I would take cover for a few minutes in the porch of the Village Hall. I noticed several people were going inside, and realising a meeting was about to commence and never able to resist meetings, I joined them.

There was a table on the platform covered with a Union Jack and a banner with the words British Israel World Federation.

The lecturer, Harold Stough, was a chubby faced American with twinkling eyes and a genial manner. I forget the title of the lecture, but never had I heard a speaker with a greater knowledge of the Bible. I saw the whole truth of the British Israel movement and what it stood for in a single flash. Suddenly the veil that had hung over the Scriptures was rent, revealing a truth so simple that I could not understand why I had not seen it before. Here, by a stroke of chance, I had had the whole mystery of the Bible unravelled and set before me in all its grandeur.

I had been attending Anglican services since coming to Orpington, drawn every Sunday by the "beauty of Holiness", the formality of the prayers, the glory of the language, but had failed to solve certain problems. For instance, I could not understand why the Benedictus commenced with the stupendous acclamation "Blessed be the Lord God of Israel, for he hath visited and redeemed his people". And why in the Magnificat was written "as He promised to our forefather Abraham and his seed forever"? And those words in the Nunc Dimittis, "to be a light to lighten the Gentiles and to be the glory of Thy people Israel".

I could have understood all this had we been in a synagogue, but what had it to do with the Church of England, the Anglican Community, the official ecclesiastical body of Anglo-Saxon Christendom? Where then were these people known as Israel?

I was to learn that night the answer to these questions. We, the Anglo-Saxons, and our kindred nations were "Israel in the Isles", the Isles of the West, referred to by Isaiah. Another thing that had always been a stumbling block to me were the references made by St. Paul to The Mystery. What was this mystery? St. Paul all will agree is known as the apostle to the Gentiles. While this Mystery was not made known to former generations of mankind, it was foreshadowed in the Old Testament and this Mystery was revealed to me in Orpington Village Hall on that night to the accompaniment of guns and bombs; the Mystery was the opening of the door of the church of Israel to the Gentiles: the incorporation of the Gentiles into the Church of the new covenant which God had made with his people Israel through the birth and resurrection of Christ who was the Redeemer of Israel though rejected by his own people. The heart of the Mystery was that the Gentiles henceforth should be joint-heirs with Israel for whom the first Covenant was still valid. The rending of the veil of the Temple at the time of the Crucifixion was symbolic of the destruction of the "middle wall of partition" spoken of by Paul in his letter to the Ephesians.

The Jews were of the tribe of Judah, but as every Bible student knew, the Northern House of Israel and the Southern Kingdom of Judah separated in 975 B.C. Judah was taken captive into Babylon for her sins, but eventually at the time of Ezra and Nehemiah some were given permission to return to Jerusalem to rebuild the Temple. Israel, also as punishment, was taken captive into Assyria and lost to history. We know now that after the exile they settled around the Caspian and in course of time migrated in waves to Ireland, to Spain, to Gaul and ultimately to The Isles of the West, the Brit Isles, where the Brits, the old name for Covenant people, settled centuries before the birth of Christ.

The tremendous promises made to Abraham were fulfilled only in the history of the Brits. Their story is written on the tablets of time. With this new slant on the old Bible I came out confused. I could grasp only a fragment of the great scroll that was unrolled that night but I knew I had found a peace of great price. The war took on a new significance. I had never doubted that we would win, but now the whole thing was lifted onto a plane that was beyond nationalism, beyond politics, beyond the mere human spectrum. This was in very truth a controversy between good and evil, the continuance of the same warfare that had been going on since the Creation. This was what Our Lord Himself had foretold. What are the gospels but the records of the workings of Divine against Satanic powers. In the words of St. Paul "we wrestle not against flesh and blood, but against powers . . . spiritual wickedness in high places."

The ministry of Christ commenced with the confrontation in the wilderness of Judeah known as The Temptation which followed the forty days and forty nights of fasting. It ended on Calvary, a seeming victory for the Adversary, but in reality it was God having the last Word three days later.

There is no need for me to attempt an exposition of the truth of the British Israel case. It is embedded in history for all who have the strength and the will to dig for it. Confirmation of its veracity are to be found in many different sciences, Egyptology, archaeology, ethnography, etymology and prophecy. It is not a cult, nor is it a denomination. Any member of a Christian church can became a British Israelite, for its teaching is based purely on a study of the Bible, not as the Church has construed it, but as God wrote it in the beginning. I saw that it was necessary to get back to an absolute fundamentalism as a starting point for this great voyage of discovery. I ran all the way home, eager to get my hands on one of my Bibles, to confirm the flash of truth I had seen that night in the village hall in Orpington, Kent.

From then on I wrote with a new fervour, a new clarity of perception. The Daily Mirror was co-operative. So far as I was concerned there was no editorial ban on any subject. The next day I submitted a verse entitled "God's Battle Axe" to which there was an immediate and warm-hearted response from service men and women on every battlefront. I had not realised that there were so many Bible students who thought along these lines. I replied to them all, encouraged to realise that there was this great company of believers stationed in our forces at home and overseas.

A new light fell, too, upon the Churchill speeches. How often this God-sent leader had spoken of "the unfolding purpose" being worked out on the tapestry of history. For all his greatness Winston bore the hallmark of the true Christian, the humility of spirit that acknowledges the sovereignty of Almighty God.

The following year came another upheaval in my personal life. My father had succeeded in advancing his retirement and six months before his sixtieth birthday he said goodbye to friends and colleagues and set about the arrangement of yet another move. He bought a bungalow in Poole. After much discussion Paddy and I decided to join him, so we let our house in Orpington and bought a house near Wimborne a few miles from Poole. I had never lived so far away from London, and a new life began for me then. I should like to dwell upon the many funny incidents that happened on the way to our settling in but must content myself with recording one.

The moving van arrived in the morning. We had stayed

at a hotel in Wimborne the previous night. There was the usual confusion. All sorts of helpers appeared from nowhere even with a war on. How different from what it is now when you are hard put to it to find anyone prepared to help. Men seemed to be swarming everywhere. Electricians were busy with floorboards. Two decorators with pots of paint seemed to be busy in every room at once. Builders were doing something to the roof, plumbers engaged on business with the drains and in the midst of this chaos, the moving van arrived. Then more were milling round in Southways, including two who were struggling with the baby grand piano. By eight o'clock they were all gone and we had just settled down in the comparative peace to listen to the nine o'clock news when there was a knock at the door.

I hastened to open it and there stood a sombre figure clad in black.

"I've called for the body," he said.

"Oh," I said, trying not to laugh. "There isn't one. You must have come to the wrong address."

"No," he said. "This is Southways."

With this I excused myself and went to consult Paddy. "It's a man who says he has called for the body," I said. "I'll just run upstairs and look in all the cupboards."

"No," I said to the man at the door who was obviously getting impatient. "There must be some mistake."

"Where's Mrs Trim?" he said. "She always had them ready for me to collect." Then the penny dropped. I remember being somewhat surprised when first being shown over the place, to see four old ladies in each of the four bedrooms. Southways must have been the forerunner of the numerous Rest Homes that have been springing up all over the country, especially in recent years.

I explained that we had moved in that day and that Mrs Trim had gone to Ferndown but I did not know her address.

Poor man, he looked exasperated. "That Mrs Trim,"

he said. "She's always moving and forgetting to inform me."

"How very careless," I said. "And how trying it must be for you."

With this he departed, tut tutting. We laughed so much that I was suddenly conscious of being hungry, so we decided to have a walk down to The Fox, an inn about half a mile away on the banks of the Stour by Canford Bridge. Here I had sandwiches and Paddy sampled the local brew of ale which bore the name of Strong. Paddy thought this to be a good omen for our sojourn in Dorset. As soon as we crossed the border from Hampshire into Dorset we had noticed the boards proclaiming You Are Now In The Strong Country, which I hoped would not mean anything vital to the enemy.

It was the first time we had had our own home in real country and I fell in love again, with my garden. After spending a year there I wrote a book about it called *The Glory of the Garden*. It provided a never-failing source of comfort to help divert thoughts from what was going on in London and Europe.

There was a constant demand for a second front. News from Russia was grim. Huge numbers of Germans were being sacrificed on the Stalingrad front and still Hitler was pouring them in. Hitler's folly was buying precious time for us. The skies over south-east London at that time were infested with V1's, pilotless planes which we called Buzz Bombs, and with V2's. At last the pre D-Day tension broke. For the whole of the previous night the planes had rumbled overhead, a constant stream en route for Cherbourg. Somewhere along the beaches the forces of liberation were massing but it was a well guarded and a well kept secret.

I passed through Southampton on the following morning on my way to London where I had an appointment at the B.B.C. to take part in a broadcast programme called The Poet And The People. All was quiet at Southampton station. None would have believed that the greatest military operation of all time was in progress.

British and American forces had crossed that morning into enemy held territory. I was glad when I could escape and get out into the streets to buy a paper. There it was. The curtain had gone up on the greatest drama of all time. There were the pictures of infantrymen wading ashore from the landing craft. A report in The Star by Gault MacGowan told of how he had seen the invasion begin at dawn. It had begun with a rain of bombs followed by a naval bombardment. The first troops were nosing inshore and jumping from the landing crafts as the tactical bombers flew in to attack the German shore batteries.

He went on to speak of another sky sign, not dramatic like the Essex crucifix, but just a beautiful rainbow spanning the whole of the combat area. A supernatural phenomenon, for it was no day of April sun and showers, it was June, and it was dawn. This surely, was the Israel sign, God's special message of hope to the Anglo-Saxon forces in their magnificent enterprise. General Eisenhower had agonised over the decision to go as the weather was rough, but later changed in our favour.

We British-Israelites believe that when the first rainbow raised its coloured arch over the water which had destroyed almost the whole human race excepting Noah and his family in the year 2347 B.C., God spoke saying "I do set my bow in the cloud and it shall be as a token of a covenant between Me and the earth." That covenant was ratified on the morning of June 6th 1944 when the miracle of the D-Day rainbow spread its glory above beaches where the men of Israel—of modern Britain—and her world wide Commonwealth were embarking on a crusade which was to free all nations from enslavement.

Every day after the D-Day brought news of victories: the deliverance of Paris, Rome, Brussels, though Rommel was to make a stand which slowed down the impetus of our first advances. But the Huns were reeling back before the massive Russian war-machine. Authenticated stories of the atrocities committed by the retreating Germans upon French civilians made sickening reading.

Looking back over my wartime file of newspaper cuttings I see that the great General Smuts of South Africa who had served in the War Cabinet had expressed the hope that when it was over, Britain, America and Russia would maintain the alliances forged in the fires of suffering. He was another Churchill. He had served in both wars, a truly great man, and well does he deserve to stand amongst the statues in Parliament Square. Had we heeded his advice we would not now be in our present plight.

I cannot close this chapter without looking backwards at two very memorable happenings of the war.

It was an evening in October. I had been standing on the front porch watching the sun setting behind the pine trees down by the Stour river. In the background the news was just about to commence. Then the news came through that Monty had attacked and was mounting a tremendous offensive in the Western Desert. We had all been deep in the trough of near despondency, impatient for the opening of the second front, hungry for news of some victory to boost our morale. Here it was; Monty was on the move, and he was moving fast. I went down on my knees thanking God and crying, "Blessed be the Lord God of Israel", words that were sung every Sunday in every Anglican church throughout the Empire. From then onwards nothing could hold him. In a speech to his men, at a later stage when flushed with victory, Field Marshal Montgomery gave God the glory, quoting the Psalm: "This is the Lord's doing and it is marvellous in our eyes".

The other occasion for thankfulness was the Japanese collapse following Hiroshima and Nagasaki, when my brother came home with his wife after three years of internment in a Japanese camp. This was in the autumn of 1945; they were only half alive, but they were home. A thousand thousand prayers had been answered.

It was during the time that I lived at Southways in Dorset during the latter half of the war that I decided to be confirmed into the Church of England. It had been simmering in my mind ever since the Bible had been opened for me in a new way in that village hall in Orpington. It seemed to me the only logical course to take, for how can one attend morning service in an Anglican church and sing the Te Deum Laudamus without feeling the pull of Canterbury, especially when singing the words "O Lord, save thy people: and bless thine heritage". And the Venite, Exultemus Domino which includes the assertion "we are the people of his pasture and the sheep of his hand". The Benedictus brings us even nearer to an emphatic declaration of our identity with the opening words, "Blessed by the Lord God of Israel, for he hath visited and redeemed his people and hath raised up a mighty salvation for us in the house of his servant David". I already possessed a copy of the Milner chart which Queen Victoria had given to the British Museum and can still be seen there by anyone interested in the descent of our Royal House from the House of David. And the Benedictus goes on to speak of "our forefather Abraham". Why were the Brits singing these particular words in their national church if they were not the Covenant people? And the words "that we being delivered out of the hands of our enemies might serve him without fear", came with a special significance at a time when we were fighting for our very existence.

And so it came about that I was confirmed in Salisbury cathedral on a December morning in 1944. It was an adult confirmation mostly of serving men and women in uniform of some kind. I remember the clattering of heavy army boots on the ancient stones. The cathedral soared above the figures kneeling before the altar. I had come a

long way from the tin hall of that South London Baptist
Church where I had caught my first vision of the everlasting glory.

18
OUTINGS AND INTINGS

*I*T WAS MY fictitious New England friend, brain-child of Mrs. Whitney, who introduced me to the form of travel which she called "inting".

You can visit a place on your feet or on wheels or wings. In fact, you cannot have an outing at all unless you go by these means, so in a sense outings are dependent upon the mobility of feet and machines. The beauty of outings through "intings" is that you can get to most places in the mind without the inconvenience and expense of travel. You know what you have to do if you want to go out but if you want to go in, that is, to travel without effort, all you have to do is relax into a quietness allowing knowledge to seep up from within, thus receiving in-sight, in-tuition and in-spiration. There is a danger of losing our capacity for this in-travel; so busy are we with our outings, putting special clothes onto the body and rushing it from place to place. Poor body! Seldom does it have time to settle itself in one spot before it is whisked off to another. It is no wonder that its nerve endings get frayed, ultimately coming to the end of its limited resources of strength.

Go out we must, but going out and coming in must be balanced; too much of the former ends in exhaustion and too much of the latter ends in the psychological imbalance of the introvert. Life keeps us on the move. It is the cost of being alive. The Creator put the going out urge into our blood. It is part of our humanhood. When God decided to create a new race to be His very own servant people through whom ultimately the whole human family was to be perfected and redeemed he first had to isolate one man from whose seed this special people could evolve. It was upon Abram that the choice fell. His command to him was direct so there should be no verbal misunderstanding. God said; Get thee out of thy country, and from thy kindred, and from thy father's house unto a land that I will shew thee. In short, Go. He went. And the whole story of the Bible from cover to cover is about Abram's outing: where he went, what he did, and how his descendants were used to bring about the fulfilment of the tremendous promises made to Abraham and confirmed through Jacob, promises that are even now being worked out on the looms of history in a fearful and marvellous manner.

The one hundred and twenty first Psalm puts the whole thing into a golden nutshell. "The Lord shall preserve thy going out and thy coming in". So intings and outings, undertaken for good purposes are blessed.

My longest and most glorious outing was the visit to the Holy Land and this I have attempted to describe briefly in chapter nineteen called "The time of my life" for so it was.

Another outing rich in blessing was the visit to Iona, the first of several. But how attempt to delineate in words the features of the face of Iona, the breath-taking loveliness of Mull seen from Iona's white shore, the wild irises in the boggy grasses, the little royal burial ground that holds the bones of Scottish kings, the lilac-tinted mist, the grey rocks, the Abbey and the wild turmoil of waves? Beautiful as they are, they are but the embroidery on the hem of the garment that is Iona. To quote Fiona Macleod,

"It is loveliness I seek, not lovely things."

We travelled by train from Euston and spent a night at the King's Head Hotel at Oban. Next morning we sailed from the little harbour. It was a bright June morning of blue sky streaked with white feathery clouds. Mountains seemed to rise all around towering out from the green water. We passed Staffa the island which had inspired Mendelssohn to the writing of *Fingal's Cave*; the tide was high, filling the mouth of the cave with spray from the breaking waves. Sailing under Mull I thought of Keats with his friend Brown, making his way to Iona on foot with the last of his diminishing strength, taking shelter in the shepherd's hut, soaked to the skin. That remembrance was a part of the Iona experience, finding a sad echo in the crying of the gulls swooping about the rocks and islets of the Hebrides.

Behind what is visible on this holy island, is the beauty that cannot be seen or touched. It is the spirit of St. Columba, the saint who came from Ireland in a coracle resolved to settle on the first island on which his eyes alighted. It was Iona, and before he died at the end of the sixth century, Iona became known through the missionary work of Columba as "The lamp that lit all Europe". After the death of Columba the Pope Gregory sent Augustine and forty monks to Canterbury, supposedly to convert England to Christianity, but he arrived to find that England already had a Christian queen, and the Christian church of St. Martin in Canterbury. Moreover, a Convocation of British Bishops had met the Augustinian Mission disowning any knowledge of the Bishop of Rome in his new role as Pope. It is the very heart and soul of pure and true religion that is enshrined in the mystical island of Iona.

All Christian nations sent a gift for the rebuilding of the old Abbey, but I am glad that I saw it before it was restored. More people come now to see the new Abbey with its books and souvenirs and its huge altar of green Iona marble, but I prefer pilgrims to tourists. Sir George

Macleod did a great work here, but something of the spirit of Columba seems to have departed from the Abbey. But not from the island, for Columba is Iona. The voice of the saint is heard in the thunder of water raging over rocks and soft winds sighing through heather.

The tale told in Iona of the old Stone of Destiny, regarded with reverence by the Gaels many centuries before the birth of Christ was no mere legend. I knew it before I ever set foot on Iona, for it is woven into the very fibre of our history, but until coming to Iona I had not realised that upon this stone Columba himself had crowned Aidan, King of Argyll. Many years later it was removed to Dunstaffnage where the last of the Celtic Kings was crowned upon it, and it now rests in Westminster Abbey under the sacred Coronation chair on which every British monarch since Edward the First has been crowned.

Few out of the thousands who pass through the Abbey daily stop to examine the iron rings let into the stone. We British-Israelites believe that these rings were to help its transport through the wilderness when the tribes of the children of Jacob (Israel) were on their way to the promised land under the leadership of Moses. We also believe that this was the very stone on which Jacob, grandson of Abraham, rested when he dreamed of the ascending and descending angels and where he wrestled with the stranger until the breaking of the day. On his return to Bethel it was revealed to Jacob that this was the very house of God. It was to form the capstone of the first Temple in Jerusalem and ultimately to rest under the Coronation Chair in London's Westminster Abbey. This Stone has a more romantic history than any other stone in any part of the world. We believe it was carried into Egypt, and in the care of the prophet Jeremiah, travelling in the company of the daughter of Zedekiah, the last king of Judah, was taken to Ireland via Spain. Centuries later, early in the Christian era it was moved to the west of Scotland, and in the ninth century to the Abbey of Scone,

from where its divinely appointed history came to ultimate fulfilment, when the cracked and battered stone
came to rest in Westminster. Not only is this stone a
visible witness to our early Israelitish beginnings, but it is
embedded into the very heart of English monarchy linking
our Davidic Throne with the traditions of Tara and Iona.
It is of interest that the great window above the West door
of the Abbey in which the twelve tribes of Jacob are
depicted is called the Israel window, lighting the nave that
leads to the Stone of Destiny.

Our outgoings to Iona led inevitably to Glastonbury
which has its own secret to disclose to the seeing eye and
the discerning heart.

The story of our pilgrimage to the Isle of Avalon is, so
we British-Israelites believe, the extension of the story of
our pilgrimage to Jerusalem, for a connecting cord runs
from Joseph's tomb in the garden of the Resurrection to
the place on Weary-all Hill where he planted his staff at
the end of his long missionary journey from Palestine to
Somerset. Joseph of Arimathea who was an influential
counsellor and officer of the Temple would have known
that he had a rightful claim to the body of Jesus, for his
mother Mary was Joseph's niece. The reason why Jesus
was born in Bethlehem, was not because Mary and Joseph
were wandering, poor and homeless, at that time, as some
sentimentalists would have us believe. They were in Bethlehem at that time because it was prophesied that they
should be, both Mary and her husband being of the royal
house of David, therefore compelled under the edict of
Caesar Augustus to be taxed in that particular city of
Judea.

I believe that a few years after the Crucifixion Joseph of
Arimathea had taken his son and twelve companions to
build a Christian church in Avalon. By reason of his
connection with the tin mining business he would have
been familiar with our West Country and would have had
many friends amongst the Jewish communities which had

settled there following the westward migration from the Caspian area after the dispersion. Some returned at the time of Nehemiah and Ezra to rebuild the Temple at Jerusalem, and this was the first time, according to Bible records, that they were ever referred to as Jews. It was a kind of nickname as they were of the tribe of Judah.

There is an otherness about Glastonbury whose beauty defies definition. Tennyson knew something of the secret of these holy legends and the well of healing. In his *Morte d'Arthur* the wounded king speaks of Avalon, or the Isle of Apples as it was first called, saying,

> *But now farewell. I am going a long way*
> *With these thou seëst—if indeed I go—*
> *(For all my mind is clouded with a doubt)*
> *To the island-valley of Avilion;*
> *Where falls not hail, or rain, or any snow,*
> *Nor ever wind blows loudly; but it lies*
> *Deep-meadow'd, happy fair with orchard-lawns*
> *And bowery hollows crown'd with summer sea,*
> *Where I will heal me of my grievous wound.'*
> *So said he, and the barge with oar and sail*
> *Moved from the brink, like some full-breasted swan*
> *That, fluting a wild carol ere her death,*
> *Ruffles her pure cold plume, and takes the flood*
> *With swarthy webs. Long stood Sir Bedivere*
> *Revolving many memories, till the hull*
> *Look'd one black dot against the verge of dawn,*
> *And on the mere the wailing died away.*

One of the loveliest things to be seen in the ruined Abbey, is the Glastonbury Thorn, the magic may tree that blooms, not only at its proper time in Spring, but at Christmas, to mark the season of the Incarnation. Many cuttings have been taken from what was left of the original tree after Cromwell's soldiers had cut it down, so that not only in Avalon but throughout the land one sees the blossom of trees which had been rooted in the soil of Glastonbury. And every year on Christmas Day, a sprig of this Eastern hawthorn is sent to the reigning monarch, which forms another link in the mysterious chain of evidence that connects our Royal House with Glastonbury and back to Jerusalem. Always the mind is turned back to Jerusalem.

Lustrous words burn like candles around the name of Glastonbury: the Grail, the Chalice Well, King Arthur and the Knights of the Round Table, the Tor, the Cruets containing the blood of Christ, Vetusta Ecclesia. Deeper and deeper we go into legend, tradition and history. All this enveloped me in a great cloud of wonder when first I went to Ynis-wytren with Paddy, but one goes on finding fresh threads of evidence to stitch into the great tapestry of the Glastonbury mystery. When I was there last Easter I made a new discovery, the small gem of Pilton a few miles from Glastonbury. Here we knelt on Easter morning for our Resurrection communion drinking from a chalice that is older than the Reformation. It is believed that one of the chapels was erected on the site of an original wattle and daub church built by Joseph of Arimathea who is known to have used Pilton harbour. We saw an iron ring in the wall to which the boats would have been tied by ropes or chains.

As the belief that Joseph brought the young Jesus here as a boy is still strong, I was reminded of Blake's poem,

"And did those feet in ancient time
Walk upon England's mountains green?
And was the holy Lamb of God,
On England's pleasant pastures seen?"

Looking up from the little river to the sheep grazing on the green hills of Somerset, that is a question one might well ask. Perhaps the feet of Jesus did walk these hills in company with his kinsman. If so, it would account for the fact that Blake's poem has become our second national anthem; and it would also throw light on the eighteen hidden years, for we hear nothing of Jesus from the age of twelve when he was lost in the Passover pilgrimage and discovered in the Temple, until his appearing at the age of thirty to be baptised in Jordan to commence the ministry. And we know too that he paid the Stranger's Tax. Why would this be if he had never been outside Palestine?

I must forego the desire to record more of my outings for lack of time and space. But before I complete this chapter I must recall one of the outings on which I look back with a pleasure that never decreases.

I was in the embarrassing situation of having received a present and not knowing what to do with it. It was a handsome haversack and I felt obliged to justify possessing it by going on a walking tour, Paddy assuring me that he had one up in the loft which he had brought with him from the Wirral.

So after much discussion we set off one beautiful summer's day for a weekend of walking in the Chilterns. We travelled to Aylesbury on the District Railway and set off towards the hills. It was idyllic. The autumn woods hung thick and bright upon the Buckinghamshire hills; gold, copper and flame they blazed in the evening sunlight. We sat on a stile watching the sunset until the valleys were black with shadow.

"By the way," I said, somewhat carelessly, "Where are we going? Where do you aim to stay?" Paddy got out his map and compass. "We'll make for Princes Risborough" he said, so away we went, haversacks on our backs, swinging our walking sticks.

It got darker and darker and there did not appear to be any signposts in sight. In our carefree mood we had strayed a long way from the beaten track and in those pre-war days there were few motor cars about.

By this time Paddy was getting very thirsty and not a little anxious, so when we came to an inn sign pointing up a muddy track to The Pink and Lily we decided to make that our destination, hoping they would be able to offer accommodation, as well as supper.

After a stiff climb we came upon the inn. It looked inviting with its lighted windows and an enormous pig lying across the doorstep.

We stepped over the pig and entered. There was a crackling fire in the ducksnest grate and an oil lamp with a red glass shade on the centre table. Paddy went to the bar and made the acquaintance of the landlord, who looked as if he had had a good day either at a market or the races. When Paddy asked about accommodation he said, "I'll have to see my Mrs about that." His Mrs duly appeared and took me upstairs to see the room with its china jug and basin on the washstand and a huge double bed with brass posts and covered in a white cotton quilt. It all looked very homely and comfortable. By the bed there was a new candle in a blue candlestick.

"I'll put supper in the parlour," she said "and light a fire. Just say when you're ready."

I was ready almost at once. The walk from Aylesbury had been so enjoyable that we had been unaware of the miles we were covering. Downstairs on the parlour table which was spread with a red checked table cloth, a high tea awaited us: a pot of tea in a willow patterned pot, two boiled eggs each, a plate of brown bred, a basin of butter, a jar of jam, a plate of ham and an enormous fruit cake. It was all too perfect to be true, but something even more wonderful and unexpected was to follow.

After we had done full justice to the meal we felt strong enough to look around. On the wall by the fireplace I noticed a framed poem neatly set out in ornamental script. I read it aloud:

"Never came there to the Pink
Two such ones as we, I think.
Never came there to the Lily
Two young men so pink and silly."
Signed Rupert Brooke.

I dashed out to find the landlord to ask him about the poem. "Oh yes," he said, "they used to come over from Grantchester, Rupert Brooke and his Cambridge friends. A fine time we used to have up here on a Saturday night."

"Well," I said, "and to think this was waiting at the end of that dark lane—and without knowing we landed here. Where did Rupert Brooke stay," I asked, "when he came?" "At the Pink" said the landlord. "We always gave him the best room. That's the one you're in," he added.

It was like something out of Alice and Wonderland with the pig still asleep on the doorstep. I advised him to take good care of the framed poem. "He's very famous, you know." "Oh, is he?" said the landlord. "Fancy that." I wondered if he knew that Rupert Brooke had died in the war, but refrained from mentioning it in case it should spoil his evening.

When we left the next morning Paddy asked the landlord how much he owed him. He scratched his head and looked very worried, as if the mental effort of calculation was proving too great a strain. "Well," he said at last. "Would three and six each be too much?" So Paddy put a ten shilling note on the table telling him to keep the change. He remonstrated, then gave in, accepting the note and assuring us that we would be welcome to come again at any time.

Another outing which flickers back across the screen of memory from time to time is our visit to Oberammergau in 1960. It did not make a profound impression; perhaps because the crowd scenes and the angry German voices reminded me too much of Nuremberg and Hitler's circus, but I brought back one or two little souvenirs which I still treasure; a wooden bread plate with the words Give us This Day Our Daily Bread picked out by poker work in German. I use it every day. I also brought back half a walnut shell which contained a cross and crucifix carved out of a matchstick.

19
THE TIME OF MY LIFE

*W*HEN SOLOMON ascended the throne of his father
David he was told by God in a dream to ask of Him
anything that he desired. He asked for wisdom and lived to
become known as the wisest man in the world, but he had
prefaced his request by saying "I am but a little child; I
know not how to go out or come in". Solomon in his
simplicity proved himself fit to receive the gift of the
precious pearl of wisdom for when you come to think of it,
what is life but this: going out and coming in? He that knows
how to go out to some good purpose and come back in peace
can be said to know the secret of happy and successful
living.

Most people have an annual "going out" that they call
a holiday. I rarely feel the urge, or if I do there never seems
time in which to satisfy it, but that has probably been
because I have not really wanted to go to any particular
place sufficiently, at that particular time, preferring the
daily round at home and the satisfaction of uninterrupted
work. Travelling for the sake of travelling has never held
any appeal for me. But sooner or later the call comes to
embark upon a journey that you feel in your bones you
must make because it is something that you have always
known you would do one day; suddenly the way opens out
and out you go. The clock of Providence has struck the
right moment, right for you.

On such a journey Paddy and I set out in the December

of 1954 for a month in the Holy Land. I have always held that every Christian should go on this spiritual "outing" at least once in his or her lifetime. Every child should be encouraged to make this the chief goal in life, the good thing towards which to strain every effort until accomplished. Vast amounts of money are flung away every year on holidaying in crowded, uncomfortable places, chasing tawdry pleasures, eating, drinking, idling, when a man or woman might go to see the greatest of all the wonders of the world: the place of the Incarnation where at Bethlehem God Almighty was reduced to something small enough to put into a cattle trough. Here is the challenge of life itself; here is a "going out" into a new dimension of reality, mysterious enough to stop a man in his tracks, wondering. Can anyone look upon Golgotha and be unchanged, or walk the Via Dolorosa without realising even if fractionally, the cost of his own redemption?

I happened upon a notice in the Sunday Times announcing that a pilgrimage to the Holy Land had been arranged, covering a period of one month, visiting Bethlehem at Christmastime. All travel, coach, sea and train plus hotel expenses in places visited for an inclusive charge of seventy guineas per person.

When I read this I knew that the moment had come. Paddy was upstairs on a ladder painting a window. I called up to him "Come down. Great things are astir. We're off to Jerusalem for Christmas." He descended ladder and stairs with all speed and in no time we had made our arrangements.

It was to be the first organised pilgrimage to the Holy Land since the cessation of the Jewish-Arab war of 1948, so from the point of view of the people who were financing it and making all the official arrangements this hastily improvised pilgrimage was indeed a hazardous venture, fraught with difficulties and barbed with problems. But we were fortunate in having for our guide and leader the Reverend Leonard Pearson of Brighton who had spent many years in Palestine as Warden of the Garden Tomb, whose father-in-law had been an eminent Hebrew scholar who had done much research on archaeological discoveries relating to Biblical sites.

Almost all denominations were represented in the crowd of about seventy pilgrims assembled at Victoria station on that evening when we set out: Welsh Methodists, Scottish Presbyterians, a sprinkling of Irish Roman Catholics, Baptists from Belfast, Seventh Day Adventists, a solitary Unitarian on the defensive from the outset, Anglicans, High and Low, American Episcopalians, and Evangelicals with two Mormons thrown in for good measure.

We stood about in groups while luggage was sorted out, trying to be friendly but eyeing each other with a certain suspicion, speculating as to theological labels. Mr Pearson drifted about vaguely, introducing himself. We were thankful that he obviously was not the hearty type. He was helpful but reserved, an Evangelical, but only a minimal part of his mind was occupied with practical matters; the rest of it lay deep in the scholarship of his own subject. He and his wife spent half the year lecturing with his travelling exhibition of rare rabbinical scrolls and treasures of interest to Bible students, and the other part of the year was devoted to the conducting of Holy Land tours. But this was the first since the ending of the Jewish-Arab war, the first to go into the new land of Israel-Jordan which had been fought over fiercely and ruthlessly partitioned.

At the time of our pilgrimage Jerusalem was still a city under military surveillance. Though officially hostilities were at an end there was a wartime feeling in the air. The drivers of the coaches in which we travelled were armed against snipers. Many times we had to crawl under barbed wire barriers and step warily over land pitted with bomb craters and the devastation left in the wake of tanks.

We went by rail to Dover, crossed the Channel that evening and travelled all through the night to Marseilles. After much fussing with forms and passports we went on board the *Artsa*, a ship which had been taken from the Germans by the Jews as part of a reparations deal. No luxury liner this, but it had been hurriedly equipped for passengers, pilgrims and refugees. These latter were emigrants from Hitler's Europe, mostly Jews, making for The Land, as they called it. It was pitiful to see the fanatical zeal with which, on arriving in Haifa, they flung themselves to the ground, kissing it and crying, "The Land, the Land". We were told that in a matter of hours after disembarkation they would be at a Kibbutz ready for immediate work.

So there we all were, tightly packed aboard the *Artsa*. The refugees were somewhere in the bowels of the ship. They were not allowed into the saloon. This, apart from being a bar, was the main assembly point for lectures, meetings and religious services. Roman Catholics and Protestants did not mingle. We celebrated our Holy Communion at 8.00 a.m. and the Roman Catholics their Mass an hour earlier.

I have forgotten most of the names of our fellow travellers except for a few kindred spirits, especially a Mrs Evans from Glamorganshire. She was a rare soul whose glowing, transparent face shone with the happiness that lighted it from within. She kept a small grocery store in the village in which she had been born and in which she had worked all her life saving her hard-earned pennies so that one day she would be able to afford to visit the Holy Land. So for her too this was the time of her life; the realisation of a dream, the answer to prayer. To be with her was to be near to something very wonderful. She lived out her simple nonconformist faith in all she did and said. There were others like her in the group but I remember her specially because of something we were to share together in Jerusalem.

There was no attempt at anything social aboard the *Artsa* for which I was relieved. From the moment we sailed out of harbour at Marseilles it was as if the outside world ceased to exist. We were all intimately gathered up into a single-mindedness, bound together by a tension that was absolute. There were no references to family interest. We were encapsulated, sealed off, centred solely within the common enclosure of our Christian faith in spite of individual eccentricities of belief, with the exception of the humanist Unitarian, who didn't count.

This was before the New English Bible had done its work of attempting to secularise and trivialise the grandeur of the Authorised Version of the Scriptures. From the hour that the prow of the *Artsa* was set in the direction of the Holy Land conversation was lively, controversial but always connected with religion. Nothing else was of any interest or consequence. We were gathered in groups all over the ship talking Christianity with a fervour that was life-giving and exhilarating because it was not organised by anybody. It was wholly spontaneous. There we were, shredding our dogmas, thrashing out our theories, arguing, discussing, gloriously diverse, flaunting our differences like coloured cloaks that we delighted to wear, completely absorbed in our disparate opinions. Surely some beneficent power had been at work to fling together such a motley crowd, intellectually divided yet bound together by invisible cords of fellowship.

Looking back I can realise now that we, in our passionate diversity had uncovered the secret of the vitality of the Christian gospel, each contributing to the health and wealth of the whole by doing his own thing, speaking his own thoughts and going his own way. That is the soil in which men like John Wesley, Pastor Blumhardt, William Temple and Charles Spurgeon took root and grew.

We spared scarcely a passing glance at the jewels of the Mediterranean as they flashed by, Malta, Italy, Sardinia, Crete, so dazzled were we by the immense prospect which lay ahead. The eye of the mind was on the far horizon where Haifa waited to receive us into Galilee.

At last we were there, and strange to relate we all had the feeling that we had come home. I suppose, it must have been because all being Bible students we were so familiar with the place names and their associations that it was our place. From childhood most of us had been there in imagination, except for those like Paddy who had actually been there before to lay wire roads for transport and pipelines for the waters of the Nile to flow across the deserts traversed before by the Israelites under the leadership of Moses.

We travelled by coach through the rugged Judean highlands along a road that snaked between cruel cliffs and terrifying chasms of pitiless dry rock. It was not hard to visualise this as the wilderness in which the Saviour fasted, and hungered and was tempted of the devil. The whole region seemed to suggest demoniac activity. But as we approached Jerusalem and the coach groaned up the last slope which brought Suliman's Walls into view, we remembered that it was Christmas Eve, and over towards Bethlehem way it was not difficult to imagine a King-sized star hanging over a stable. For the Jews it was Chanukka, the Feast of Lights and every door was lit with little candles.

The first thing I saw in the new Israel was a red U.K. pillar box bearing the letters GR, a relic from the days of the Mandate which supposedly the Israelis had not yet had time to remove. This was a sight that warmed my heart for one of the many reasons for wanting to visit The Land was to look for marks of identity between Britain and ancient Israel.

We were welcomed at the hotel by a host who informed us that the Mayor would be coming to see us later that night. After a meal we all went to the Christmas Eve Carol Service at the Y.M.C.A. and as we stood there singing good old favourites like *Good King Wenceslas, While*

Shepherds Watched, Hark the Herald Angels Sing and *It Came Upon A Midnight Clear,* it was all so familiar that the Jerusalem mirage had faded and we were back in Britain. When it was over and we were out in the streets of Jerusalem under the Christmas stars, the magic returned. The silent night was indeed a holy night and over the hills but a few miles away we could hear the bells of royal David's city.

I stood bewitched at the window of our room gazing out over the roofs, the domes and the towers of the Holy City. You could not only see its beauty in the light of the stars, but you could feel the power of its fascination and the throb of its timeless pulse. The very stones cry out, so deeply do its roots thrust down below the surface of what is seen that its past is beyond measuring. I looked across the old walls in the direction of the Temple area where David's son Solomon had built the first Temple of fir, olive wood, cedar and gold on Mount Morish a thousand years before the great star hung above the Bethlehem stable. My thoughts slid away to A.D. 70 when the later Temple and the whole city was destroyed by Rome under Titus, as foreseen by Christ. No wonder He wept as He looked upon it, envisaging its destruction.

The following morning we Anglicans went to Holy Communion in St. George's Cathedral and back to a breakfast of sardines, milkless tea or lemonade. We were doing it the hard way which is the only way to see the Land. An easy luxury tour would not have seemed suitable. Small deprivations and discomforts were a small price to pay for so great an adventure. It is not possible to give a photographic account of all we saw on our enthralling journey. All I can hope to do is to snatch at what comes floating within reach hoping it might convey something of that wonderful month. But the result must be fragmentary, mere glimpses of and impressions which can never be conveyed or adequately described.

Fortunately on my return I wrote four booklets on the

subject of our pilgrimage while still fresh in my mind and it is upon these that I must rely for the refreshment of memory. They were published by Henry Walter of Worthing, but now out of print. The titles were: The Hills of Galilee, The Bethlehem Story, Nazareth and Pilgrimage to Jerusalem.

Since our visit the map has undergone more changes. There was the war that arose out of the Israeli attack on Egypt across the Sinai desert followed by the Anglo-French invasion of the Suez area in an effort to separate the combatants and ensure the safety of the Canal. A few years later came the five day war by which the Israelis re-drew the boundaries which gave them back their rights over the Old City.

When we were in Jerusalem the Arabs were in control of the vital sectors, but tourists were permitted to enter it for a period of forty-eight hours by way of the Mandelbaum Gate. This was the house through which we had to pass. For most tourists it took several hours to get through the various rooms where they were vetted by officialdom having to produce visas, passports, certificates relating to place of birth, particulars of vaccination and other proofs of identification.

It was fortunate for us that Leonard Pearson was such a well known figure in Palestine with firm friends amongst Arabs, Jews and Israelis. He was trusted and respected wherever he went so our passage through the Mandelbaum Gate was comparatively speedy.

Once through the Mandelbaum Gate we stepped out of the Christian calendar back to the beginnings of a story which would have been beyond the wit of a mere human being to conceive, a story originating in the mind of God Himself, spanning the whole chronicled history of mankind. No wonder that the true history of this place and its people are to be found not in any ordinary book but in that collection of dramas, thrillers, historical romances and mystery stories which we call the Bible.

Our first sight of the thirty-five acre area on which the Temple stood left us speechless. Nothing now was left of the glorious Temples which were the wonders of the world with their golden roofs and treasures of marble, sapphires and pearls, nothing but the original pavements on which they had stood, the whole expanse being large enough to accommodate every minster and cathedral in England. The foundations of the first Temple, Solomon's, was hewn out of the solid rock of the Mount Moriah, and there now stands the Dome of the Rock, known also as the Mosque of Omar.

I felt vaguely resentful of the pride with which the Arab guide showed us over this fabulous edifice. On entering we had been asked to remove our shoes in order not to soil the priceless Persian carpets. I had come here to see our ancient Israelitish beginnings and to look upon the sacred places of Christendom. But why was this Mohammedan Mosque flaunting its glory up here on Mount Moriah looking out towards Calvary? I should have been even more surprised had I been told that I should live to see the day when the Mosques of Islam would be raised in our own cities, including London.

The Crusaders of the Middle Ages had been moved to attempt the rescue of our Christian shrines from the hands of the infidels but without success. It was going to take a world war to bring back the cross of Christ to the place where it was first planted. And it was a great thought that Paddy, my uncle and thousands of other Britons were going to have a part in that historic deliverance.

There is a huge slab of bare rock in the Mosque, surrounded with golden railings, an incongruous sight thrusting up from the magnificent flooring. It was on this rock that the Jewish sacrifices were made in the great days of Herod's Temple. The blood from the lambs ran through a channel out to the Kedron Valley. And it was here on this naked ledge of stone that Abraham raised the altar which he intended to use for the sacrifice of his son

Isaac. The lad was spared. God had only been testing the faithfulness of His servant Abraham. But as the Arab was telling us the story with which we were all familiar, it occurred to me that this was a rehearsal of the scene that was to be enacted over nineteen hundred years later when, a short distance from Mount Moriah, the Lamb of God was to be sacrificed on Calvary.

I should like to linger over a description of our days at Tiberius, Nazareth, Capernaum, Bethlehem, Joppa, Cana and Carmel, but throughout the pilgrimage "Time's winged chariot" was at our heels as it still is. Yet I cannot leave without allowing myself one or two flashes of recollection.

There was the evening walk by the Sea of Galilee. We were at Capernaum. I still treasure the leaf picked from a eucalyptus tree growing near the ruins of the synagogue where Jesus healed and taught. I also have a precious box of tiny shells picked up from the shore where He preached from the boat. I recall too how we stood at the entrance of the tomb in which Lazarus had been laid. I remember the Church of the Loaves and Fishes, The Wailing Wall, and the roses in the Garden of Gethsemane.

At Nazareth we attended a service in the Baptist church conducted by an Arab Christian. How restful it seemed to be in a plain, almost austere church again, after all the glitter and the glamour of ecclesiastical splendour. My eye fell on a painting over the Baptistry; it was a simple scene by Jordan. Of course. How stupid of me not to have seen the connection at first. Jordan, that blue brook in the picture was where it all started, the ministry that was to change and redeem the world, when Jesus left Nazareth going down into Judea to be baptised of his cousin John in the little river Jordan.

Another surviving memory of our going to the plain of Megiddo, or Armageddon as it is in the Hebrew, standing in the long shadow of the prophecy of things to come. This is the Valley of Decision where in the latter days all the nations of the earth shall be gathered for battle in what is referred to as the "terrible Day of God Almighty". Events are outstripping prophecy, and now in this our own day we are witnessing the beginnings of what was foretold so vividly by the prophets, Ezekiel, Isaiah, Joel, Haggai, Micah and others, prophecies which were confirmed by Our Lord when He said, "When ye see these things come to pass, lift up your heads for your redemption draweth nigh." The Saviour never leaves us comfortless. This was His message to Israel in the Isles, and to all who acknowledge His kingship.

How near we come to missing the most marvellous thing of all when our thoughts are bogged down in a welter of detail. That is why we should pray every morning to be led by the Spirit, remaining inwardly alert for the guiding word. That morning we had started out at six o'clock as we had a full programme ahead. The precious forty-eight hours allotted to us were running out. We had to see the Church of the Holy Sepulchre, even if we were Protestants, for it had been founded by Helen, the mother of Constantine, a British princess from Colchester. In the third century she had come upon what she believed was the true cross and well it might have been. We had spent several hours that morning examining excavations, walls and tombs. The Church of the Holy Sepulchre did not impress me except as a historical memorial to the piety and faith of the remarkable woman who had conceived the idea of building it. I found it oppressive as if the weight of the millions of pounds worth of jewels packed within its walls weighed upon the mind with a heaviness that somehow excluded the gentle presence of the Saviour.

So when we came out into the sunshine many of us were physically weary. The warm sun of the Palestinian winter was overpowering at times for us, accustomed as we were to biting winds and sunless Christmases. So when Mr Pearson announced that we must see The Garden Tomb and the site that had recently been excavated to discover the actual position of the old North Wall, he looked a little deflated at our lack of enthusiasm. None of us had heard of The Garden Tomb, or if we had, we were not aware of its significance. I heard Paddy murmuring into my private ear, "Oh no, not another tomb." We had been scrambling over rocks and ascending or descending steps since sunrise. Paddy, I was sure, must be not only tired but extremely thirsty. How near we were to missing the opportunity of standing in the place of the greatest miracle that was ever wrought. But some guiding angel was at our elbows pushing us gently forward towards what looked at first sight like a heap of stones surrounded by ancient olive trees with a huge skull-shaped rock in the background. It was only a matter of a few minutes walk from the Church of the Holy Sepulchre, so we followed Mr Pearson.

Half way he stopped, telling us to stand for a moment on the planks which had been put across the deep chasm recently opened up by the archaeologists. We walked to the site, picking our way somewhat nervously amongst the rubble. "Now look down," he said, "and you will see the top of the Old North Wall. Look with your eyes and with your minds. Look so that you will always remember, for this is the last time that you will ever be able to do so. Next week, this excavation is to be closed by order of the Vatican."

Within a few more minutes we were at the gate of the Garden Tomb. A strange hush pervaded the place, though so near the road. The Roman Catholics amongst us had evidently been forbidden to enter by their priests before leaving home. I suppose they imagined that the existence of the Garden Tomb invalidated the claim of the Church of the Holy Sepulchre to be the true site of Calvary, but to come here with an open mind and to have the backing of Biblical and archaeological evidence is to know without proof that this is the very place of the Lord's burial. Its geographical position at the northern end of Mount Moriah at The Place of Stoning used by the Jews to stone blasphemers provides further evidence of its validity, for Christ went to His death on a charge of blasphemy. Mr Pearson had published several books on this subject and he had ample time to investigate when living there as warden during the war. But what need of further evidence is there when you look up at the skull-shaped rock above the opening to the tomb and when you acknowledge the undoubted fact that it stands outside the old Wall now buried out of sight. The Church of the Holy Sepulchre does not meet this requirement, being well within the Second Wall, but this need not detract from its value as a memorial and a witness to be maintained as such for the sake of its antiquity.

But it is by what it does to the heart that you know you stand in the holiest place on earth when you stand here on Golgotha and step down into the semi-daylight of the tomb that Joseph of Arimathea had had hewn out of the rock for the interment of his own body. Joseph was a man of wealth and influence, a Counsellor and a Temple official. He was also the uncle of the Virgin Mary. Being a member of the family enabled him to go to Pilate and beg the body of Jesus, knowing that he had the right.

There is no time for me to go more deeply into this, except to relate an incident that occurred when we were leaving. The others had gone and for a few moments I was left alone there with Mrs Evans. This is something that I never recollect without a feeling of disquiet. If anyone but that good woman had asked me to do this thing I should have refused without hesitation, but this dear soul with the radiant face, exuding love and adoration for her Lord, asked me if I would be willing to sit on one of the seats hewn from the rock and on which, at the resurrection, two angels were seated one at the head and one at the foot of the tomb. "But would it not be an act of sacrilege," I asked, hoping she would withdraw her request. "No," she said, and she said it with such confidence that I agreed. "For one moment then," I said. And there we sat for one holy moment where the angel had said to Mary Magdalene, "Why seek ye the living among the dead. He is not here; He is risen."

We were both in tears. Before leaving we turned to take a last look at the loculus on which a gleam of daylight rests all day because of the unique window in the roof, not to be found in any other Jewish tomb. If it were not for this window, the disciples would not have been able to see what they saw; the empty tomb and the grave-clothes lying in position with the napkin in its separate place.

We stumbled out into the garden looking up at the niches above the entrance where the Emperor Hadrian had placed objects of Venus worship in later years to discredit it as a place of Christian veneration. We cast an eye over the heart-shaped baptismal pool, another testimony to its Christian origins, and then hurrying under the cool shades of the olive trees we joined the group at the gate. But it was obvious that a Presence had moved among us. There was hardly a dry eye and no-one seemed inclined to talk.

Mr Pearson made an effort to re-assemble us, telling us to follow him closely and on no account to lose touch with one another as we were about to enter the narrow bazaars where heavily laden donkeys pushed against the pedestrians and Arabs and Jews stood at the entrance to their shops soliciting custom in a good humoured but persistent way. Before passing the man on duty at the gate of the garden I had asked him who owned the Garden and to my astonishment he had said, "It belongs to a Society in London. It was discovered by General Gordon towards the end of the last century and Lord Brabazon of Tara had organised the purchase of it to be held in perpetuity by trustees in Britain."

It suddenly occurred to me that I had not seen Paddy for a long time. The experience in the tomb, the lingering under the olives and then going back to make my enquiry of the gatekeeper had put everything out of mind. I hurried to catch up with the others who were moving through the bazaar slowly holding on to each other. Still no sight of Paddy, but I assumed that he would have found his own way back to the hotel.

On arriving at the hotel he was nowhere to be seen, nor had anyone seen him. Mr Pearson assured me that he would turn up, probably by taxi. The thought struck me that he would probably not know the name of the hotel as it had an Arabic name; I didn't remember it. When two hours had elapsed he appeared. He had missed us when we were mustering to go from the Garden Tomb to the bazaar which led by a devious route back to the hotel. Mr Pearson had been right. Once separated from the group you are in danger of being lost. Paddy had taken a taxi not knowing the name of the hotel but having some idea as to where it lay, having spent a few weeks here when in the army and being good at maps. But he hadn't been clever enough to outwit the taxi driver who, knowing him to be a tourist, took him for a ride to the far side of the Mount of Olives. As Paddy had climbed the Mount of Olives on foot in a snowstorm on Easter day during the Allenby Campaign of the first world war, he recognised it and knew he was a long way from the hotel. Unfortunately he could speak neither Arabic nor Hebrew, but at last by much waving of Israeli pound notes which were the equivalent of our ten shilling notes, and displaying of empty pockets he managed to convey that if he did not get him to his destination soon there would be no money left to pay his fare. As this possibility dawned the driver made a U turn and in no time they were hurtling into the courtyard of the hotel.

"I must have a drink to soothe my nerves," he said, "and it's got to be something that will make me think I'm in The Royal Oak at home." With this he ordered a pint of English beer. "Very expensive," said the waiter. "Imported from England." "Never mind," said Paddy. "It will be worth every penny."

And so all was well. And all was well with me because I had made the most tremendous discovery. Britain, which I believed to be "Israel in the Isles", was the custodian for all time of the world's greatest treasure.

The month was nearing its end and we were on our way to Haifa. On the way we called at Lydda airport. This was the birthplace of our own St. George and this was where he was martyred under the Romans for his Christian faith on the 23rd April which was also Shakespeare's birthday and death day. His flag with its blood red cross on a white field is flown from all public buildings on St. George's Day. He was adopted by Richard the Lionheart to be England's patron saint, and strange it was to come upon his birthplace here in Lydda.

We embarked in the late evening and sailed as the harbour lights were dimming into the darkness and the hills of Galilee were sinking into a deep violet haze.

Leaning on the deck rail we watched till the last faint outline of the hills had disappeared. We knew we were saying goodbye to something we should never see again and suddenly a deep sadness seemed to spread itself like a mist. We felt we were leaving behind us all that gave meaning to life and charged it with a supernatural significance.

It was arranged that we should stop at Naples in order to see Pompeii. Everything now was an anti-climax, superfluous, unconnected. I did not like Pompeii. It gave me the same sort of feeling that I experienced at Megiddo.

Before re-embarking I bought a very pretty necklace of blue and gold beads which I often wear, and have never had to have re-strung. The back streets of Naples were poverty stricken, full of children and washing. A funeral passed with a black carriage drawn by six black horses. I was glad when it was time to go back to the ship. Now the cords that bound us to the Holy Land were loosening with every mile we began to think of home.

Joe Sessions, our good friend at the local, was waiting

for us with his car at Victoria station early on a January morning. The windows of his Sussex inn looked across the village green to our sixteenth-century cottage so he had kept an eye on it while we were away. He would not hear of our going back to the cottage until we had had a good breakfast in the lovely old beamed dining room, where a log fire blazed and Lucy, his wife, sat pouring coffee, eager to hear all our news.

We were thankful to have reached home in safety after our adventures. Outwardly, everything looked the same, but inwardly we felt that life could not ever be the same again. We had had in very truth the time of our lives.

20
LEAN ON THE CEILING

As I LOOK BACK over the years covered by this sketchy survey of landmarks passed on the way, I sometimes wonder at the miracle of my own survival. The very grain of history has been grounded out "exceeding small" through the mill of the personal experiences of those whose memories can span two world wars. We did not realise it at the time but when we came to Woodmans, a few miles from Battle, we were entering a ten year period of quiet waters. I should like now to offer some general thoughts.

Standards of living are determined by standards of thinking and have nothing to do with possessions, achievements or any of the social trappings by which the superficially-minded are prone to judge their fellow creatures. You cannot raise a person's standard of living by putting more money into his pocket; his standard of living is determined by his habits of mind, his inner spiritual convictions and his whole attitude towards persons and things.

The first generation of inveterate televiewers to emerge during the fifties were, in many cases, the first victims of what I call Thingery, the lust for Things, not because of their beauty or their usefulness, but because of their popularity. There is no harm in buying anything you are able to afford, but the evil of Thingery is that you may be tempted to buy something you do not really want and cannot really afford just because somebody else has it.

LEAN ON THE CEILING

The happiest people I know are those who have least of this world's goods. They only are free in the real sense of the word; but it's not as easy as that. My sympathies go out to the owners of great historic mansions when I think of what it must entail in the way of upkeep, having regard to what it costs in these days to maintain even a small two-up and two-down cottage such as I live in today. Some misguided persons imagine me to be rich having read somewhere that more people buy my books than the books of any other writer of verse! That may be true. My publishers refer to me as "The Patience Strong phenomenon", the one-woman industry, but no-one in this heavily taxed country is allowed to be rich even if he wanted to be, nor is he or she allowed full freedom to give away his or her earnings or a part of them. I have never been interested in money, fame or food. I have never employed a secretary except for about a month a few years ago, when I heard of a girl who would like to do some evening work, and who, I thought, might help with the correspondence, but I knew after the first week that it was not going to relieve me in any way. The effort of getting her organised used up more time than it would have taken to do it all myself, so after this brief experience I never again entertained the idea. My mother always used to say, if you want anything done, do it yourself. How true! And it is surprising how many things you are able to do yourself. It is all a question of deciding what is important and what is non-essential. My work has always been my first concern and everything else has had to fall into place behind it. If you have a single-minded devotion to anything you must learn to simplify your life, not allowing domestic or social duties to claim more than their share of your time.

Numerous letters arrive from readers wanting to know what sort of a person I am, but how can one describe oneself? I just live from day to day, thankful for everything in life that is lovely and of good report, to use the words of St. Paul. My greatest pleasure in life is to walk alone, chiefly in the afternoon after a morning at the typewriter or pen in hand, knowing that the morning's work reposes in the local pillar box.

Some find their divinest moments in great music, poetry or silent meditation. There are many wells of joy set beside the traveller's way through the wilderness of this world, but for me Nature is the well where spring the waters of everlasting inspiration. My daily walk through the fields is more than a walk. For all my adoration of Keats it is with Wordsworth that I keep company when talking to trees and listening to the voices of brooks and birds,

> *"While with an eye made quiet by the power*
> *Of harmony, the deep power of joy,*
> *We see into the life of things"*

To the cynic that may sound pantheistic, but behind all the visible forms of beauty there stands the formless reality of the Creator of heaven and earth.

Perhaps that is one of the best reasons for being glad that my bones were made in England: I can read Shakespeare, Keats, Wordsworth and Tennyson in the original.

Woodmans was a lovely little sixteenth-century cottage perched on a hill a few miles from Battle. It was a good time to be launching out on another decade. Petrol rationing was coming to an end and I took driving lessons so that I could transport myself from A to B without too much loss of time, but I never looked upon driving as a pleasure; it was a necessity if one lived in the country, and I never craved for any but the smallest and cheapest car. Paddy did not wish to drive, so never owned a car. He pedalled his way through the lanes.

It was my first experience of living in a house which had an aura, a personality stronger than that of the human beings who lived in it. You felt almost afraid to plan an alteration. First you had to get the approval of the entity which was Woodmans. After all, it had stood there since the days of the first Elizabeth so was entitled to respect and consideration.

The previous owner had opened up the attic and dispensed with the ceiling of the bedroom raising it to the ridge of the roof so that the beams framing the dormers sloped sharply up. At this point they formed an angle with a cross beam about five feet from the floor and Paddy discovered by chance that this made a surprisingly comfortable place in which to rest even though standing. I woke one morning to see him standing at ease with his arm resting along the protruding beam. When I asked what he was doing he said "Leaning on the ceiling", which is exactly what he was doing, because the chunk of oak jutting out at that angle had been part of the original ceiling. When in Egypt during the army days he had once been compelled to sleep in a flooded gully for a week because there was nowhere else to go. This had left him with a rheumatic condition of the hip which had developed over the years, but leaning on the ceiling gave him relief as it took the weight off the affected nerve. From that position it was possible to look out across miles of green fields full of grazing sheep. Thereafter it became his special corner and it gave me the idea for several Quiet Corner poems on these lines: when wrestling with some evil thing stretch towards something beyond your reach. Lean on the ceiling. Lean on God for you can stretch no higher.

Every spring turned the Woodmans garden into a fairyland of blossom created by a group of old russet apple trees. Those ten years at Woodmans were eventful without being disturbing. Happy, interesting things happened. There was our first visit to Iona, the island of Celtic crosses, white sand and green seas, the holy isle known as "the lamp that lit all Europe", Druidheda, beloved of the Druids. We saw the ruins of Columba's Abbey before it was restored. But you do not have to read about Iona. You have to see it, feel it and love it.

Shortly after Iona came my meeting with Mary Whitehouse and those first gatherings in a London hotel before the Viewers and Listeners Association was formed. Few people realise how Mary has worked to rid our society of the pornographic poison that trickles day after day through all the channels of communication. It was in reading Mary's book, *Cleaning Up TV* that I was reminded of the translation of the inscription on the dedication panel in Broadcasting House.

"This Temple of the Arts and Muses dedicated to Almighty God by the first Governors of broadcasting in the year 1931, Sir John Reith, being Director General. It is their prayer that good seed sown may bring forth a good harvest, that all things hostile to peace and purity may be banished from this house and that the people, inclining their ear to whatsoever things are beautiful, and honest and of good report, may tread the path of wisdom and uprightness."

Fifty years later, it is no easy task to separate the good seed from the wild oats of evil and violence that come out of this building every day and night not excluding the seventh. Those who prayed that their Temple would be devoted to the pursuit of peace and purity would turn in their graves if they could hear and see the moral squalor, the vulgarity and the profanity now disseminated from what was to be a temple of learning, a broadcasting house for the elevation and not the degradation of future listeners and viewers.

It was from Woodmans that we set out for Jerusalem to have in very truth the time of our lives, and it was while we were at Woodmans that King George VI died at Sandringham and the second Elizabeth ascended to the throne. I remember presenting each child in the village with a Bible which bore his or her initials in gold lettering. I hope that some of these Bibles are still in daily use.

The Rector asked me at that time to undertake the supervision of the Sunday School which was held in the little parish church of St. Mary Magdalene. I was assisted by Heather Morgan whose father was the village schoolmaster. At first it was hard going trying to enrol new members and there was one Sunday when the church was empty and I remember saying to Heather, "This calls for definite action. In the parable of the great supper when none of the invited guests turned up the Lord of the feast said, 'Go out into the highways and byways and compel them to come in.' Come on, Heather," I said. "We're going to snatch the first child we see." So out we set and the first child we saw was a small boy of about three staggering tipsily around a grave in the churchyard while a couple, presumably his parents, were occupied with the arrangement of flowers. In a matter of seconds I had lifted him up and he was being carried off under my arm in the direction of the church, struggling, kicking, screaming, and making every sort of violent protest. This drew the attention of the parents and Heather hastened to reassure them that we were only taking him into the church. They recognised us, and seeming satisfied that he was not being kidnapped, returned to the peace of the grave.

Fortunately, while all this was going on, another lad had arrived whom he recognised and suddenly there was a great calm, as little Johnnie's attention was engaged in watching me get the pedals of the harmonium working which I had to do by hand in a kneeling posture. As soon as it clanged into action we started to sing *Onward Christian Soldiers* in which he joined, not tunefully but with enthusiasm. The battle was won. When the parents came for him he was reluctant to go and was only pacified by the promise that I would call for him next Sunday morning. Thereafter he proved to be the most regular attendant and remained in the Sunday School long after I had left the district. Christmas parties for the Sunday School were given at Woodmans every year and summer outings by coach to Hythe where tea by the water and a rowing boat on the canal were thrown in for good measure.

Shall I ever forget climbing up the winding stone stairway into the tiny belfry to ring the single tone bell which had served to call the people to prayer for a few hundred years? On the old wall in the porch there was a record of past Rectors going back to the early thirteenth century and in a niche by the font a pre-Reformation silver chalice and platter. The chalice, I understand, is not now kept in the church.

I seldom pass this little wayside church without remembering the year when the Feast of the Epiphany fell on a Sunday. I was walking in the dark to Evensong down the steep slope from the green to the Mill House by the brook when, like the Gentile Kings of the Epiphany, I saw a great light as my head hit the road. A pedal cyclist had been freewheeling downhill and failed to notice me. Fortunately the old fur coat I was wearing because it was a cold night had padded shoulders, then fashionable. Had it not been padded, the injury to the shoulder might have been more serious. An ambulance had been sent for as my head and face were streaming with blood. Early Christian Science training then stood me in good stead as I lay on the grass verge looking up at the January stars, knowing that He who had made and arranged them in their cosmic pattern was more than capable of doing a small repair job on me.

After leaving me at the hospital in Hastings Paddy spent the rest of the night at the kitchen sink washing the blood out of my coat. I still wear it in cold weather. Some things never seem to wear out.

It was my first and only stay in hospital and it lasted a month but was an experience, interesting and enriching.

The hospital was housed in what was once the old infirmary. The Health Service had not yet got fully into its stride. The spirit of personal service and devotion to duty had not yet been submerged under a blanket of officialdom.

LEAN ON THE CEILING

At ten every morning, by order of the Sister in charge, the door of the ward was closed. Everything stopped for a ten minute withdrawal into the precincts of prayer. Vacuum cleaners were switched off, dustpans and brushes were put on the floor, radio sets silenced, eyes closed and hands folded. This was a dramatic and moving experience. One could almost hear the wings of the angel of healing passing over our heads. There was a power stirring amongst us that was greater than any that might have been latent in the pills and tablets of the medicine chest.

The extraordinary thing was that no time was wasted by the institution of this service of silence. Nurses and ancillary workers seemed to spring into action with a new vigour as if they too had drunk deeply of some life-giving potion, but the patients seemed reluctant to come back into the busy world of vacuum cleaners, thermometers and hospital routine. It was as if they knew where their real healing lay and could not easily shake off the effects of this heavenly drug of silence. A long time elapsed before anyone felt inclined to switch on a radio set.

It was in one of these drugged silences that the starry-eyed woman who was literally dying happily of cancer in the next bed suddenly passed me a small booklet called *Wells of Comfort*. "I want you to have this, dear," she said with a radiant smile. "You might find in it just the sort of comfort you need." I thanked her and looked at it; it was one of mine. I wished afterwards that I had told her I was Patience Strong, the writer of that little booklet, because she would, I think, have enjoyed the joke. She died that afternoon.

As a member of BUPA I could have gone into a private ward, but though I longed to be quiet I was afraid of hurting the feelings of those who were treating me with such loving care.

If I had followed my selfish inclinations and asked for a private bed, I should have missed that lovely moment of spiritual intercourse with that dear soul in the next bed.

She told me she was concerned about leaving the little shop which was her world. Her husband might not know that she kept the candles and the bootlaces in the left hand drawer under the counter.

Her eyes, sunken into her head with suffering, were lit with the light of a beautiful faith. I remember thinking, this is how everyone should die, happy, hopeful, believing.

Looking back across the latter part of our time at Woodmans is like opening a photograph album and seeing blank pages. Though the coming of each day was wonderful, in retrospect it seems there is little to remember; but that is good because it means that there were few sorrowful images to project onto the screen of memory. We tend not to remember the long calm days of uninterrupted work with no intrusions when days merged into days leaving no impressions behind.

I had switched from the Daily Mirror to the Sunday Mirror; that meant one verse a week instead of six, but strange to relate, this did not mean there was more time to spare for other things. I still hurried on in the same frenzied rush of never having time to spare for other things no matter how I tried to cut down on commitments. I was, of course, still doing the weekly for Woman's Own and a prose column for Tit-Bits under the name of Faith Forsyte, plus the annual production of four calendars and periodically adding to the stocks of birthday and Christmas cards. Once, sometimes twice a year, I would do a book for Mullers, sometimes these consisted of collections of verses and it was during this period that I wrote *"The Morning Watch"*, a book of devotional daily readings which was followed by *"The Kingdom Within"* along similar lines.

Amanda came for a few days every season from Leatherhead where she was staying with her son who had returned from America at the outbreak of war. I greatly enjoyed those visits and we walked many miles together in the Sussex lanes. Her brain was as keen as ever and her step just as light as she skimmed along beside me hardly seeming to touch the ground. In 1956 on Christmas Eve she died at the age of 89 after a brief illness and I shall never cease to thank God for that stimulating friendship. When I was told of her illness I went at once to the nursing home in Epsom to which she had been taken. When she saw me she quoted from a poem we had recently discovered in the Science of Thought Review.

> *"Clay moulded round a star*
> *Cannot withstand the furnace lit within"*

She died an hour or so later so those were probably her last words and very fitting they were, for all who came into contact with that vivid personality were conscious that the fiery life in her flashed from the furnace lit within, the furnace of faith in the goodness of life and the omnipotence of Divine power.

At the funeral, a few days later, Paddy and I were struck by the aptness of something said by the clergyman who conducted the service and who had never met Amanda in his life. He concluded with the words "Now she has gone off on the greatest adventure of all." Little could he, a stranger, have known that life to Amanda had been one continuous adventure, for though circumstances encapsulated her life within the limits set by family responsibilities, she lived every day as if it were the last, joyously, expectantly, as if on mental tip-toe. She rose at five every morning so that at the very edge of the day, she was alert to catch its glory, before the first freshness had been used up; while thoughts were still sprinkled with the dew of heaven, as she would have said.

As we were coming away from the cemetery on that cold but bright morning I said to Guy, "I know now what she meant when she used to quote those words of Plato, 'You can bury me if you can catch me'." No-one ever did catch up with Amanda in the sense of possessing her. That I suppose was at the root of her antipathy to being a mother. She had said to me once, that when she knew she was to have a child, she knew too that she would never again be free from the agony of love's demands.

Life, I knew, would never now be the same for me, but I had all her letters in that strange artistic writing of hers and that greatest of treasures, the book she had brought to me in response to the telepathic message at the psychical receiving station twenty years previously: the Patience Strong book by Mrs A. D. T. Whitney of America.

If I had been asked to pinpoint what it was that gave Amanda her infinite capacity for enjoying life for the sake of life itself I suppose I should have said that it was because she seemed to have within her a fountain of thankfulness; not for what life brought her, for she stripped herself of all worldly possessions so that she could trip along unencumbered. It was not, then, for what life brought to her but for what she brought to life. Being countrybred on a Norfolk farm she loved the parks and gardens of the London suburbs through which we walked together for so many years. We would go to the lake in the gardens of the Public Library in Bromley watching the swans and the last of the sunset light falling upon the upturned faces of the flowers. When it was time to go she or I would break the silence with a Wordsworthian quotation.

> "and this prayer I make
> Knowing that Nature never did betray
> The heart that loved her; 'tis her privilege—
> Through all the years of this our life—
> To lead from joy to joy."

And the joy that was in her was no mere sentimental feeding upon beauty. It seemed to spring from her interest in people, most often from strangers. In tearooms, in buses or in shops she would fall into conversation with the stranger and they would go out into their own lives again feeling that life was better than they had believed. She had the gift of communication combined with the unique capacity for making others realise their potential. No person was unimportant, no encounter insignificant. Everything that happened was charged with destiny, drama, meaning. Somehow she had the gift of making life appear more than life size. "Nothing matters" she used to say, "except that everything matters."

From the time that her husband died and the three sons were launched on their careers she was able to enjoy life in a new kind of way. She who had spent more than half her life preparing meals for others was able to feed on the secret manna of what she digested in the libraries and meditated upon in the long silences of her life of full satisfaction in a bed-sitting room. Later she lived with her son and his family but the bed-sitter period was the one that yielded most delight, living on manna and drinking the heady wine of freedom.

> *Bid your friend a fond farewell*
> *But not a last goodbye.*

Those two lines come at the end of a poem written for another old friend who died twenty years later in the Isle of Wight. She lies in the old burial ground of the little Norman church of St. Lawrence and many happy hours I spent in Rose's garden under the cliffs, telling her about Amanda. It has always happened in my life that when I lose one friend I find another. Time is kind, and the more friends one gathers, the dearer grow the memories of those who have gone on ahead into the mystery of death and the greater mystery of the life beyond.

Five years after the departure of Amanda, on a day of bright March sunshine my father died, spade in hand, at the age of 79. Many years before, his brother Charles had died in the same way, spade in hand, and Ernie his youngest brother was to go in like manner two years later. But in what better way could any man wish to go than to be found by the angel of death working on his own patch of English earth? Charles had been at work on a new plot to which he had come on that same day, to a new home in Hampshire. Ernie had been shovelling snow from the path that led up to his cottage on a hill in Somerset. My father had died of a fatal heart spasm while attempting to dig out an old hydrangea root from his garden in Sussex. Each died in an attempt to do something which was beyond his physical capacity to do but each of these three brothers died trying. For all three the end was sudden and comparatively painless. They did not have to drag out their last days on the bed of an invalid under a ceiling enclosed by four walls. They breathed their last breath out in the open under the sky. That is what they would have chosen to do. At the core of every grief there is always something for which to be thankful. So passed my father, a lover of gardens, a lover of the earth and of walking; a good man, a wise man and a loving father.

As we were moving quietly through the strange no-man's-land of grief in the half-light that follows upon a bereavement, Time was carrying us across the boundary of another decade, driving on into the sixties and beyond, for Time never rests. We both realised that the shape of our lives had changed. We three had been bound in a close relationship ever since the death of my mother twenty-one years previously and it seemed to be meant that we should now spread our wings yet again and cross the border into Kent. This, we thought, would be our final move. After months of abortive viewings we came upon a tumbledown lodge by a high pair of ironwrought gates to the drive of a Victorian mansion which had been converted into a preparatory school for boys.

The lodge was a neglected hovel but we decided to set about turning it into a home. Its redeeming feature was a pillared porch which required no restoration. The exterior was of red brick and sand-coloured stone. A new room was added and for this a dense clump of conifers had to be removed; also, to my sorrow, one or two beautiful old beeches which were obstructing light and sunshine. I was sorry about this but shed no tears over the gloomy evergreens. It was a tragic day for Britland when conifers were introduced into our landscape, the unEnglish, unlovely trees which are now ruining some of the loveliest views in the kingdom.

I was soon to become aware of the fact that the mullion windows, though facing south and west never caught so much as a glimpse of the sunsets which blazed upon the windows of houses on the other side of the road. Aspect is the most important factor in the choosing of the site for a home.

At last the lodge was ready for partial occupation and was now an ornament and not an eyesore by the once grand gates at the entrance to the drive.

But a number of small disasters had led me to wonder if we had taken on too big a task in the transformation of hovel into home.

On the first Sunday we were there I set out to walk to Evensong at the parish church, a mere mile, but it was dusk and being unfamiliar with the ground, on reaching the gate I assumed it was level unaware of the step down. It was an unpropitious start. I gave my ankle a severe twist and was compelled to limp back to base, fearing this would slow down my movements for at least a few weeks. Actually, the inconvenience lasted a few months. The following day the builder arrived with the final bills for payment. In answer to our enquiry as to why the amount was so much in excess of the estimate, it transpired that, unknown to us, the work had been handed over to another firm and the original estimate scrapped. This held up the completion of the remainder of the work still to be done.

Then came Christmas. My brother and his small daughter Sonia had stayed with us at the lodge on Christmas night, but on the morning of Boxing Day he was unable to find his car which he had left outside because the path to the garage had been glazed with ice. It had snowed heavily in the night and after prodding all the likely places where snow had accumulated the little red mini was discovered under what looked like an igloo. So, without further delay, they set off on the hazardous journey to Chislehurst.

After seeing them off I remembered pausing to look up at the not unattractive façade of this odd little homestead. It wore a bonnet of snow over its steep roof which made it appear like something on the stage of a pantomime. I almost expected to see one of those windows open and the head of Snow White or a Babe In The Wood appear. I remembered the lines I had written for the man who was painting the outside of Southways during the war. He had just rescued an old cottage from extinction and was wanting a few meaningful words to carve over the lintel before moving in. So I gave him the following:

> *Reverence God,*
> *Respect man,*
> *Preserve property.*

When the painting job at Southways was completed he presented me with bellows made of oak and scarlet leather on which a design of acorns and oaks had been carved. This must have been all of forty years ago but those bellows have put life into many a dying fire and they are still hanging at my hearth by the original red leather loop.

As I stood there on that white morning looking up at the lodge I felt that it had not been a time-wasting hobby, this passion for moving around, restoring what had been neglected, always leaving a place better than we found it, structurally and aesthetically. There had certainly been no material gain in this work-pleasure hobby as any will attest who have ever been bitten by the preservation bug.

The fun and the satisfaction of it lie in the doing. But there was a severity about the lines of the lodge when not wearing its snow bonnet and I was uneasily aware of a faint sense of foreboding. So I went indoors to light a fire; always a good thing to do when suddenly life turns cold.

For the next three months the snow continued to flutter about the iron gates hardening around the newly planted roses and after what seemed a hopeless waiting March brought the daffodils thrusting through the crust of the frozen earth. By the time they were ready to dance my life with Paddy had come to an end. There were still to be eighteen more months which meant one more winter and two summers, but it was on the wintry winds of our first spring in Kent that I caught the first notes of the finale of the music of our romantic marriage, the first notes of the last movement.

On an evening in the March that followed the white Christmas at the lodge, Paddy was injured in an accident. A seventeen-year-old motor cyclist came roaring round the unlit bend in the road which Paddy was crossing on foot making for the point at which he thought I had left the car. Actually, I had already moved it to what seemed a more convenient position.

My friend, Laura, whom we had just left, heard the smash and rushing out into the road she snatched at a white cloth lying across a chair in her hall on its way to the laundry basket. Paddy's guardian angel was surely with him that night, for Laura stood in the road signalling to oncoming traffic with the God-sent tablecloth. She had the presence of mind to telephone for the ambulance before running out of the house. When at last it dawned upon me that there had been an accident I stepped out of the car to see Paddy lying in the road a few yards from the car on the opposite side. The motor cyclist had been flung across the road but was unhurt.

The ambulance arrived within minutes to take us to the hospital in Tunbridge Wells. Paddy was concussed, having sustained serious injuries to head and limbs. The orthopaedic surgeon was sent for and spent the rest of the night working skilfully and successfully on his patient while I sat in a nearby waiting room holding on to him in silent prayer. At last a nurse appeared to say that the operation had been completed and about four in the morning they ordered a taxi to take me home.

I remembered standing in the darkest hour before the dawn looking up at the iron gates with Paddy's blood stained clothing over my arm. The trousers and coat were in shreds. A memory of Iona came back and I found myself thinking of the day when we had bought that roll of cinnamon-coloured tweed woven on a cottage loom. The cap, made from that same roll of tweed had not been marked.

When at last he came home, though crippled, he still retained his humorous way of dealing with the problems which every day presented. Within a year we both decided that we should sell the lodge and move into a bungalow, and with the end of the year took possession of Meadow Cottage. The windows looked out upon a breath-taking view of orchards, oast-houses and sheep. It was only ten minutes walk from the lodge along the same road, but here was the window of which I had always dreamed, with a south-westerly aspect. And here it was that we lived out together the last sunset hours of our shared life.

In the May following that fateful September I decided to visit Bad Boll near Stüttgart with Enid Heyworth who for over thirty years had been matron at Dr Nesfield's nursing home in Kent. Bad Boll had been the home of the famous Pastor Blumhardt, healer and preacher, the uncle of Dr Nesfield's mother who had been a missionary in India. As, through the extraordinary powers of this extraordinary doctor, Paddy had been spared the suffering he would have had to endure under orthodox treatment, I had always wanted to see the place to which so many had travelled from all parts of the world in search of healing for mind and body. And so it was that the opportunity arose and it was an experience never to be forgotten. But this is not the place for the telling of it for fragments of it have already been told in *Dr. Anonymous*, so called because at that time it was not permitted to name in print the name of a living doctor. So I wrote my brief account of the life of Vincent Nesfield. Inadequate though it was, it was my sincere and grateful tribute to a dear friend, a natural healer and surgeon and fighter under the banner of truth. This was published in 1967, and when he died a few years later I was pleased that I had made the effort to get at least a little of his long life onto the printed page. The writing of *Dr. Anonymous* had involved me in many weeks of research at the British Museum in connection with the Blumhardt story which proved to be as fantastic as that of Dr. Nesfield's though in a different setting and a different period of time.

On completing this piece of work I felt in need of a few days by the sea and it was then and there that a strange thing happened. I was hurrying along the seafront at St. Leonards, revelling in the unseasonable warm sunshine of the first day of November. So remarkable it seemed to me that such a day should come in such a month that I made a note of it in my diary. Unknown to me Guy, eldest son of my friend Amanda, whom I had not seen since the day of his mother's funeral ten years previously, was also making a note in his diary with reference to the date and the exceptional weather. He had always been meticulous in noting recordings of barometers, thermometers, times and temperatures. He also was walking that day on the same seafront, having brought two friends from where he lived near Epsom to keep an appointment in Hastings. We must have passed one another, probably looking in different directions, for we had both been at the same place at the same time as confirmed later by entries in our respective diaries. Perhaps it was as well that we passed each other at that moment, unaware. The timings of fate are always accurate.

I suppose there is really no escaping from the past. You think you have left it behind then suddenly it catches up and falls into step with you becoming once more a part of the present, actually or in thought. As I have so often observed, everything that happens happens because it must. This is not a form of fatalism, an easy way out of difficult situations, abandoning oneself to the merciless precision of an unalterable destiny. It is rather a recognition of the fact that human beings whose minds are tuned to a particular degree of sensitivity are drawn inevitably towards the people and the places to which they have unconsciously been gravitating. Final decisions and their results lie within the realm of the will which is always left free to act for good or ill. Whichever way things shape, the piecing together of the scattered bits of life's jigsaw is part of a never-ending process of spiritual unfoldment. Consciously or unconsciously we strive against fragmentation knowing that ultimately our peace lies in the achievement of wholeness.

We missed the moment for a re-meeting on that golden November day but on a December morning of the following year I was hastening through the gates of the cut that leads off Fleet Street by the Law Courts, on my way to the Womens' Press Club when I saw Guy standing at the top of the short flight of steps at the end of the passageway. Except for the silvery hair, he looked very much as he did in the old days, slim as a blade, a neatly rolled umbrella in his hand, a newspaper under his arm, trilby hat and dark overcoat. Feeling again an upsurge of the old ecstasy of Amanda's companionship I rushed up the steps and kissed him. "I see you are still using that old music case," he said with a critical glance at the battered leather case in which I had always carried music and papers given to me by my parents on my seventh birthday. "I see you are still reading the Daily Express," I retorted. We might have been back in the fog of that night in 1927 when we had first met at a political meeting. He had always been passionately interested in the current political situation and as we lunched together later that morning we hammered out the same old questions as if a world war and half a lifetime had not intervened since those summer afternoons when we sat watching cricket at the Ravensbourne Club in Lee. Within a few months we were married. Blake's golden string was unwound to its full length.

Guy had recently retired and was living alone at a pleasant flat near the river at Surbiton. I could not endure the thought of living under unquiet skies so he joined me at Meadow Cottage in Kent. The twelve years of our marriage were dimmed by his progressive ill health, an inherited lung condition. No doubt this had been affected by the almost fatal bout of pneumonia which he had developed after that long wait for me in the fog outside the hall in which we had met but not spoken. I often thought of that but I had not known that he was waiting for me to come out of the meeting. I had imagined he had gone home immediately after leaving the hall.

Much happened during those twelve years. The Patience Strong rose was introduced. The book *The Other Side of the Coin* was written and published following my visit to South Africa in 1974. Then there was the day when we went to the Guildhall and I received the Freedom of the City of London but the thing that I remember most of all was the day when it was arranged that I should present my poem on Keats at Hampstead to be hung in the room he had occupied during the unhappy years of his illness and his hopeless love for Fanny Brawne who lived in the next house. It was from this place that he went with Joseph Severn on September 13th 1820, to die in Rome. The loving friend who accompanied him on the voyage nursed him all through that fatal illness and remained with him faithfully until he died the following February in the sad little room on the Spanish Steps. It was in this room that I wrote *The Broken Bloom* in 1970.

There have been extensive alterations to the house in Hampstead and I believe the name has now been changed from Wentworth Place to Keats House, but I have not had time recently to go there. That is one of the things to which I look forward, to stand once more in the room in which Keats knew that his days were numbered, when he saw the blood on the sheet, and said to his friend Browne, "That is arterial blood."

I remember coming out of the Keats-Shelley Memorial House, that cool sad little death chamber on the Piazza di Spagna and stepping into the gold blaze of the Italian sun. The Bernini fountain was playing at the foot of the Spanish Steps as Keats and Joseph Severn would have seen it play more than a hundred and fifty years ago. I sat on the stone steps making a few alterations to what I had written in The Room and made my way to the beautiful little English Protestant cemetery where Keats and Severn lie side by side within a few steps of Shelley's heart, buried here under a tree because it would not burn with his body on the sands off Leghorn where he was drowned in 1822.

If it had not been for my meeting with Guy on the steps it is unlikely that I should ever have had a Christmas in Rome. His daughter had married an Italian who lived there. So it was here that we spent our first Christmas together. I had always longed to see the church of Santa Pudenziana under which lie the ruins of the magnificent Palatium Britannicum known in A.D. 58 as the Palace of the British where the royal Silurian family lived when Caractacus was in residence. His daughter, the British princess Gladys, later to be re-named Claudia was married at the age of seventeen to a Roman Senator, Rufus Pudens, whom she had met in Britain, referred to in the Pauline writings of the New Testament. It is a story of such romance and tragedy that it would be impossible for me to relate it at this point, but it is all there in the history of the early Christian church for any who care to look for it. To me, it is thrilling to recall that Linus the brother of Claudia was a British prince, the first bishop of the first Christian church below ground in Rome. The first above ground was in Glastonbury established by the Apostle to Britain, Joseph of Arimathea in A.D. 53, whose arrival in Avalon would have been welcomed by the indigenous Culdee Church, and who for many centuries had been awaiting the birth of Messiah.

Standing in that quiet little corner of the English Protestant cemetery in Rome I felt that John Keats had made that small plot of Roman earth into something that belonged to all the world. I read again the words Keats had wished to have upon his memorial stone. "Here lies one whose name was writ in water." De profundis. Out of what bitterness of heart had those words been conceived! I turned away with mingled feelings of pride and pity, fingering the poem in my pocket.

On the return flight from Rome Guy and I shared an experience which was never to be repeated or forgotten. Our small plane, while passing over the Alps, was caught in the immense conflagration of the sunset. The summits blazed with gold and crimson streamers of light under a pearly ceiling of cloud, flushed softly with the reflected glory of the dying day. Such beauty seemed to bring us to the outer courts of heaven itself, and I hoped that for both of us death, when it came, would be like this.

21
ROYAL SERVANT

$\mathcal{I}$ AM HAPPY to be able to say that as these last chapters
are being written my old Royal typewriter is still
coping efficiently, on duty every day with the exception of
Sundays. It may have lost something of its once smart
appearance but it works, and still takes first place in my
working life.

Had its owner been less conservative it would, I suppose, have suffered the indignity of being consigned to the
scrap heap long ago and replaced with something more up
to date, but I like the feel of something old and
trustworthy under my hands. An affinity of affection exists
between us which goes deeper than the superficial rapport
between the user of an object and the object used. My
utter dependence upon it has invested it with the aura of a
friend. Just to see it standing in its familiar place on the
desk warms my heart no matter how much of the world's
turmoil has filtered through with the eight o'clock news.
So long as the Royal servant stands ready to serve I too
must be ready for anything that comes at me via the
letterbox.

Conscious of the fact that I am a heavy tapper, I must
admit to having ill treated this shabby defenceless little
machine. A doctor once told me that the force exerted
upon the keys of a typewriter during the course of a day's
pounding was considerable as was the expenditure of
nervous energy used up by the pounder. Poor little port-

able! It is not deserving of the hammering it gets, day in and day out, from one year's end to another.

Prior to my sister's death I had used an old Oliver, but after commencing the Quiet Corner feature in the Daily Mirror I decided to take the Royal into daily service, and so it was that we set out together as a partnership which, in four years' time will have lasted for half a century, making allowances for the five years it was exiled in a dark cupboard having had a death sentence pronounced upon it by a typewriter salesman who was out to boost the continental machine. My Royal was made in New York, and sold in England. It is a sad thought that the Royal typewriter is no longer marketed in the U.K. Its very name should inspire us to do something about the manufacture of typewriters.

With Paddy's help I tapped my way through the war and managed to cope with about fifty letters a day in addition to the daily verse for the Daily Mirror, the weekly for Woman's Own, the yearly calendars and greetings cards and a book twice yearly for Mullers.

After the end of the war I hammered my way through another twenty years of producing Quiet Corners in a world that was anything but quiet until a day came when the Royal servant refused to serve. I feared I had worked my old friend too hard and too long. It would have to submit to examination by an expert. The consultant shook his head at the very idea of restoring the patient to health. "Sorry," he murmured, "but it's obsolete. Now what you want is a nice new machine." "That is just what I don't want." I protested. "I want this one put into working order," to which he replied that as typewriters were not now made in the U.K. it would be impossible to get spare parts. In short, the Royal had had it. I went from one to another and at each was given the same diagnosis of the patient's trouble. So eventually I gave up trying and went home with three typewriters on the back seat of the car: the obsolete Royal and a pair of portable Olympias, one for use and the other for a spare in case of breakdown.

The Olympia seemed tinny after the solidity of the Royal but I tried to make the best of it. A year or so later, Mr Allen, who came to help in the garden and to do odd jobs in the house on Saturday mornings, asked me what I had done with my old typewriter. I said that I still had it, but it was now retired collecting dust in the attic. He was the local scout master and his duties included writing and distributing notices in connection with scout meetings. He wondered if he could get it to work for use at the scout hall. I drew it out of interment in the loft and handed it to Mr. Allen with a pang of misgiving. I had not really given up all hope of a miraculous metamorphosis of the battered old blue body that had withstood the worst hammerings of the worst years, to say nothing of a few near misses in the blitz.

A few days later I was dusting my desk which meant moving the Olympia, when for the first time I discovered the "Made in West Germany" sign on its base. So out went the Olympias, one to Sonia, my niece who, I hoped, would one day take up her pen and write following in the footsteps of her father and her aunt. The other I placed in a cupboard feeling that it would be useful to somebody, some day.

In the meantime I had to equip myself with another machine and was persuaded to buy a Hermes, Swiss made. This was disastrous. I found myself making errors; t, h and m seemed to be crowding too closely under my flying fingers, although the arrangement of the keyboard was unchanged. This I was told was the continental type of lettering. I was half way through the book on the subject of practical psychology published later by Mullers under the title of *Life Is For Living* and it caused me a great deal of inconvenience and irritation. So in desperation I accepted the kindly offer of my friend Katy Gillum who had volunteered to type the ms for me.

Gloomily I looked into the future wondering how I was

going to cope. Suddenly, I remembered what Amanda had said so often in moments of crisis. "Everything is possible. Believe the unbelievable. Dream only what you wish to be true." And that night I dreamed of my Royal servant. The following morning I decided to see Mr Allen and enquire as to its fate. The next evening I walked to his cottage and found him working in his garden. "Is it possible," I asked, "that you still have my old Royal?" "Yes," he said, "it's in the loft. I wasn't able to do anything with it." Then I knew what I had to do. "Let me have it back," I said, "and I'll give you a new Olympia." He came home with me bringing the Royal servant and relieved me of the Olympia still in the cupboard where I had placed it a year or so previously.

Still hoping to find something as good as my old blue Royal I replied to an advertisement in Exchange & Mart in which a standard Royal was offered for sale second hand. The owner was willing to deliver from Chislehurst, so arrangements were set in motion and the typewriter brought to the door, but my heart fell when I saw the long carriage from which I deduced that the machine had been designed for legal work. However, I agreed to take it as the vendor had made a special journey to bring it and I comforted myself with the thought that it was a Royal so at least the keys would be in the same position as those to which I had been accustomed. More great expectations were dashed. It was too large for my requirements, so I set in motion a request for a typewriter mechanic to call. In due course a young man appeared with a catalogue of smart continental machines which I refused to consider, but as he was leaving the room his eyes lighted on the old Royal resting, as if weary and abandoned, on a shelf in an open cupboard. "What's that?" he asked. I proceeded to tell him the sad story of its relegation to the shelf and as if rising to the challenge he said, "I'll see what I can do. I shall be passing this way in a day or two. Keep on eye on the woodshed."

With these cryptic words he went off with the Royal servant, and sure enough there it was a few days later, standing on a pile of logs between the dustbin and the mangle with a note attached. "Can get replacements for anything except steel parts."

This to me was nothing less than a miracle. And there it stands to this day, restored to its rightful place on my desk giving Royal service, a mute testimony to the validity of the belief that one thing leads to another, and if in faith you hang on long enough you will come to the point at which you are able to clutch at the last link in the chain of circumstances.

22
THE TOUCHSTONE

*M*OST OF MY TIME is taken up with the letters that come
in daily and to which I reply personally. Some, if
not most of them are from readers with problems of one
kind or another. Chiefly they are requests for copies of
verses published during the war period, treasured for years
but lost owing to a removal or sometimes a bereavement. It
is not always easy to trace these missing items as the files in
which all my published verses are pasted cover nearly fifty
years. This often means that I must search through the files
several times before being able to trace the elusive title, but
with patience and perseverance I am usually able to track it
down. It is a sad day for me when I have to disappoint a
correspondent because he or she remembers only a few
lines and is unable to recall the title.

Seldom is it necessary to wait more than a few seconds
or minutes for the first words of a poem, but I often have
to spend considerable time in cogitation over replies to
letters, some of which are written out of the depths
of very real trouble and I feel the responsibility of being
asked not only to give an opinion on the matter but to
advise. This is not always easy to do, especially when a
marriage is in jeopardy and all the circumstances are not
known.

There are times when I receive letters which pose no
problems of any kind but are simple expressions of thanks

for my writings over the years and these are a joy to receive. One in particular springs to mind. It was from a mother whose son was in prison for robbery with violence. There is usually a story behind a story and behind this boy's record lay a history of antagonism between himself and his step-father. The mother visited him every week but was unable to establish any point on which they could form a harmonious relationship. No doubt he had felt excluded when his mother made a second marriage. One day when she was visiting at the prison she happened to leave behind the Woman's Own which she had bought to read on the train. A few days later she received a letter in which the boy asked her to bring him another copy when next she came. This went on for several weeks and she noticed there had been a change in his manner. Whereas previously he had been abrasive and critical he now thanked her for coming, and began to talk of his fellow prisoners, telling her that he had made a friend and that together they had been discussing the Patience Strong verses in the Woman's Own which she had brought for him. A friendship sprang up between the two boys and eventually they asked the chaplain to join in their discussions. The result was that within a few weeks they had asked to be confirmed. When the other boy was released he persuaded his parents to take his friend into their home when his time came to be free. So the story had a happy ending for the four people involved, the mother, the chaplain and the two boys. This takes me back to the thread that seems to be running all through this chronicle, the thread connecting lives with lives leading through a chain of events which on the surface may appear to be insignificant. As I have written before, one thing leads to another. Through the seemingly accidental circumstance of that mother buying the Woman's Own with the intention of reading it on the journey home and forgetting to take it with her she, without realising it, had set something in motion which was to bless them all. There was another occasion on which a prisoner was moved to make a wooden cross about ten inches by four which he sent to me on an impulse after reading something of mine in the Daily Mirror. From Stafford prison there came also a painting of the crucifixion and a note of appreciation. These are amongst my greatest treasures.

But most of the letters received have been on the subject of religion. What do you personally believe? they ask. Do you belong to any particular church? How can it be that God answers prayer? Do you believe in an after life? Do Christians truly believe in the second coming of Christ as they declare Sunday after Sunday throughout the world in the recitation of the Apostles' Creed? And what are your views in regard to spiritual healing?

These are deep and difficult questions to answer. Religion is such a personal thing with its roots reaching down into the core of life itself; and in a sense it is more important than one's work, home, friends or family. It is, for me, a world that must be explored entirely alone, for in the last analysis we are all utterly alone with our problems. Fellowship exists around the edges of religion, but at its centre you stand in a stark confrontation with the Eternal, the Other, the One reality in a nebulous infinity of space and time. We have the law and the prophets, but these are only guides and teachers helping us grope our way through the wilderness of secularism with a few ethical rules to keep us on the right track. If the Eternal had not been incarnated as the Christ, men surely by now would have destroyed themselves with the hopelessness of living in an unredeemed world.

There has not been space within the limits of a letter to go into the metaphysical and theological dimensions of life in an attempt to reply to the question "What do you believe?", but this book provides me with a little more ground for venturing out upon the finding of an explanation drawn from my own experience. There are many roads to truth and all roads must at last converge at the point where God made Himself into something small enough to be put into a cattle trough.

The impression I have gathered from most of these letters is that people, particularly since the war, are afflicted with aimlessness. My diagnosis for this would be that unknown to themselves they are famished for the bread of life. Jesus said, "I am the Bread of life; he that cometh to me shall never hunger. The bread of God is he that cometh down from heaven, and giveth life unto the world. I am the bread of life; he that cometh to me shall never hunger. I am the living bread. If any man eat of this bread he shall live forever. The bread that I will give is my flesh, which I will give for the life of the world." Thus spake the Master.

And what is this mysterious bread that gives a man life by feeding his soul? It is not grown in a field, to be threshed, ground in a mill and garnered in a barn. Jesus *is* bread. He Himself is life, sustenance, manna. If we attempt to live without that mystical bread we die spiritually. And where can I get it? asks the hungry man. Many semi-starving half-alive people in these days are ready with their own answers. All you have to do, say some, is to do unto others as you would be done by. That is a good answer, but it is not good enough. That is humanism, but it is not Christianity. Jesus said "Only believe."

No man has a right to call himself a Christian unless he believes that Christ is the bread of life. There is no other answer to those heart-searching questions. It is as simple as that. All you have to do to open the gates of life is to believe in the miracle of the Incarnation. That is the divine simplicity of the whole Christian gospel. "If ye have faith", said Jesus . . . "nothing shall be impossible unto you."

In these latter days in which we endure the tribulation which must come before "the terrible day of the Lord", our faith will be bested as it was prophesied that it would be.

To those who appeared to be lost I always gave the same direction for there is no other that can be given. Look to the Bible, for it contains the pearl of truth, the Word of life. The Bible is the touchstone, the jasper by which life is tested for the gold of truth. It flashes a light on all subjects and all times for all men everywhere. Britain is uniquely blessed for in the Authorised Version of the King James Bible we have access to the crown jewels of the King of Kings.

Much has happened in the last few years to discourage the faint-hearted. The church is assaulted on all sides. The wine of Cranmer's liturgy has been watered down by reason of the recent introduction of Alternative Services, or the go-as-you-please type of religion. The singing of the Te Deum Laudamus, the Benedictus and the Jubilate Deo, provide good foundation stones under the feet of the congregation when the people are there not to please themselves but to please God.

Throughout the world in the Anglican church the people cry "Blessed be the Lord God of Israel; for he has visited and redeemed his people and hath raised up a mighty salvation for us in the house of his servant David; as he spake by the mouth of his holy prophets which have been since the world began, that we should be saved from our enemies and from the hands of all that hate us." And how much the Benedictus meant to Christians during the war when we flocked into our churches and cathedrals on national days of prayer pleading with the Almighty to "deliver us out of the hands of all that hate us"! And we were. The prayers of the nation, led by the monarch, did not go unanswered.

Our need is just as great now as then for there is little comfort in the present scene, political and ecclesiastical. Shakespeare was not only a poet but a prophet. The words of John of Gaunt, in the second act of Richard II, have a prophetic ring reminding one of prophets like Ezekiel, Hosea and Amos.

THE TOUCHSTONE

"England, bound in with the triumphant sea
Whose rocky shore beats back the envious siege
Of watery Neptune, is now bound in with shame,
With inky blots, and rotten parchment bonds:
That England, that was wont to conquer others
Hath made a shameful conquest of itself."

We are beset by grievous problems and we flounder helplessly in "a sea of troubles" all of our own making because we have refused to put everything to the test of the touchstone of the Bible. All the answers to all the questions are there in the Book. We have made our own difficulties by disregarding the commandments in Old and New testaments. The laws laid down in Holy Scriptures cover every field of human need for they contain the laws of farming, hygiene, food, health and every social and moral problem with which we have to wrestle. Racial and sexual problems are discussed also.

Politically the outlook is grim and the future misty in a world under the shadow of the nuclear bomb. What crumb of hope have I to offer to those who write to me at a loss to know where to turn and what to believe?

To this question I would give the only answer possible and that is, open your Bible and read. There you will find not only a crumb of hope. You will find more than a crumb. The very bread of life is there for the taking.

Through the sound of the quaking of the earth and the strife of human tongues a voice comes ringing down the centuries. The Christian knows that these things must be before the fulfilment of the prophecies. First the time of great tribulation must come upon us. But said Jesus "When ye see these things come to pass Lift up your hearts, for your redemption draweth nigh." What a promise and what a hope! The nations of the earth must be tried in the furnace of adversity because by their sinfulness they have made their once lovely world into something evil and chaotic.

But the promise holds. He shall come again "with power and great glory." Could there be a more wonderful note on which to end a letter, a book or a life?

23
FROM THE HARVEST OF THE YEARS

IF YOU STAND VERY STILL

If you stand very still in the heart of a wood – you will hear many wonderful things – the snap of a twig, the wind in the trees and the whirr of invisible wings.

If you stand very still in the turmoil of life and you wait for the voice from within – You'll be led down the quiet ways of wisdom and peace in a mad world of chaos and din.

If you stand very still and you hold to your faith you will get all the help that you ask. You will draw from the silence the things that you need: hope and courage and strength for your task.

This little verse established itself by being sent from one country to another enclosed with letters finding a home at last in a chapel in the redwoods of California where it was recorded, as it happened to be the very thing the builders of the chapel had been hoping to find. Visitors to the chapel in the woods can now hear this record at the press of a button.

First printed in the Daily Mirror and published by Muller in *The Quiet Corner*, 1937.

THE DAY WE MET

If I could live one day again, a day out of the past – I'd choose the day that we two met, for when my mind I cast – across the landscape of the years, it stands out bright and bold. The memory is evergreen, although the tale is told.

A lovely summer afternoon, a blue and golden sky. A garden by the water and a white sail moving by . . . and someone coming up the path I'd never seen before – walking straight into my life to stay for evermore.

Harbours of Happiness, Muller, 1954.

LIFE IS FOR LIVING

Life is for living so live it and see – what a thrilling and wonderful world it can be – when you let go of the things that annoy – and start to discover the secret of joy; life is too good to be squandered, too brief – to waste upon grievances, grudges and grief.

Life is for giving, so give of your best. Keep nothing back and your days will be blessed . . . Give time and give money, give thanks and give praise – It will return in mysterious ways. Life was not meant to depress or destroy. Life is for giving and giving is joy.

The Windows of Heaven, Muller, 1963.

THE CROOKED CROSS

The Swastika, an ancient sign now stands for blood and hate. The symbol of a pagan creed, that glorifies the State. It drips with tears, the tears of those who would not bend the knee – to shoddy gods: the enemies of truth and liberty.

Martyrs, rebels, Jews and Gentiles, locked in living hells – broken, beaten, hounded into camps and prison cells. The Swastika! The crooked cross! The ghoulish travesty – of that dear cross of the redemption wrought on Calvary.

Windows of Hope, John Miles, 1940.

THE RAF

On wings of fire they ride the storms of war in heaven's height – striking at the enemy and putting him to flight – Full into the face of death through flame and shot and shell – Outnumbered but unmatched they flew into the jaws of hell.

Daring and courageous in the teeth of fearful odds – they fight their way to glory with the valour of the gods . . . with cool control, with peerless skill and bravery sublime – they fight to win for us the greatest battle of all time.

Thoughts From The Quiet Corner, John Miles, 1940.

THE COUNTRYMAN

This is what he dreamed about beneath the desert sky: brown earth breaking on the plough and white gulls wheeling by . . . . This is what he fought for on a beach in

Normandy: parish church and village green, his English legacy.

These things did he know and love. He lived and died for them . . . Speak no word. The evening thrush will sing his requiem.

Magic Casements, Muller, 1950.

GRIEF GROWS OLD

The light goes out of life for us, the world turns dark and drear – when God calls unto Himself the ones we hold most dear. His ways we cannot understand because we cannot see – the pattern He is weaving on the looms of destiny.

But God is good and grief grows old. Time plays its gentle part – laying healing hands upon the red wounds of the heart. The secret scars grow fainter with the passing of the years – faith returns as joy comes back to wipe away the tears.

Gleams of sunlight steal in through the windows of the mind. Hope revives, the future beckons. Once again we find – Life has something good to offer. Grey sky turns to gold . . . Memories remain, but sorrows end – and grief grows old.

Wayside Glory, Muller, 1948.

THE LODESTAR

You are the lodestar of my life. Your love is like the guiding light – that brings the mariner to harbour through the darkness of the night . . . The great ships set their course for home and on that constant star rely – Led by the eternal lamp that hangs upon the northern sky.

FROM THE HARVEST OF THE YEARS

You are the dream I have pursued across the oceans of
the years. You are my hope and my salvation; in your dear
arms I know no fears ... You are my star of fate and
fortune, steadfast, unfailing, changeless, true. Safely I'm
brought to quiet havens when in thought I turn to you.

Blessings of the Years, Muller, 1944.

DEAR GUARDIAN ANGEL

Dear guardian angel, walk with me. My guide and my
companion be. Prevent, preserve and intervene – where
there are dangers unforeseen.

Dear guardian angel, close remain, my wayward spirit
to restrain – when blindly I go blundering – away from
your protective wing.

Dear Angel, when I'm called to take – the journey that
we all must make – Your final blessing be bestowed – and
lead me down the homeward road.

The Harvest of a Quiet Eye, Muller, 1969.

GIVE ME A QUIET CORNER

Give me a quiet corner and a little time to hear – the
singing of the birds from dawn to dusk throughout the
year ... Give me a chance to think things out before it's
time to go – Give me a place where I can sit and see the
sunset glow.

Give me a window with a view that flows to meet the
sky. Give me a garden where the trees can feel the winds
blow by ... Give me good days and sleep-blessed nights
when I have closed the door – and anyone can have the
world. I'll never ask for more.

Give me a quiet corner, Muller, 1972.

PROTECTION

Between myself and the power of darkness I will place this day – the lantern of the Word of God to light the unknown way.

Between myself and the evil that is rampant everywhere – I will build a wall of faith behind a moat of prayer.

Between myself and the unseen forces that encompass me I will set the saving sign: the cross of Calvary.

Crumbs of Comfort, Muller, 1962.

THE MINISTRY OF BEAUTY

Bloom lovely rose at my windowpane. Put on your glory; heal my pain. Open your bud to its full bright flower. This is your mission and this your hour.

Who would have thought when the snow lay deep – that you would awake from your winter sleep – putting forth petals of fiery red, rising like Lazarus from the dead.

Out of the dark you have come again. Much has been taken, but you remain – to hearten, to calm and to comfort me – through beauty's silent ministry.

The Harvest of a Quiet Eye, Muller, 1965.

THE SCHOLAR

There was a moment when his wings were caught in webs of fire – and in that blinding flash of time he saw a "dreaming" spire . . . He saw green lawns, the library, the chapel and the hall – and sunlight poured like golden wine upon an old grey wall.

Over cliffs of flaming cloud he plunged his wounded plane – seeing Christ Church Meadow through a mist of April rain . . . Outsoaring and outdistancing the thrust of agony – feeling again in bone and vein the Oxford ecstasy.

Over The Ridge, Muller, 1944.

THIS BE THEIR EPITAPH May 1945

From the clean hands of the young we take the gift supreme: the gift of life and liberty, the right to work and dream . . . We take what they have won for us, a thing above all price. What do we offer in return for that high sacrifice?

These have served their generation, wise beyond their years – following the flag of faith through mud and blood and tears . . . We shall remember, though once more we learn to live and laugh. They were the saviours of the world . . . This be their epitaph.

Daily Mirror, 1945

I can imagine my friend Amanda wishing to have the last word in this chronicle in which our lives were so closely intertwined. And so she shall. As has been recorded, one summer evening in 1935 when, unknown to her, I was trying to think of a suitable pseudonym for my new feature, she brought a book to my door entitled *Patience Strong* and out of that same book there has just dropped a poem in her handwriting written by Ethel Beatrice Page, published in the Essex Review of 1947. Amanda had all her long life been a plucker from the hedgerows of experience and a prodigious keeper of scrapbooks. When this was first plucked from the hedgerow of the Essex Review, Amanda would have been surprised to know how applicable it would be in the nuclear age of 1981, when Christians who understand the language of the Bible are awaiting the fulfilment of what Tennyson describes as "that divine event to which the whole creation moves".

BALANCE

The God who balances sun and star will balance men
   however far
From off their course they swing,
Whatever chaos to the earth they bring,
The God who beckons winds and tides will beckon men.
Immortal love from some clear shining place
Will draw all true souls home in time and space.

INDEX

INDEX

Campbell, Guy (son of Amanda), 85, 88–91, 106, 146, 220, 228, 238
Christian Herald, 151
Churchill, Sir Winston, 58, 165, 176
Cleaning Up TV, 215
Connie, *see* Stelling, Mrs. Connie
"Constance Camelia", 15–19
Covenant people, 181
Crew, Rupert, 151–2

Daily Mirror, calendar advertised in, 161; "*God's Battle Axe*" in, 176; Patience Strong no longer writing for, 151, 219; Quiet Corner in, 144–5, 150, 234; read by prisoner, 240
Day, Maude Craske, 27, 128–9
Drummond, Frederick, 26–7, 39–40, 45, 51–2, 70, 73–8, 81–2, 150

Edward VIII, King, 132–4
Elizabeth, Princess (later Elizabeth II, Queen), 126–7, 133, 215

Father (of Patience Strong), aged by Connie's death, 142; army service of, 6–8, 28, 51; cigars given by Patience Strong to, 120; death of, 222–3; eldest of ten, 8; fire-fighter, 163; goodbye kiss for Patience Strong, 7; London office of, 7; marriage of Patience Strong approved by, 102; Patience Strong taken to dance by, 38, 41; piano playing and, 27; Providence believed in by, 120; religious freedom accorded by, 34; retirement of, 176; return from war, 33; walking loved by, 62; wife comforted by, 142
"Forsyte, Faith", 219
France, 94, 104, 165, 180

Garden Tomb, The, 204–9
George V, King, 28, 126, 132–3, 157
George VI, King, 133, 164, 215

Germany, 28, 130–3, 164–5, 178–80, 192–3, 227–8, 235
Glastonbury, 187–90
God, acknowledged by Churchill, 176; beauty and, 213; bread of, 241; Broadcasting House and, 215; Covenant made by, 174; David's dream of, 194; Hand of, 164–5; in time of need, 117; Incarnation of, 195, 240; people of, 184; pleasing, 242; prayer answered by, 240; presence of, 129; rainbow sign of 179; table-cloth sent by, 226; terrible truths and, 136; thanks to, 220; *see also* Jesus Christ, Providence *and* religion
Guy, *see* Campbell, Guy

Holy Land, The, 184, 195–209
Homeopathy, 136
Hunt, Holman, 43

Iona, 184–7, 227

Japan, 133, 181
Jesus Christ, birth of, 187, 195; body of, 187, 206; Bread of Life, 241; Capernaum, at, 203; charged with blasphemy, 206; Glastonbury and, 189–90; ministry of, 175, 190, 203; number thirteen and, 104; promise by, 123, 243–4; prophecies confirmed by, 204; Sermon on the Mount, 243
Jews, 174, 188, 197, 199, 201, 205
Jo, *see* Stelling, Jo

Labour Party, 45, 49, 58–9, *see also* politics
London, 42–3, 86, 102, 165, 169, 178

Mason, Emma (step-grandmother of Patience Strong), 15–20
Meditation, 125
Montgomery of Alamein, Field Marshal, 1st Viscount, 180
Montgomery, Doreen, 151–2

INDEX

INDEX

INDEX

INDEX

World War I, air raids in, 12; armistice at end of, 89; bitterness after, 33; cinema visits during, 11; day of prayer in, 28–9; father of Patience Strong in army during, 6–8, 28; Guy and, 89; Paddy's service in, 79–80, 104, 111, 208; rationing during, 28; songs of, 23, 25; Stephen's hatred of, 48–9; uncles of Patience Strong in army during, 8–9

World War II, Anderson shelter of Patience Strong, 167; Aunt Ada's "time of her life", 169; brings out the highest, 167; Buzz Bombs in, 178; Chamberlain's broadcast, 133; character of Patience Strong's verses changed in, 162; Clare's denuded sparrow, 167–8; confirmation during, 181–2; D-Day, 178; Dunkirk, 165; evacuation of home by Patience Strong, 169; father of Patience Strong a fire-fighter in, 163; German attack on Russia, 172, 178; Germany's early successes in, 164–5; God's rainbow sign, 179; Great Britain alone in, 163; Hand of God in, 164–5; Japanese collapse, 180–1; Jo's death in air-raid, 65, 139; King's 1939 Christmas broadcast, 164–5; letters to Patience Strong during, 166; "London can take it", 165, 169; Mary Borden's service in, 94; Montgomery, Field Marshal, 180; Paddy an air-raid warden in, 163, 167; prelude to, 130–3, 162; service of Patience Strong in, 166; Smuts, Field Marshal, 180; songs of, 23, 25–6

Wright, Lawrence, 27, 53–5, 57, 66–7, 119–23